Pénélope Bagieu

EXQUISITE CORPSE

:01

First Second

NEW YORK

First Second

English translation by Alexis Siegel
English translation copyright © 2015 by First Second

Published by First Second
First Second is an imprint of Roaring Brook Press,
a division of Holtzbrinck Publishing Holdings Limited Partnership
175 Fifth Avenue, New York, New York 10010
All rights reserved

Cataloging-in-Publication Data is on file at the Library of Congress

ISBN: 978-1-62672-082-7

First Second books may be purchased for business or promotional
use. For information on bulk purchases please contact Macmillan
Corporate and Premium Sales Department at (800) 221-7945 x5442
or by email at specialmarkets@macmillan.com.

FIRST

EDITION

Originally published in 2010 in French by Gallimard as *Cadavre exquis*
French edition © 2010 by Gallimard
First American edition 2015
Book design by Colleen AF Venable

Printed in China
10 9 8 7 6 5 4 3 2 1

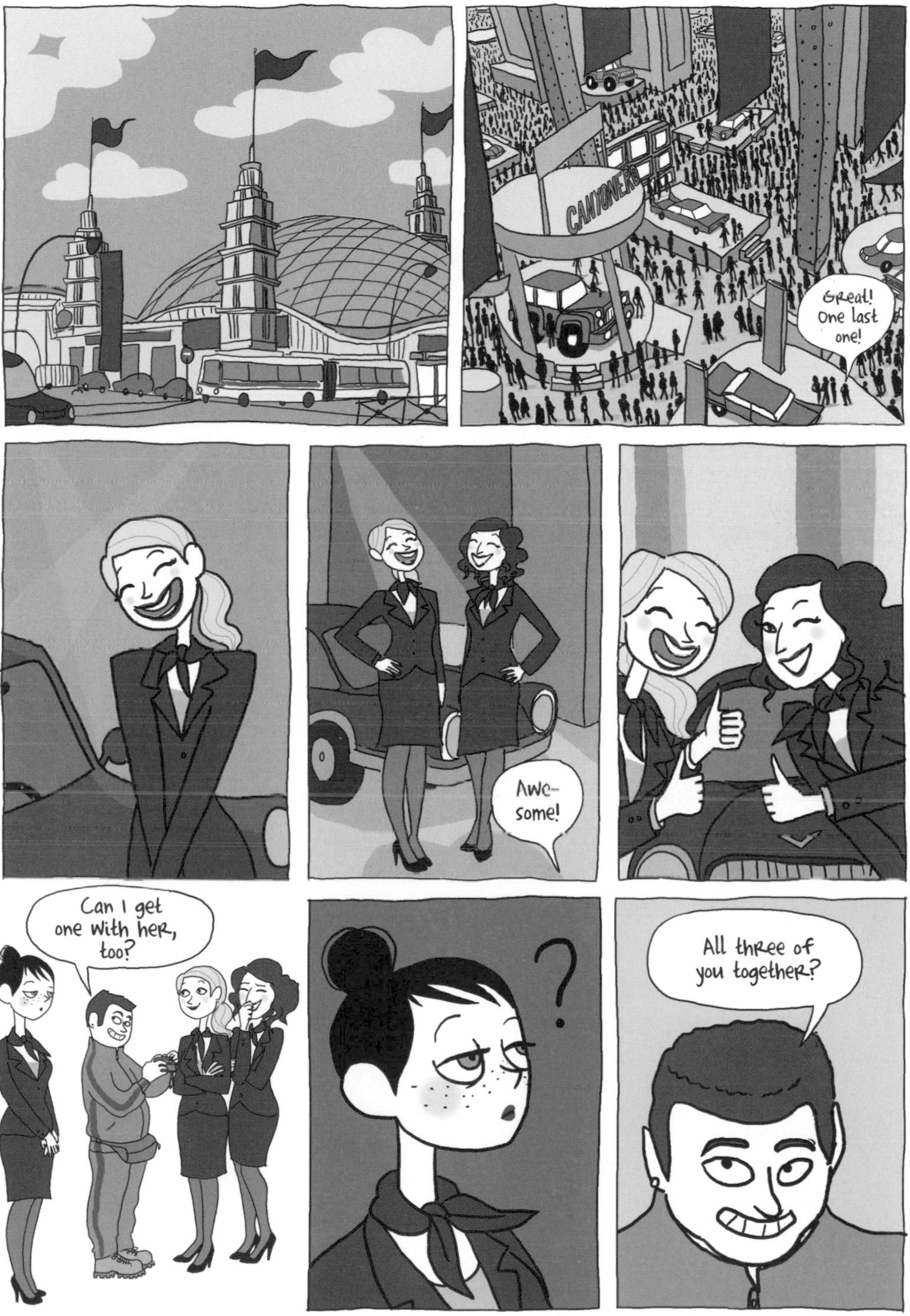
CANYONERO
Great! One last one!
Awe-some!
Can I get one with her, too?
?
All three of you together?

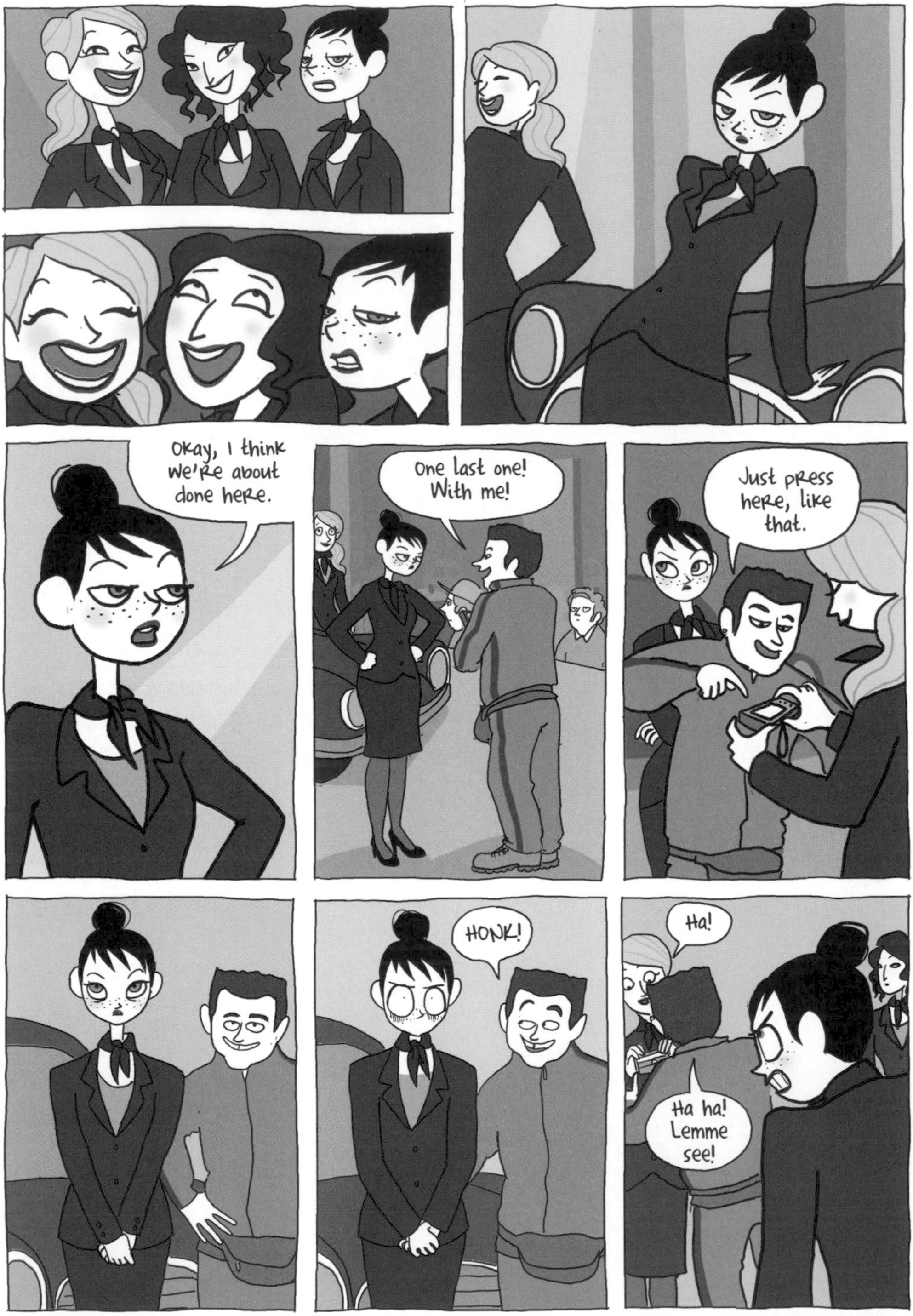
Okay, I think we're about done here.
One last one! With me!
Just press here, like that.
HONK!
Ha!
Ha ha! Lemme see!

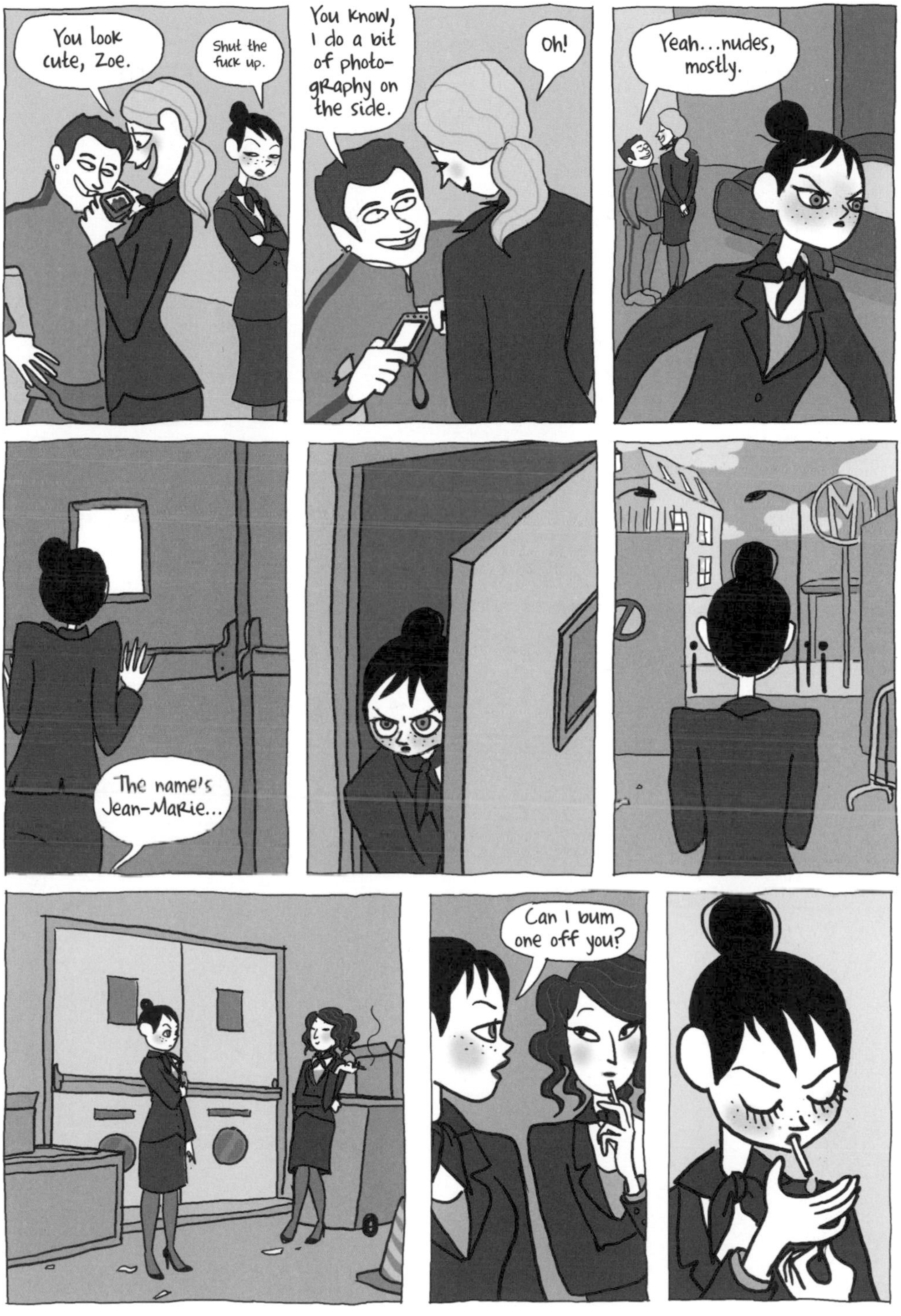
You look cute, Zoe.
Shut the fuck up.
You know, I do a bit of photography on the side.
Oh!
Yeah...nudes, mostly.
The name's Jean-Marie...
Can I bum one off you?

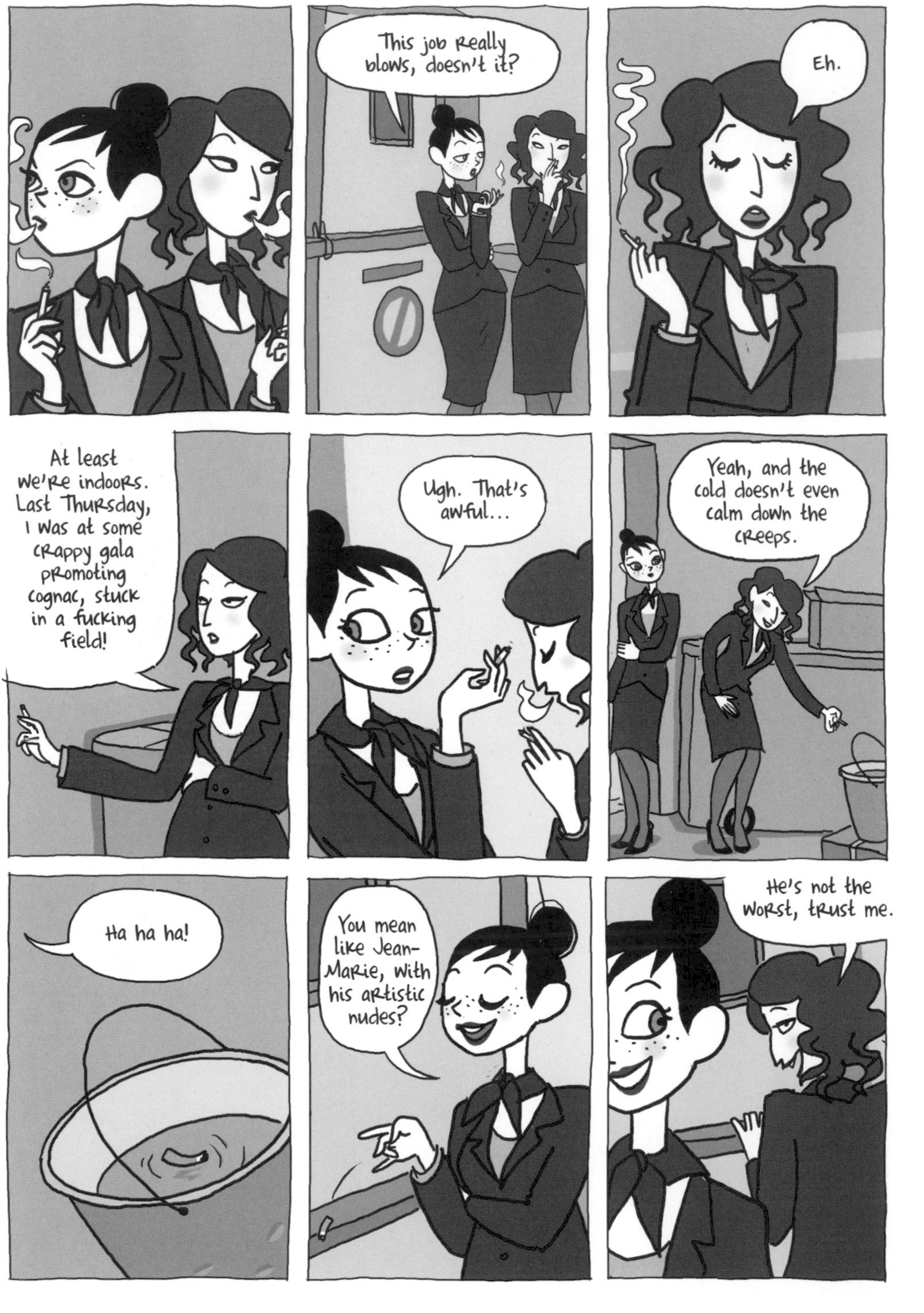
This job really blows, doesn't it?
Eh.
At least we're indoors. Last Thursday, I was at some crappy gala promoting cognac, stuck in a fucking field!
Ugh. That's awful...
Yeah, and the cold doesn't even calm down the creeps.
Ha ha ha!
You mean like Jean-Marie, with his artistic nudes?
He's not the worst, trust me.

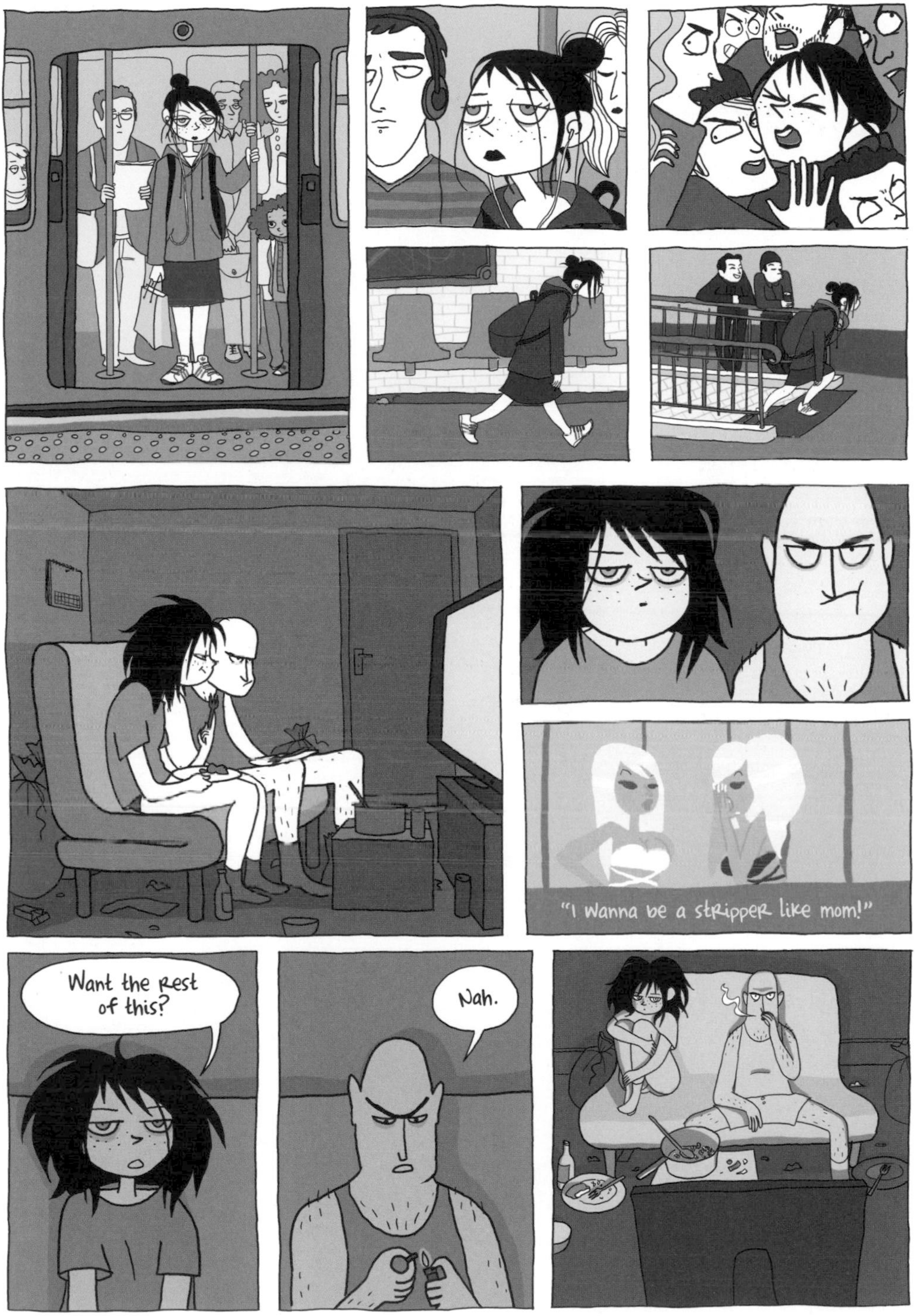
"I wanna be a stripper like mom!"
Want the rest of this?
Nah.

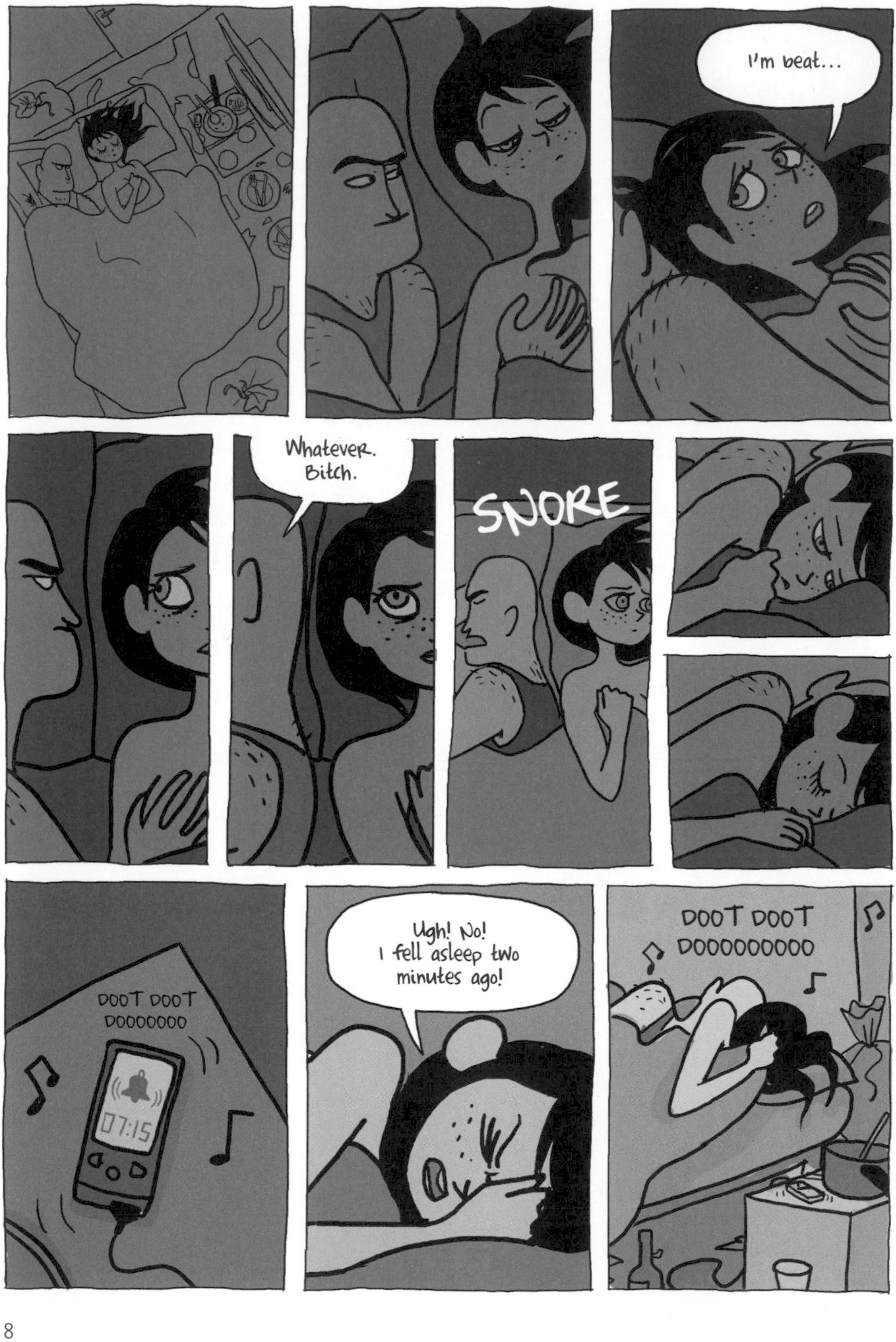

I'm beat...
Whatever. Bitch.
SNORE
DOOT DOOT DOOOOOOO
Ugh! No! I fell asleep two minutes ago!
DOOT DOOT DOOOOOOOOO

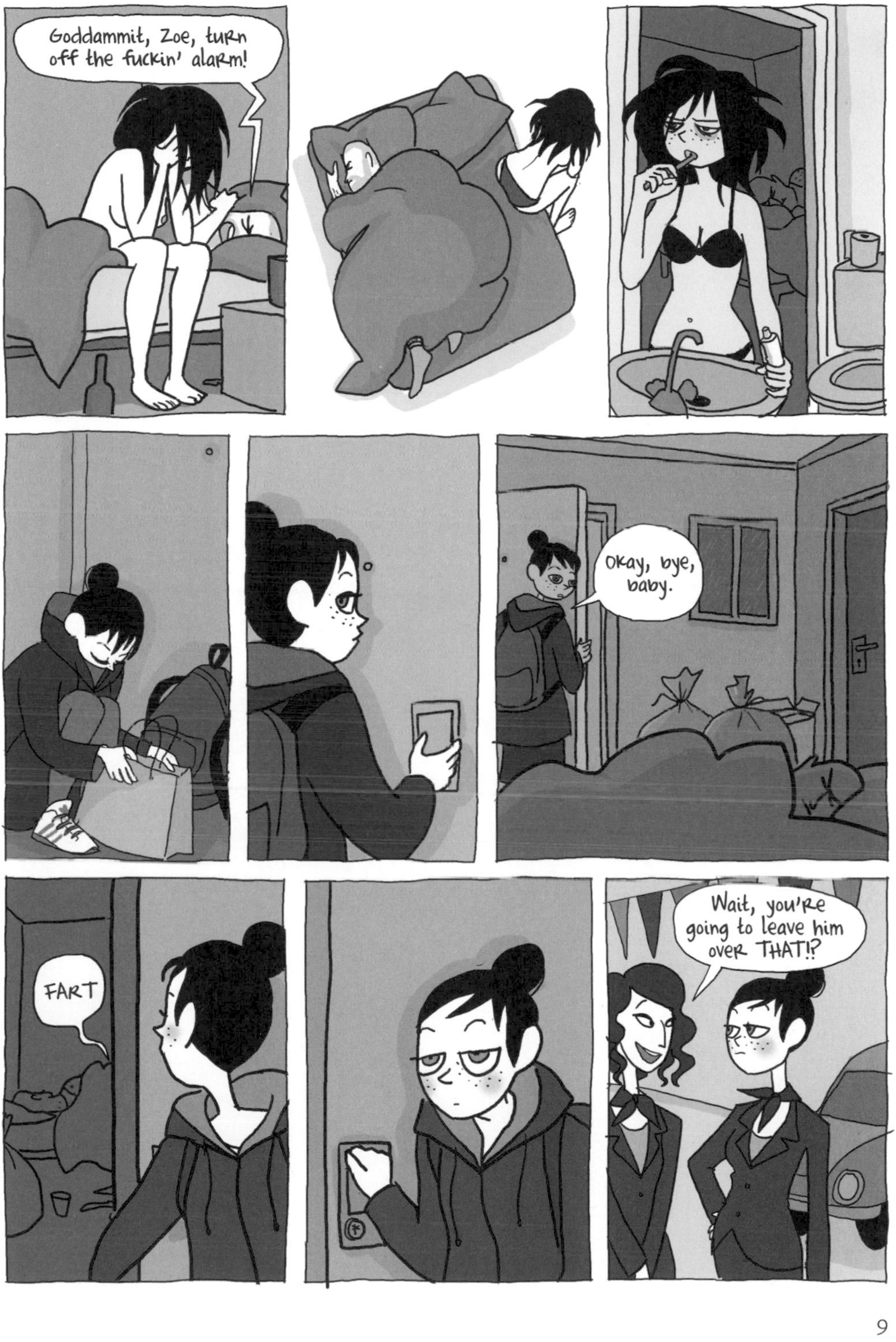
Goddammit, Zoe, turn off the fuckin' alarm!
Okay, bye, baby.
FART
Wait, you're going to leave him over THAT!?

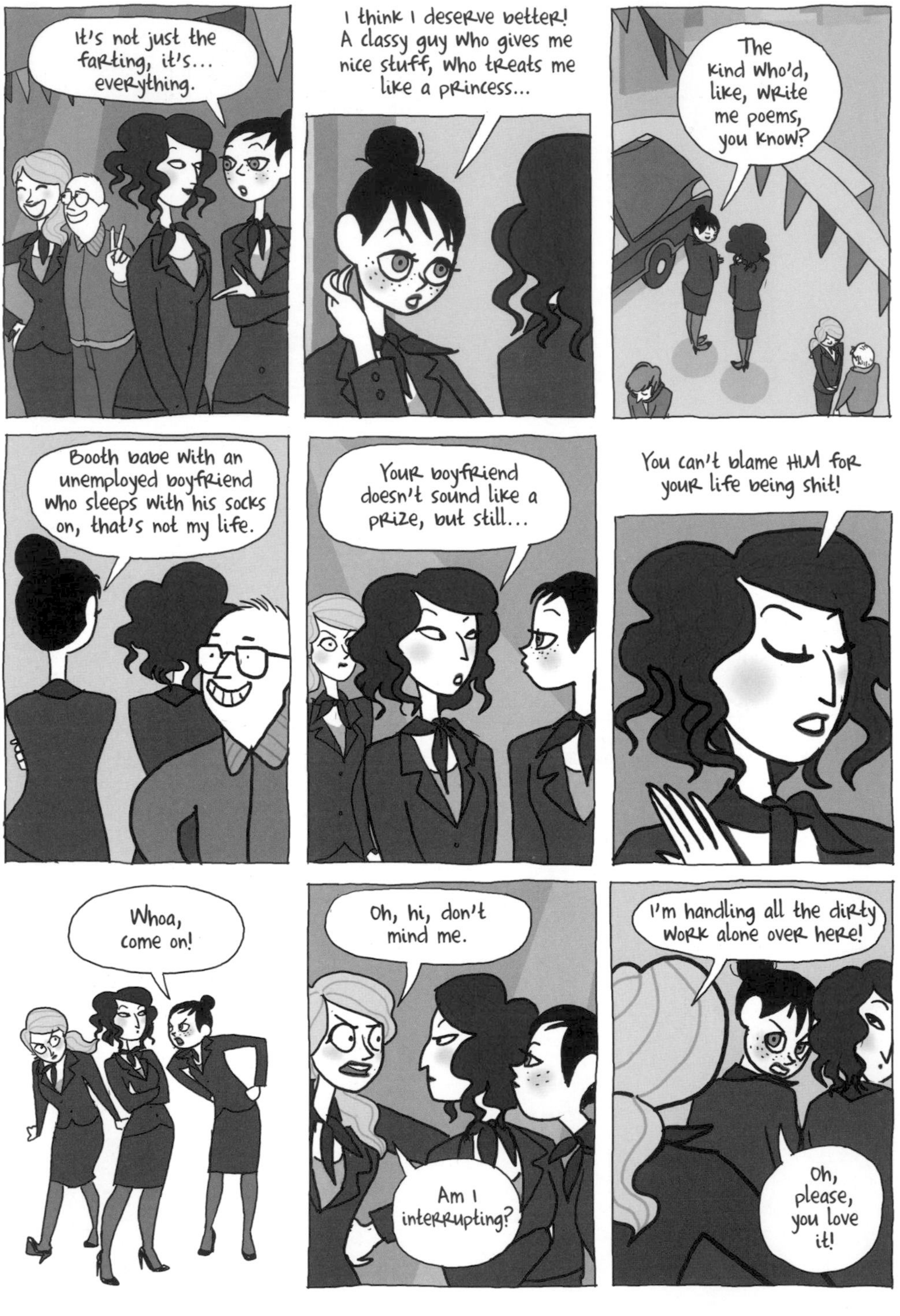
It's not just the farting, it's... everything.
I think I deserve better! A classy guy who gives me nice stuff, who treats me like a princess...
The kind who'd, like, write me poems, you know?
Booth babe with an unemployed boyfriend who sleeps with his socks on, that's not my life.
Your boyfriend doesn't sound like a prize, but still...
You can't blame HIM for your life being shit!
Whoa, come on!
Oh, hi, don't mind me.
Am I interrupting?
I'm handling all the dirty work alone over here!
Oh, please, you love it!

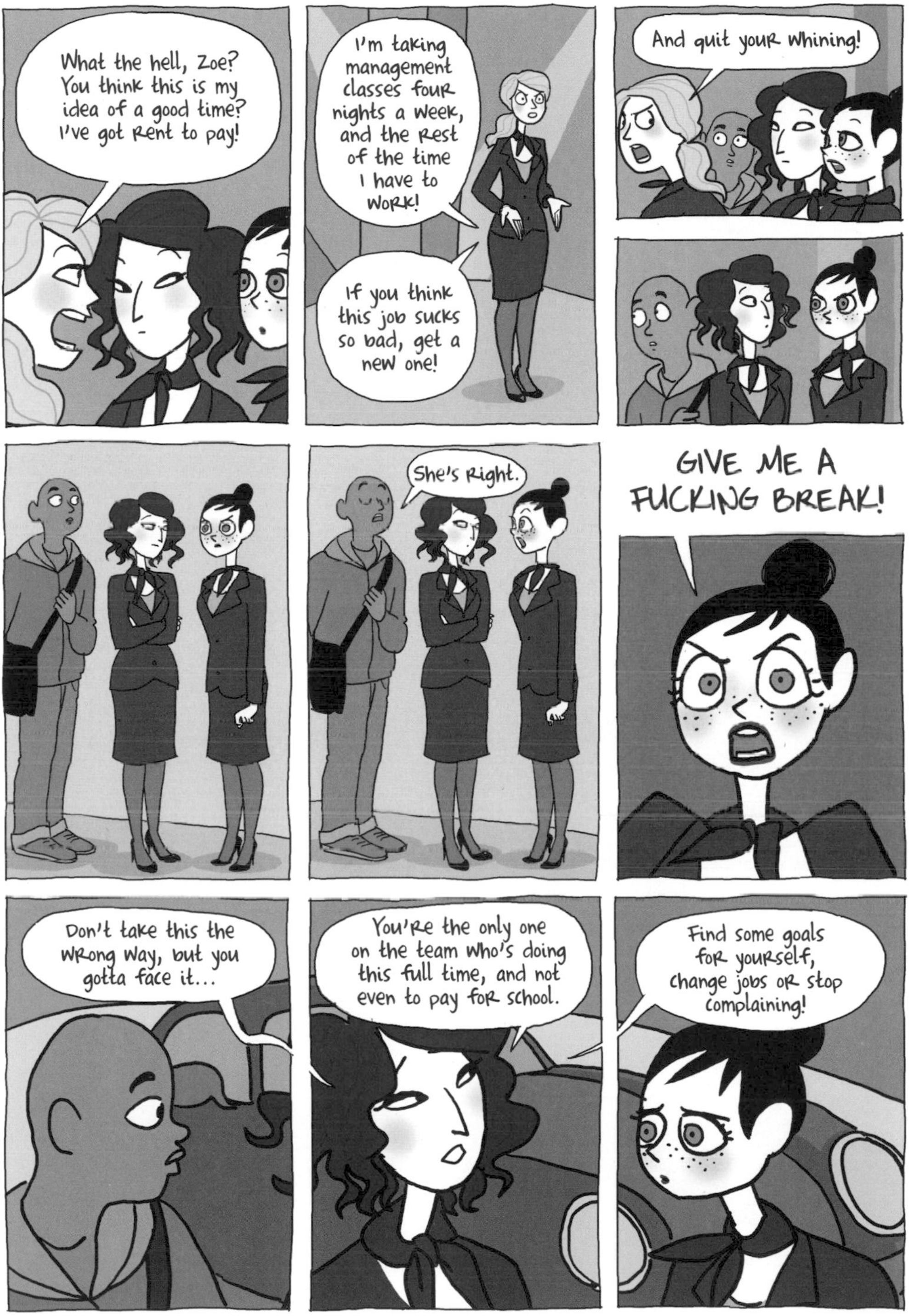
What the hell, Zoe? You think this is my idea of a good time? I've got rent to pay!
I'm taking management classes four nights a week, and the rest of the time I have to work!
If you think this job sucks so bad, get a new one!
And quit your whining!
She's right.
GIVE ME A FUCKING BREAK!
Don't take this the wrong way, but you gotta face it...
You're the only one on the team who's doing this full time, and not even to pay for school.
Find some goals for yourself, change jobs or stop complaining!

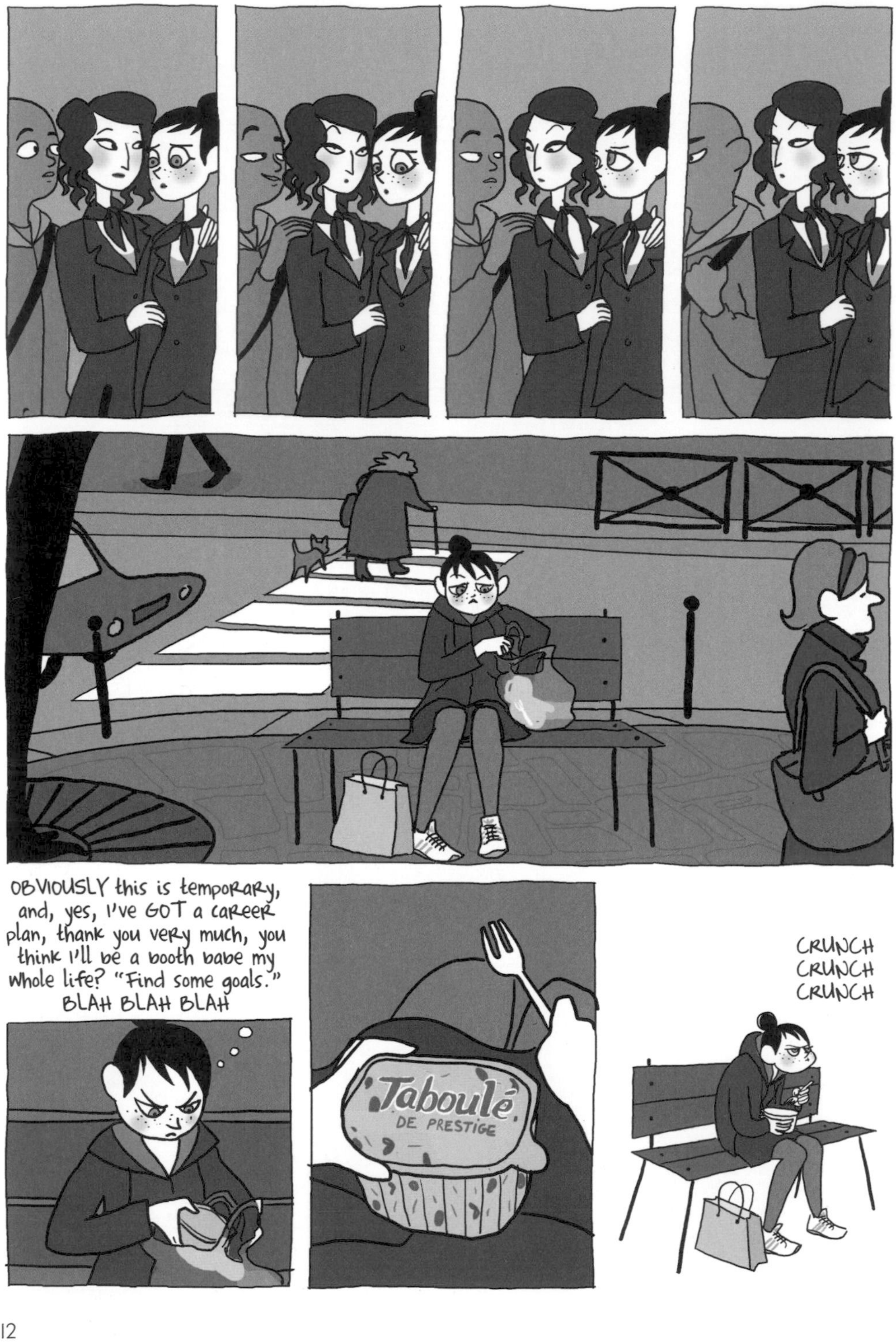
OBVIOUSLY this is temporary, and, yes, I've GOT a career plan, thank you very much, you think I'll be a booth babe my whole life? "Find some goals." BLAH BLAH BLAH
Taboulé
DE PRESTIGE
CRUNCH
CRUNCH
CRUNCH

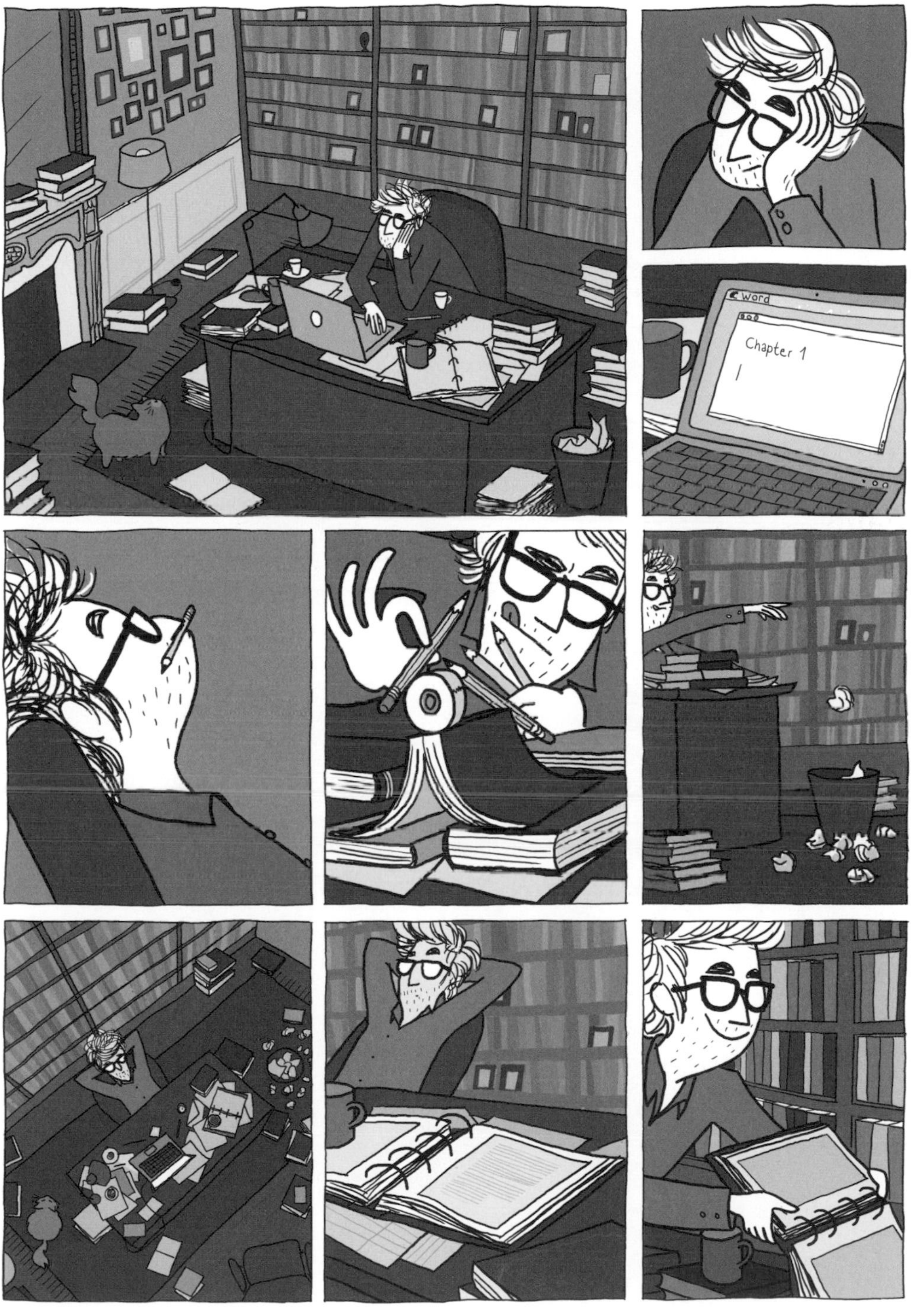
Word
Chapter 1

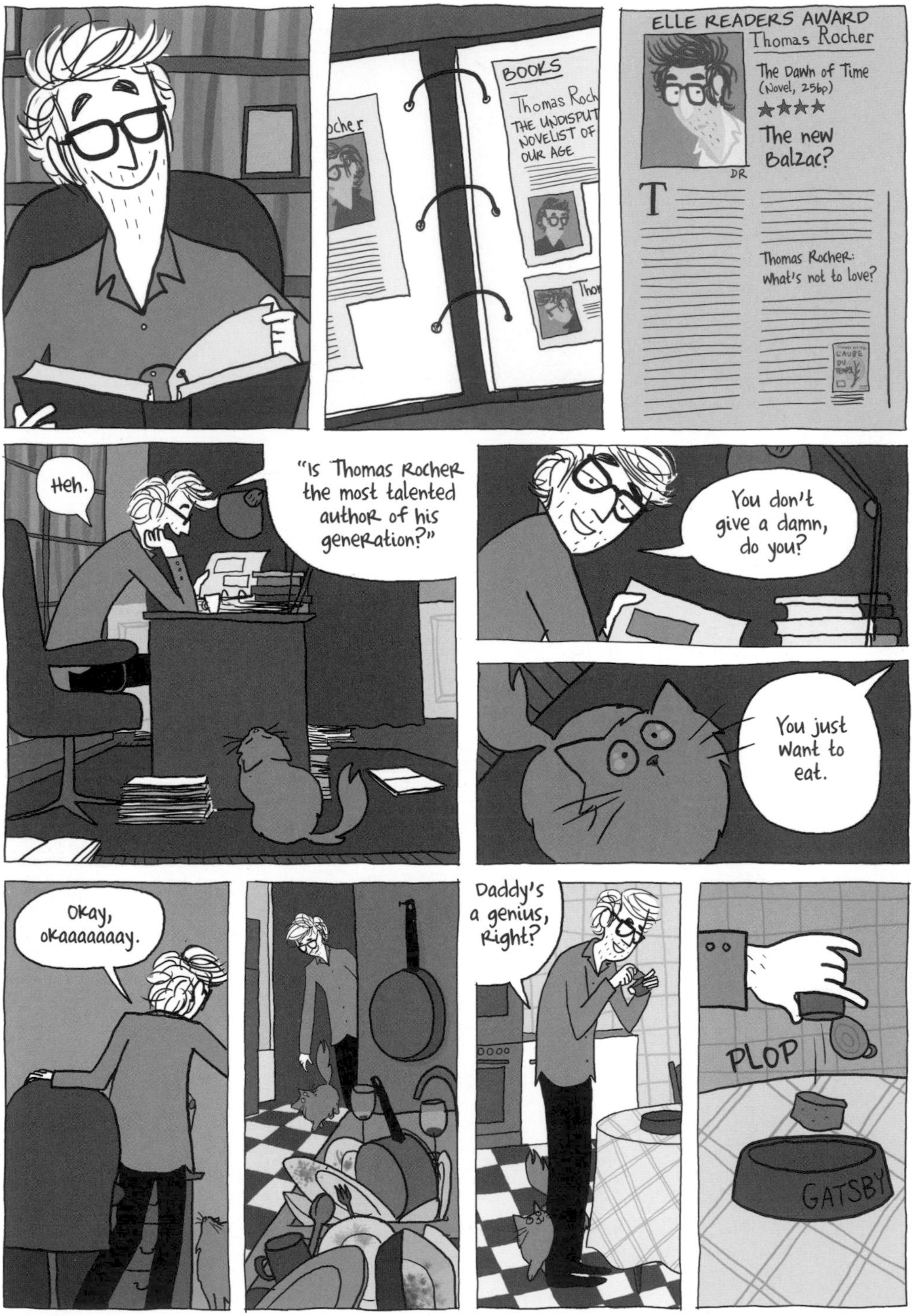
BOOKS
Thomas Roch
THE UNDISPUT
NOVELIST OF
OUR AGE
ELLE READERS AWARD
Thomas Rocher
The Dawn of Time
(Novel, 25bp)
★★★★
The new Balzac?
DR
Thomas Rocher: what's not to love?
Heh.
"Is Thomas Rocher the most talented author of his generation?"
You don't give a damn, do you?
You just want to eat.
Okay, okaaaaaaay.
Daddy's a genius, right?
PLOP
GATSBY

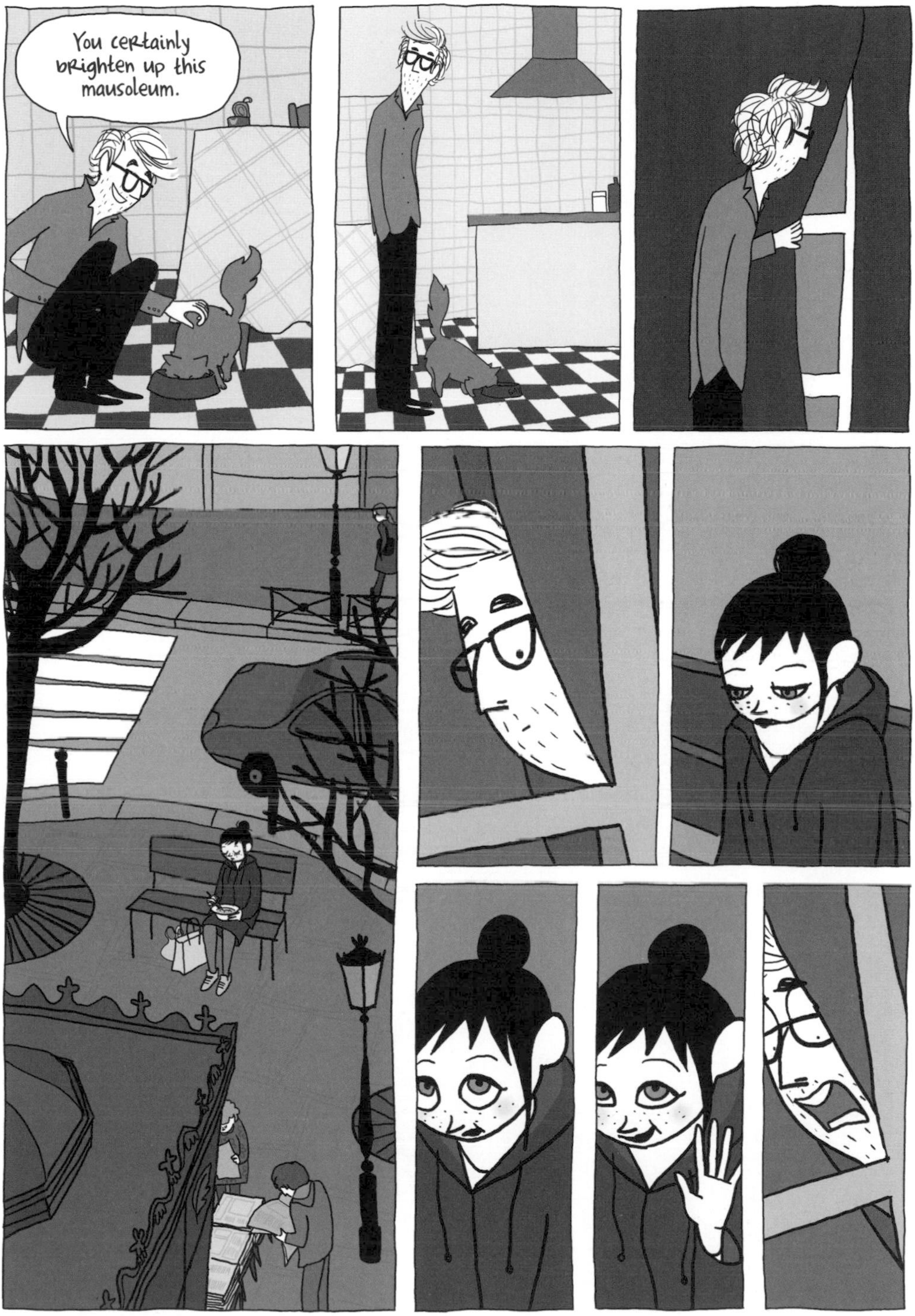
You certainly brighten up this mausoleum.

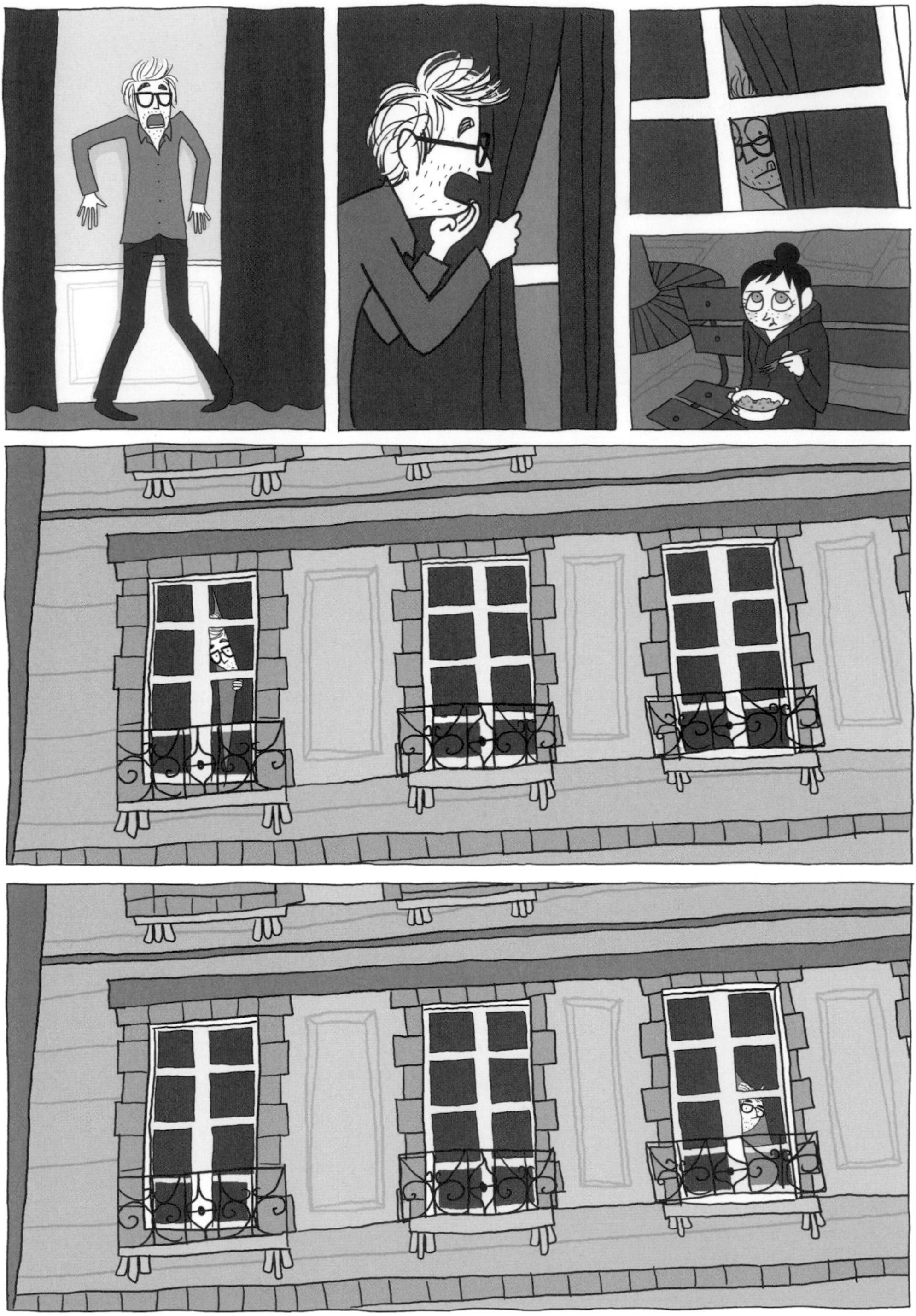

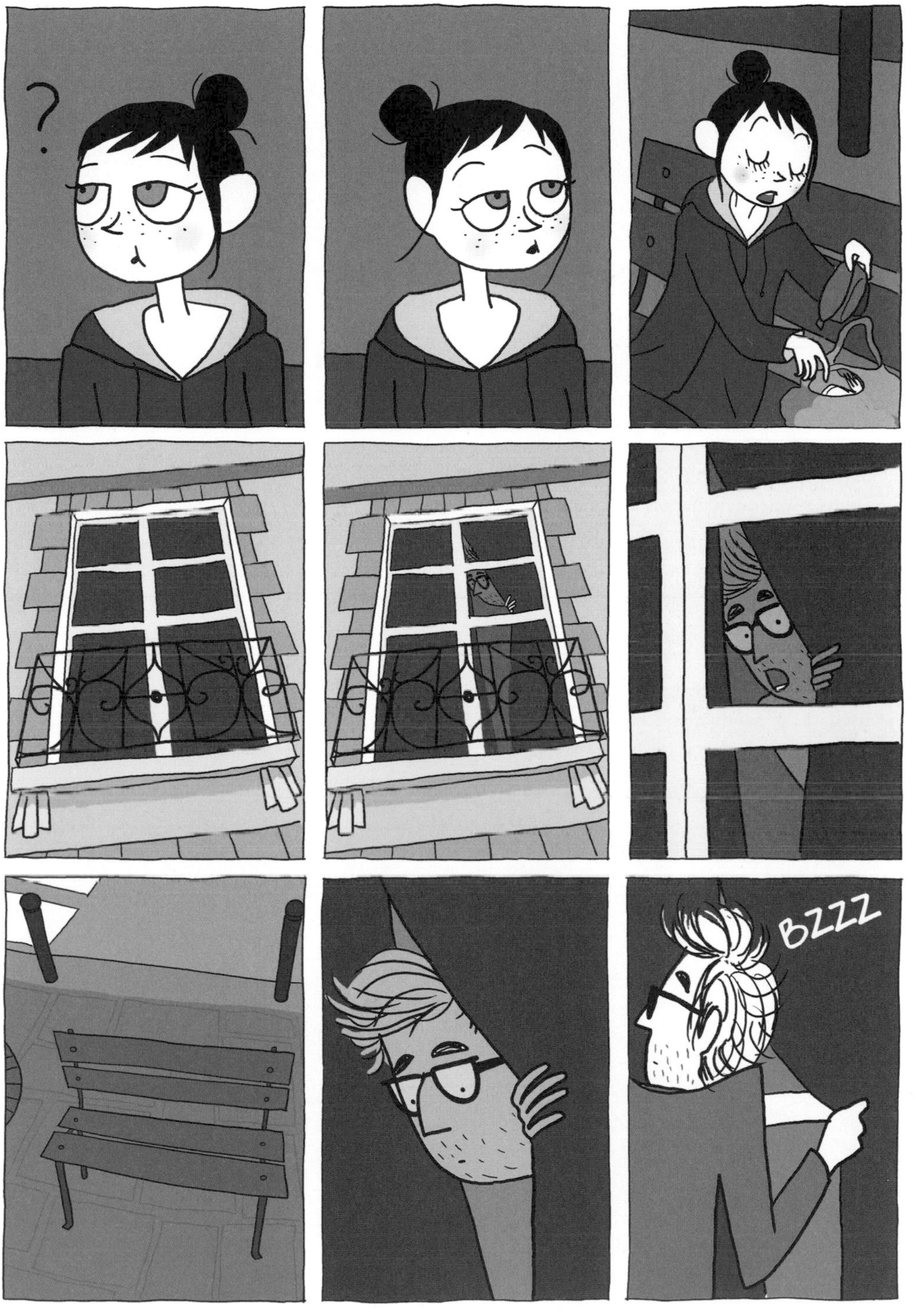
?
BZZZ

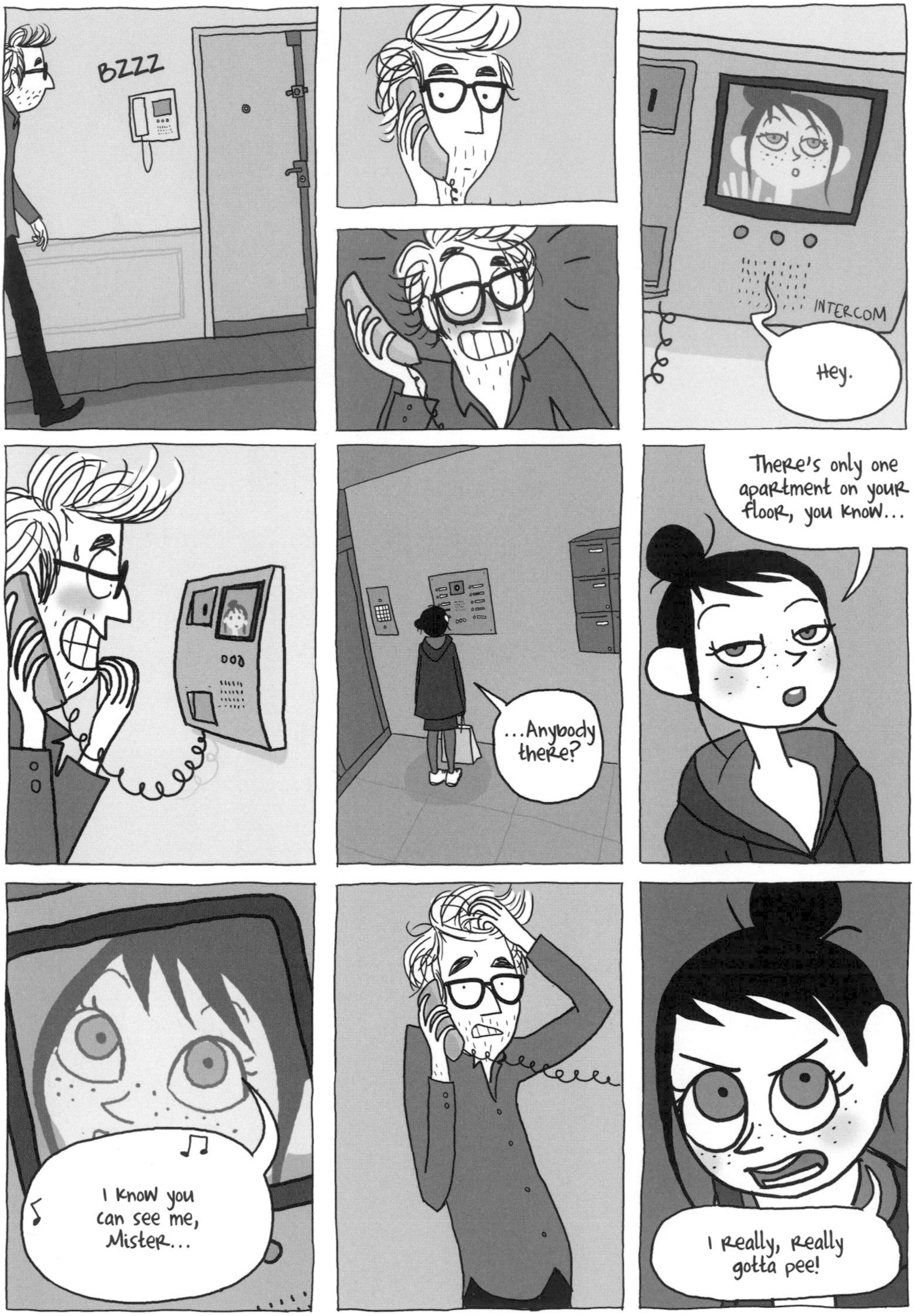
BZZZ
INTERCOM
Hey.
...Anybody there?
There's only one apartment on your floor, you know...
I know you can see me, Mister...
I really, really gotta pee!

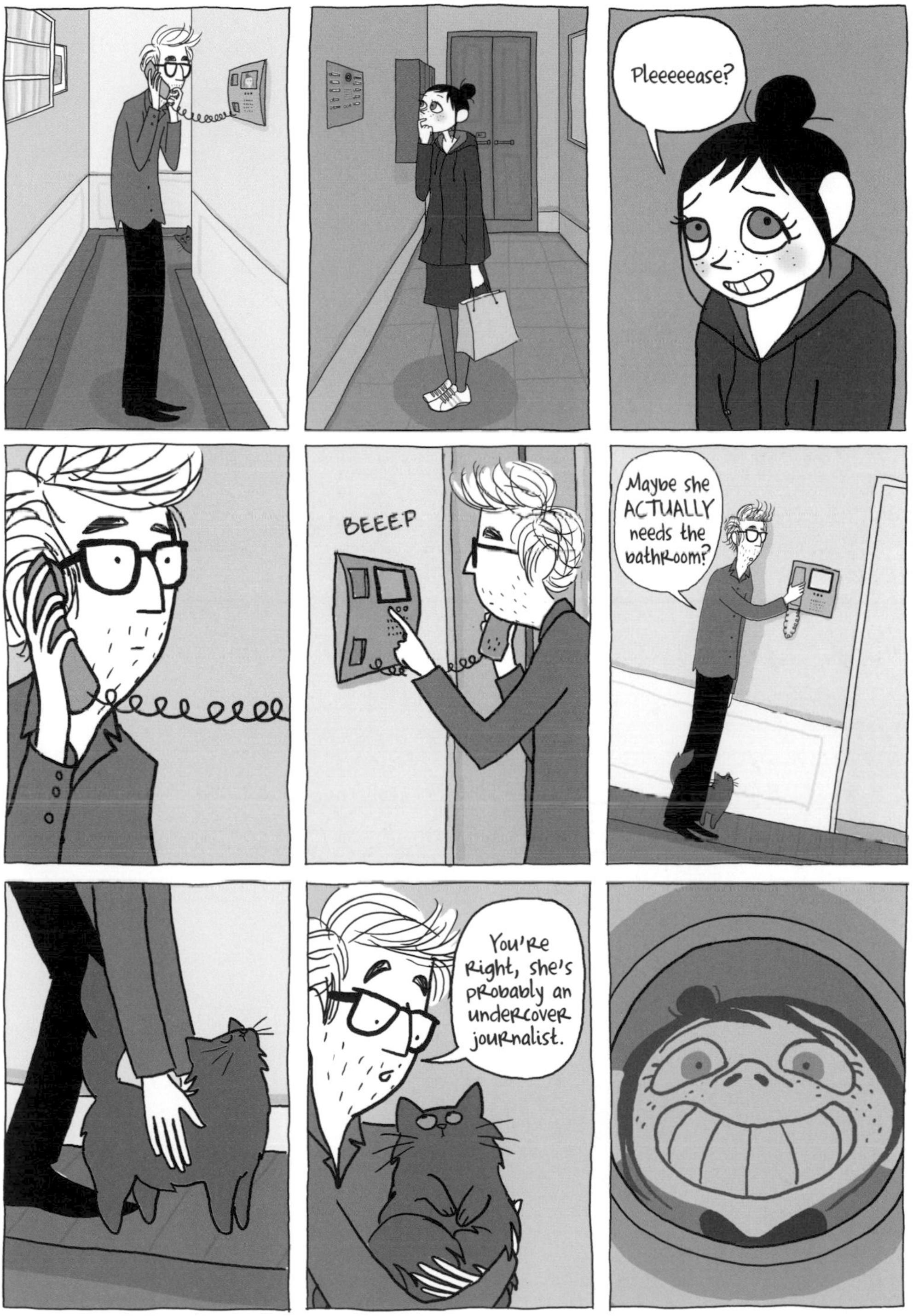

Pleeeeease?
BEEEP
Maybe she ACTUALLY needs the bathroom?
You're right, she's probably an undercover journalist.

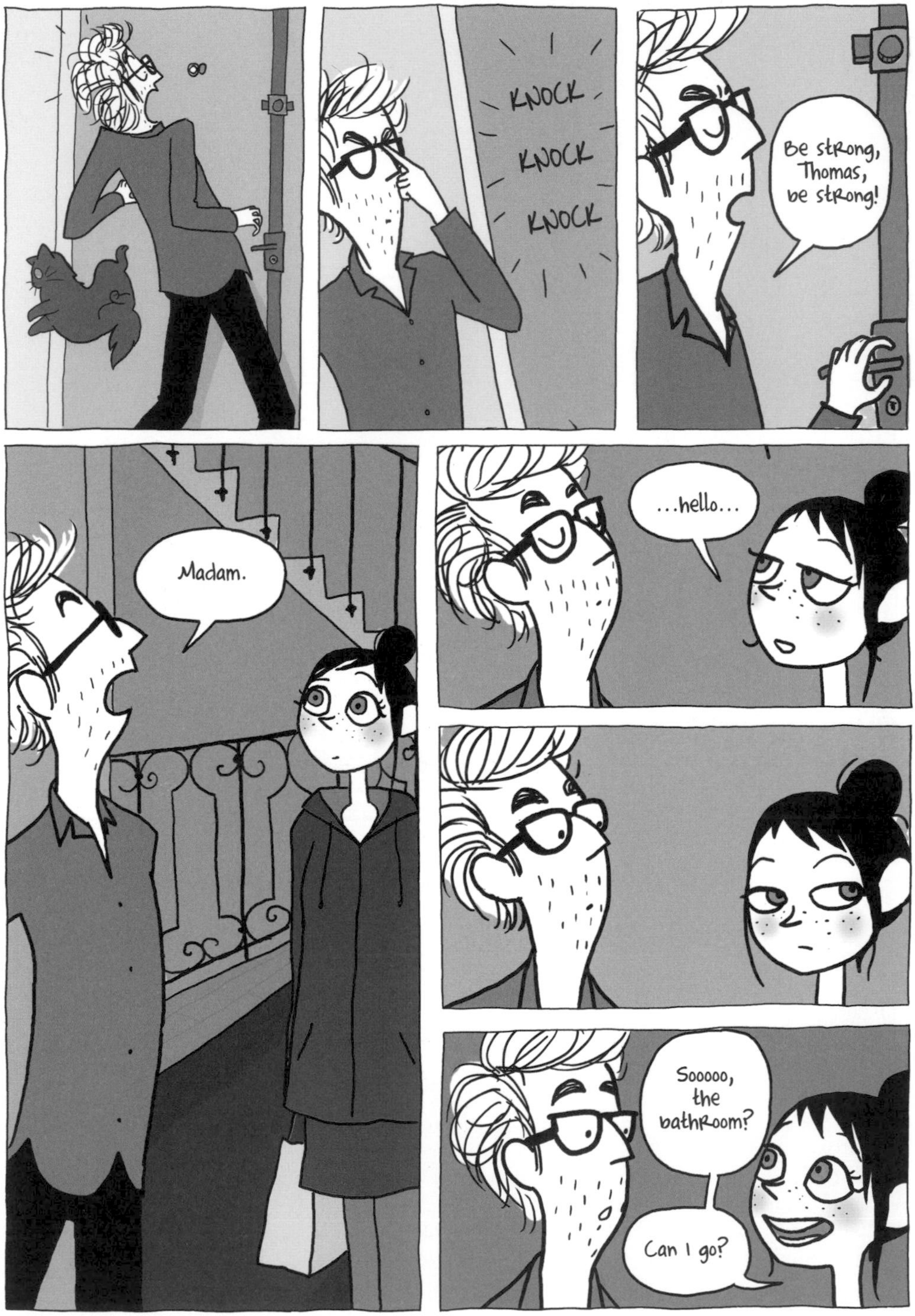
KNOCK
KNOCK
KNOCK
Be strong, Thomas, be strong!
Madam.
...hello...
Sooooo, the bathroom?
Can I go?

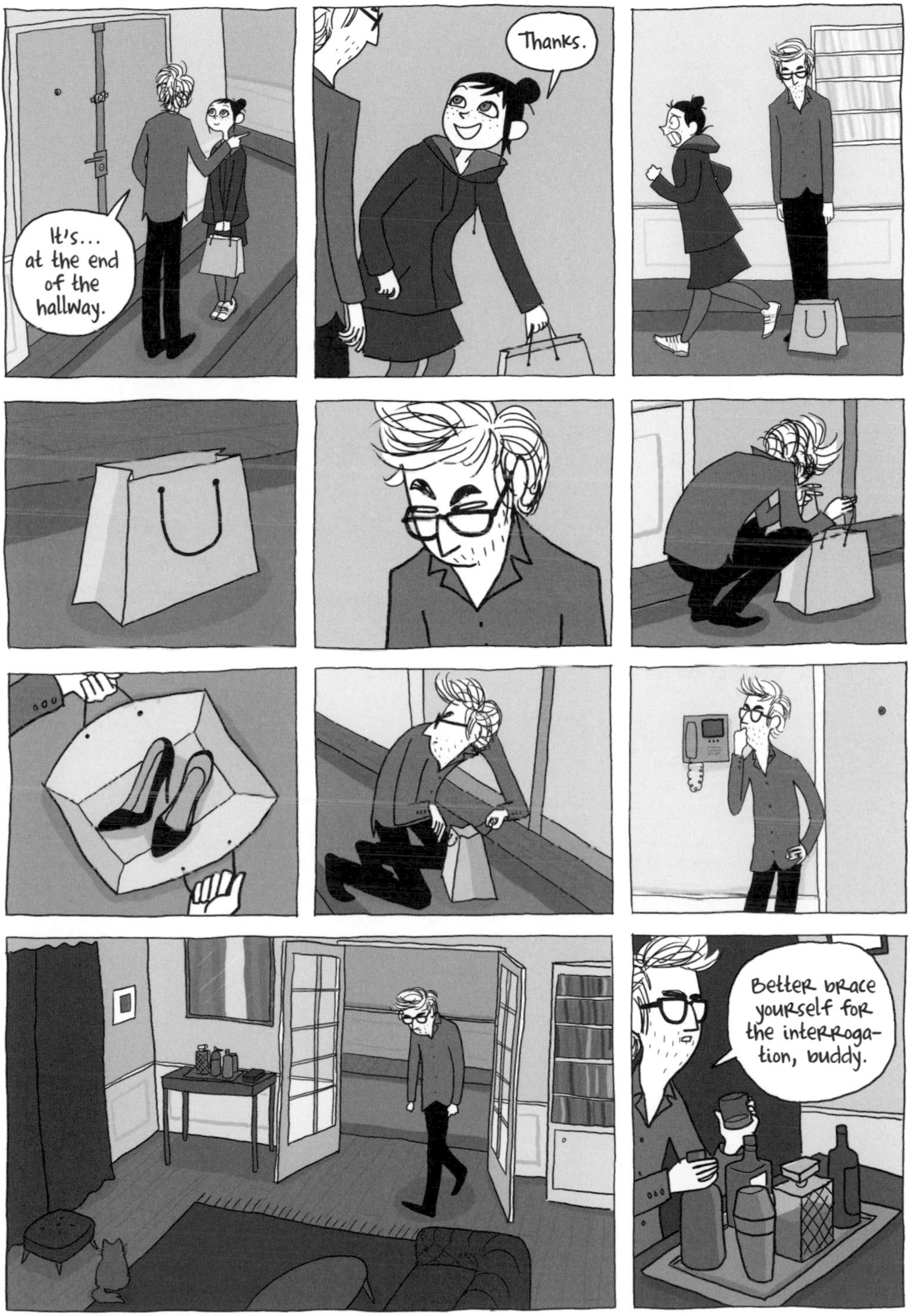
It's... at the end of the hallway.
Thanks.
Better brace yourself for the interroga-tion, buddy.

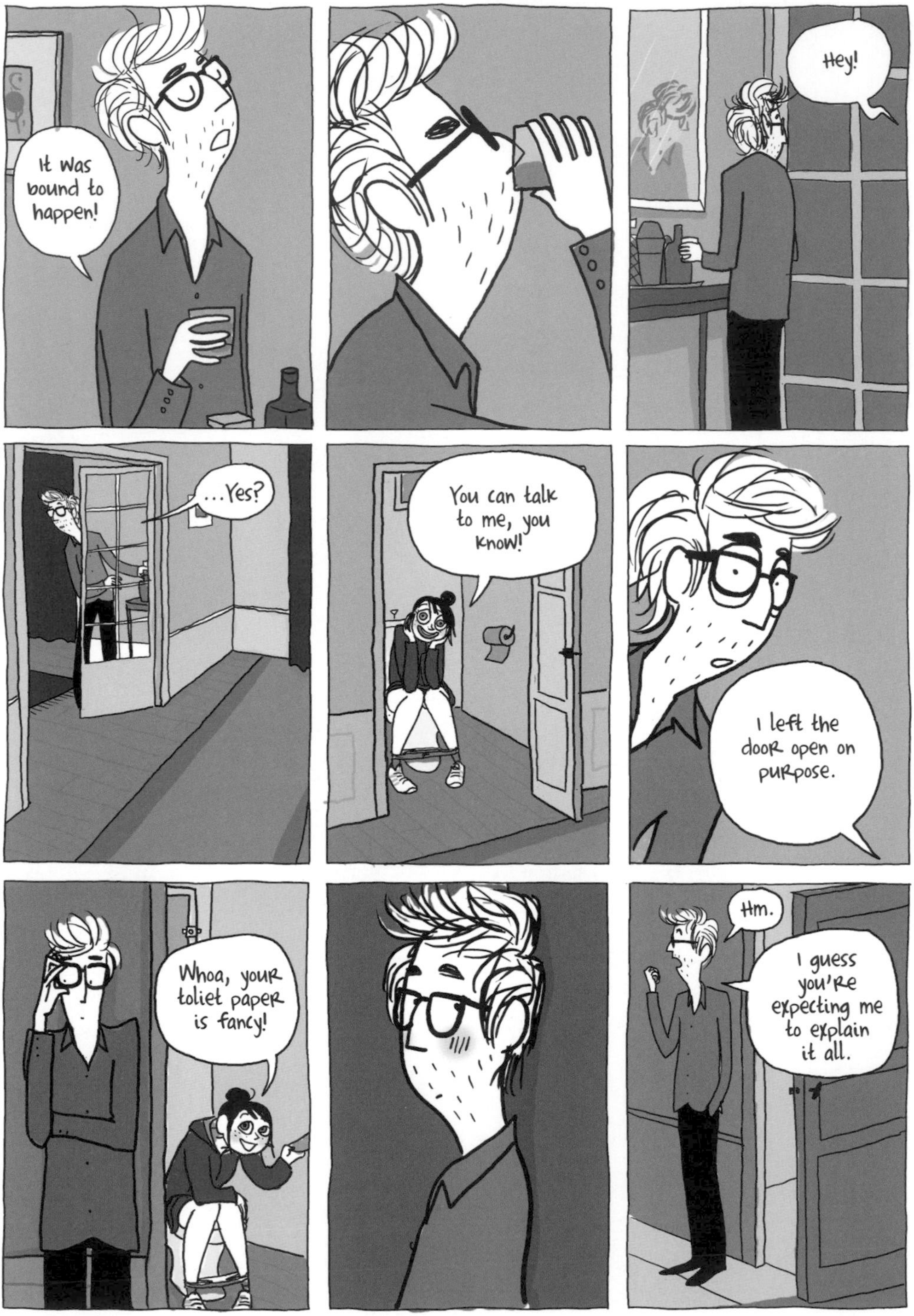
It was bound to happen!
Hey!
...Yes?
You can talk to me, you know!
I left the door open on purpose.
Whoa, your toliet paper is fancy!
Hm.
I guess you're expecting me to explain it all.

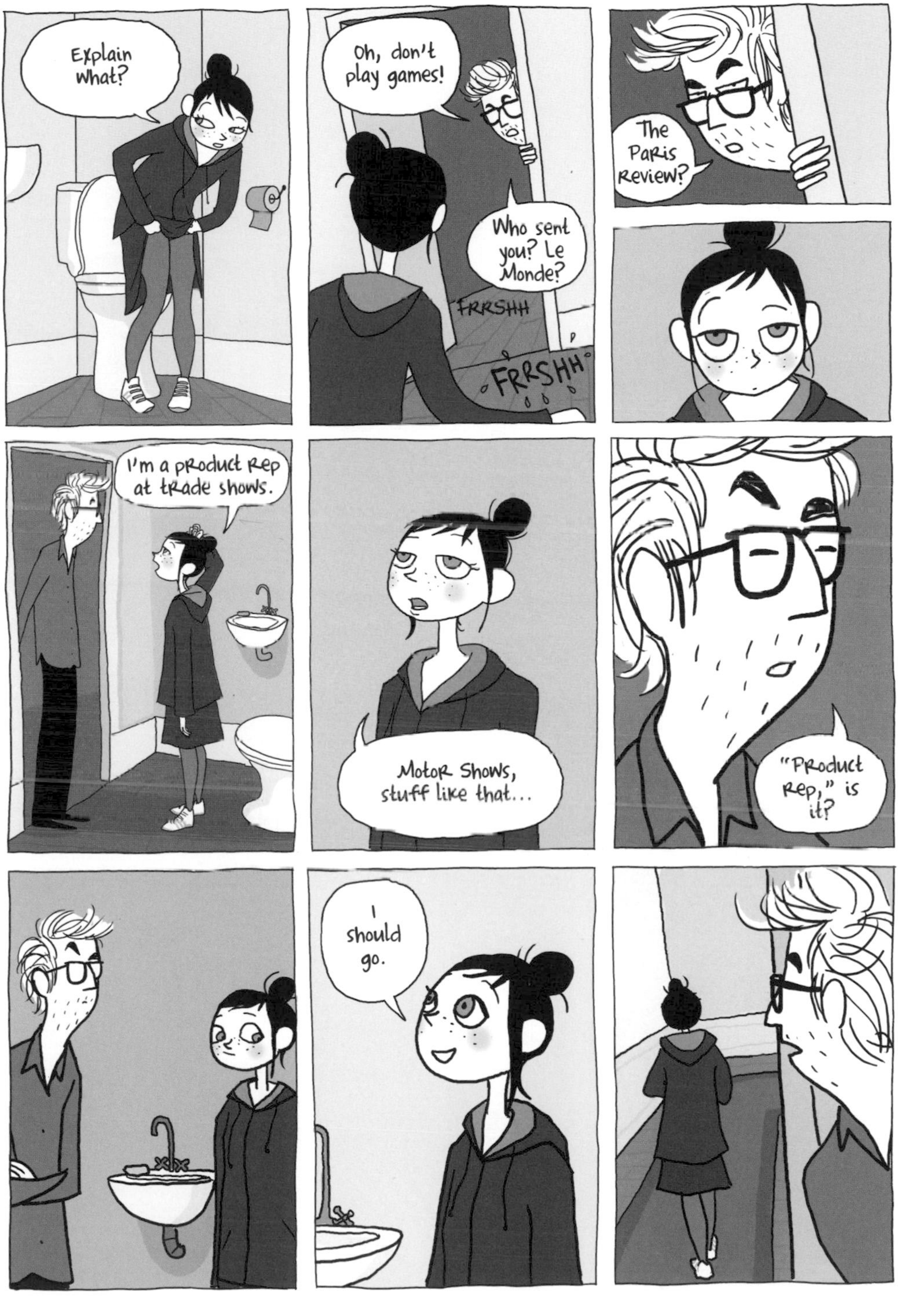
Explain what?
Oh, don't play games!
Who sent you? Le Monde?
FRRSHH
FRRSHH
The Paris Review?
I'm a product rep at trade shows.
Motor shows, stuff like that...
"Product rep," is it?
I should go.

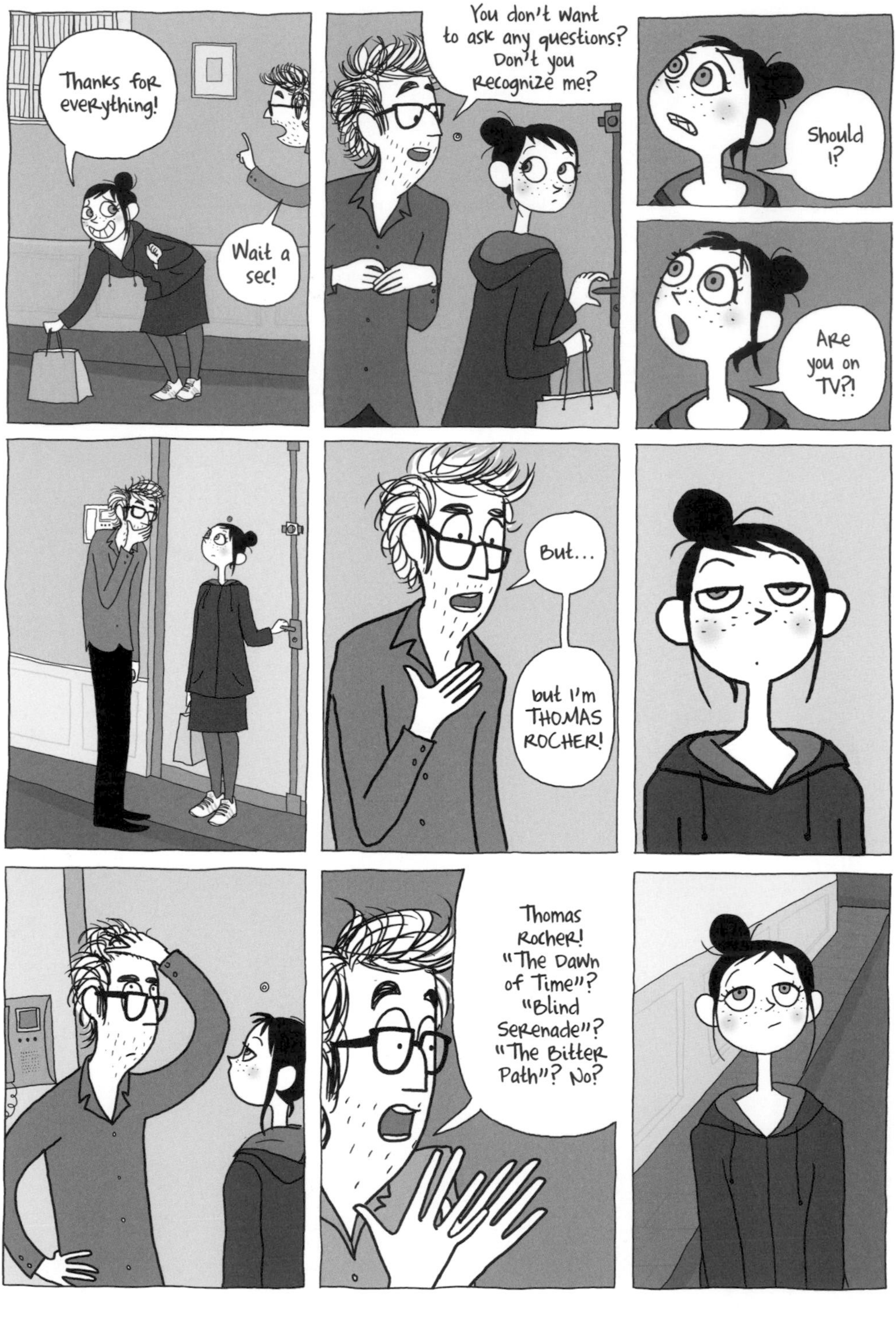
Thanks for everything!
Wait a sec!
You don't want to ask any questions? Don't you recognize me?
Should I?
Are you on TV?!
But...
but I'm THOMAS ROCHER!
Thomas Rocher! "The Dawn of Time"? "Blind Serenade"? "The Bitter Path"? No?

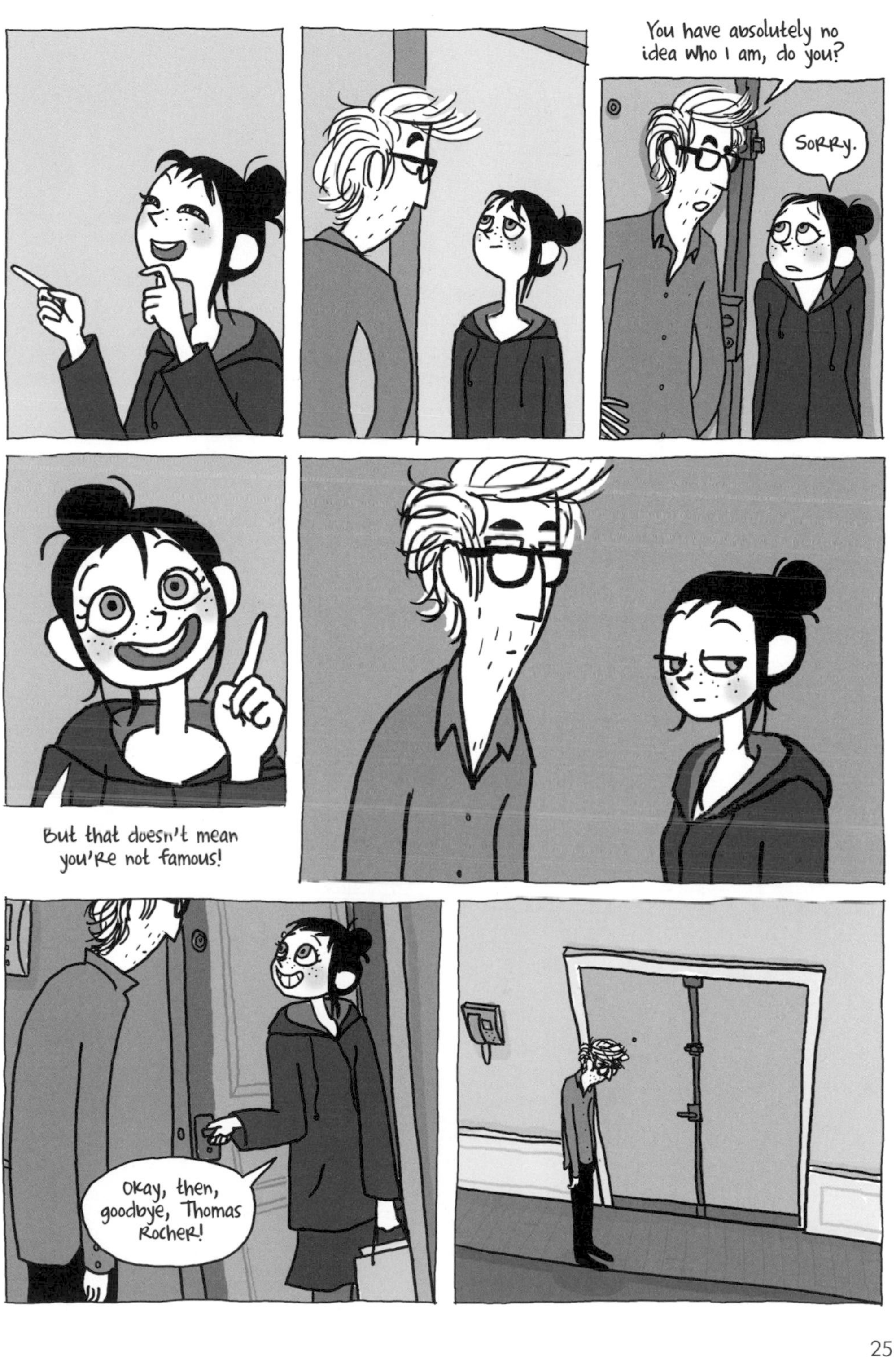

You have absolutely no idea who I am, do you?
Sorry.
But that doesn't mean you're not famous!
Okay, then, goodbye, Thomas Rocher!

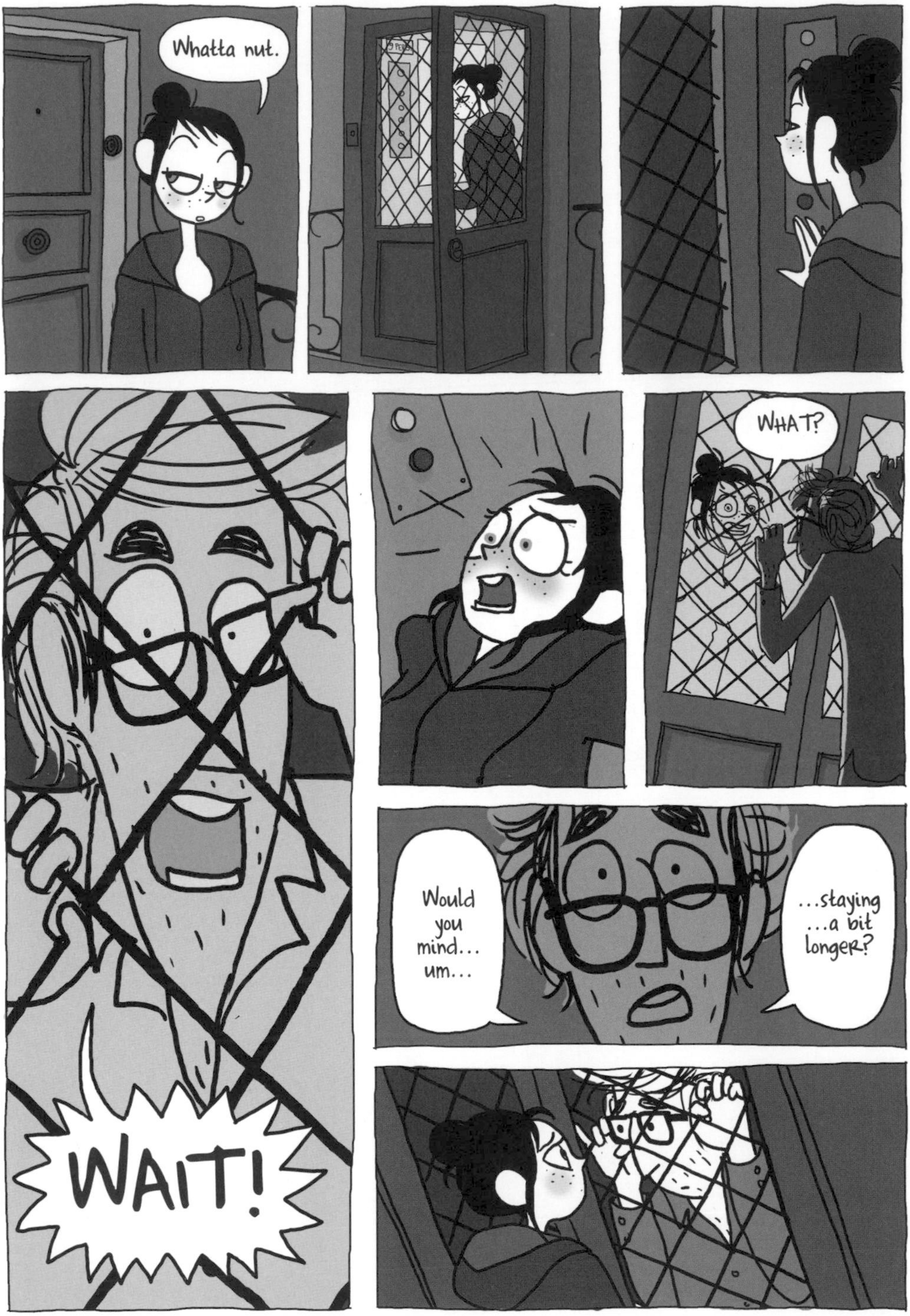
Whatta nut.
WAIT!
WHAT?
Would you mind... um...
...staying ...a bit longer?

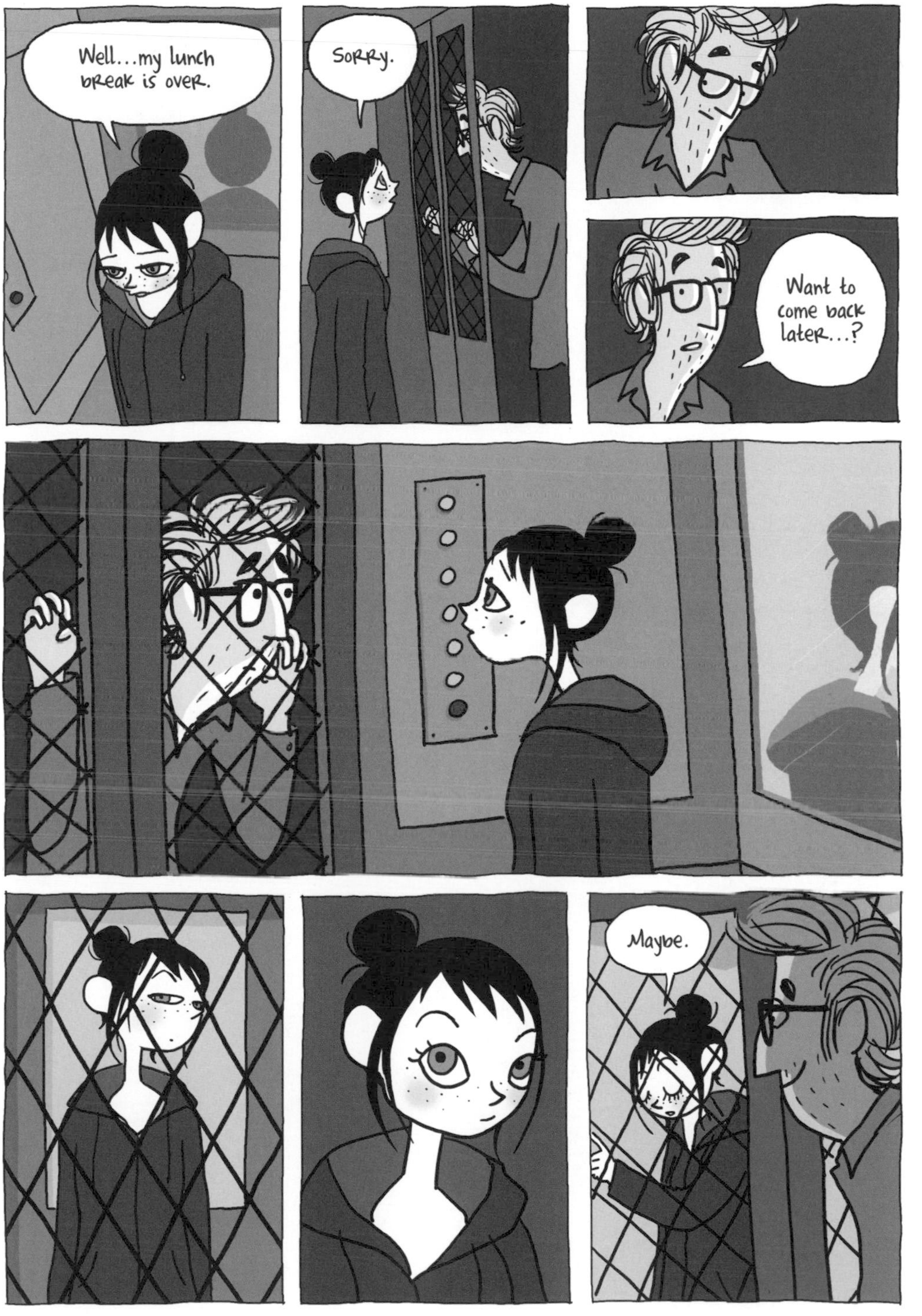
Well...my lunch break is over.
Sorry.
Want to come back later...?
Maybe.

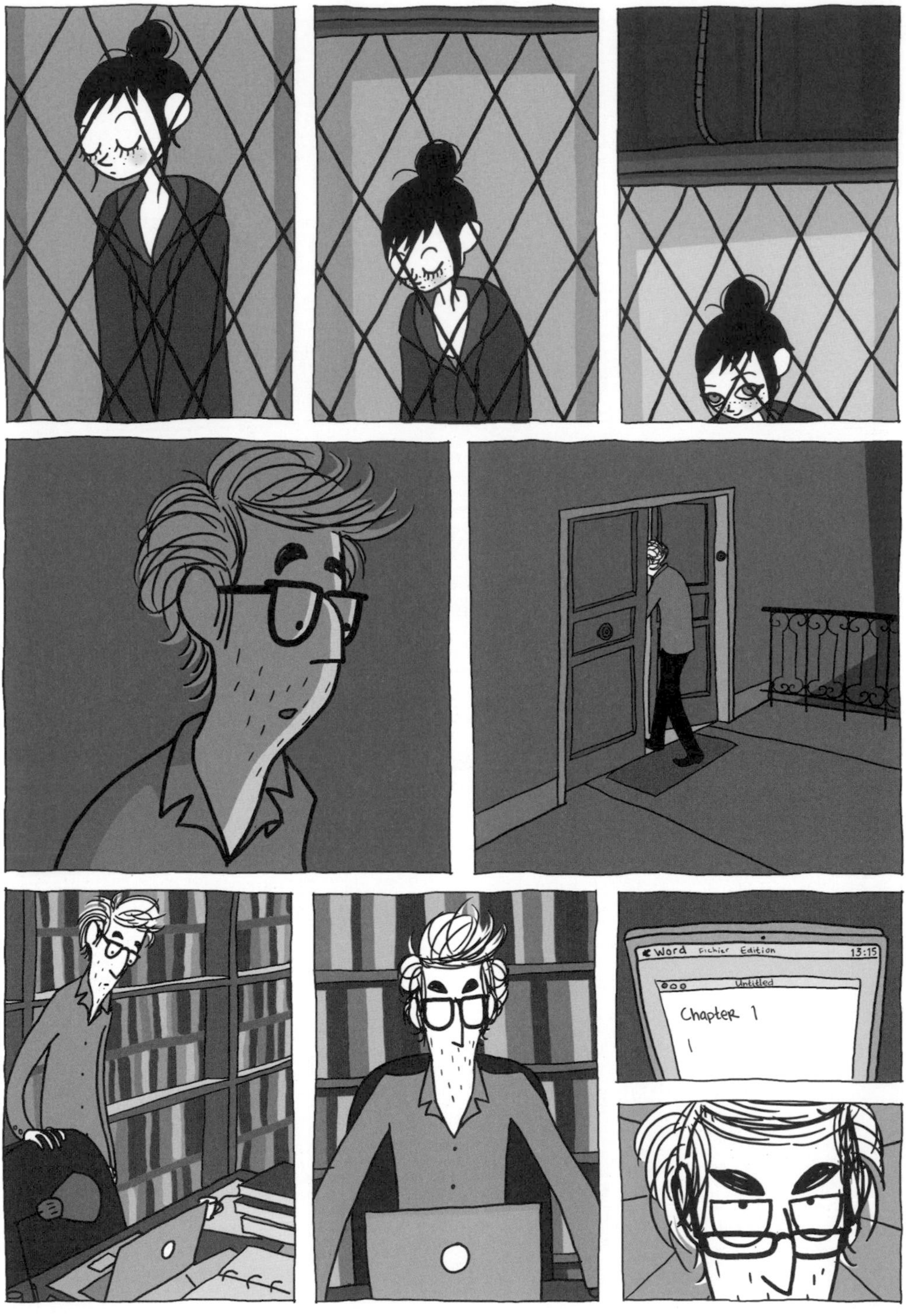
Word Fichier Edition
13:15
Untitled
Chapter 1

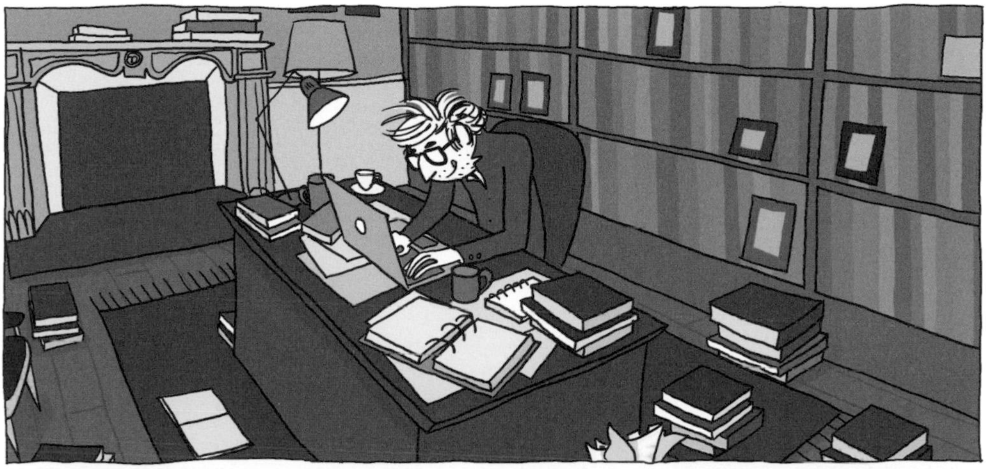

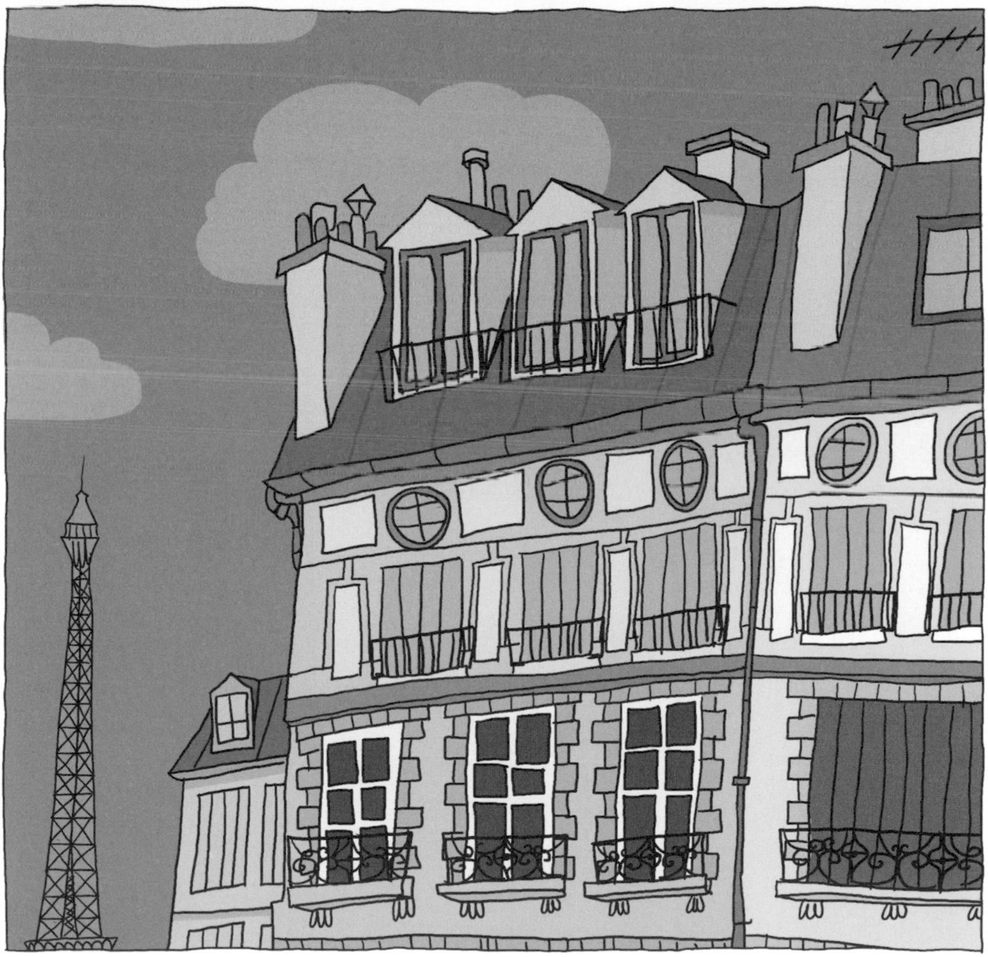

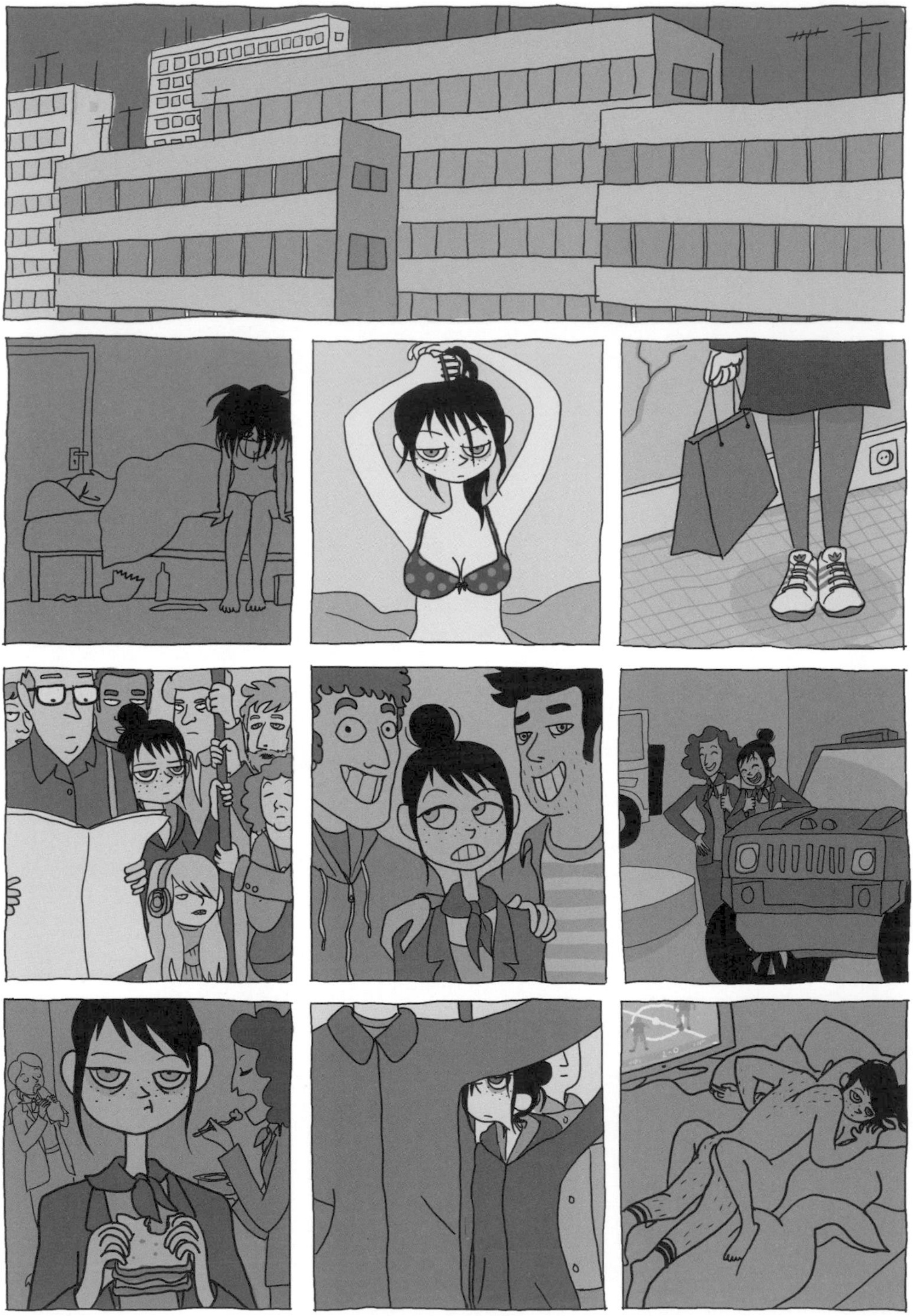

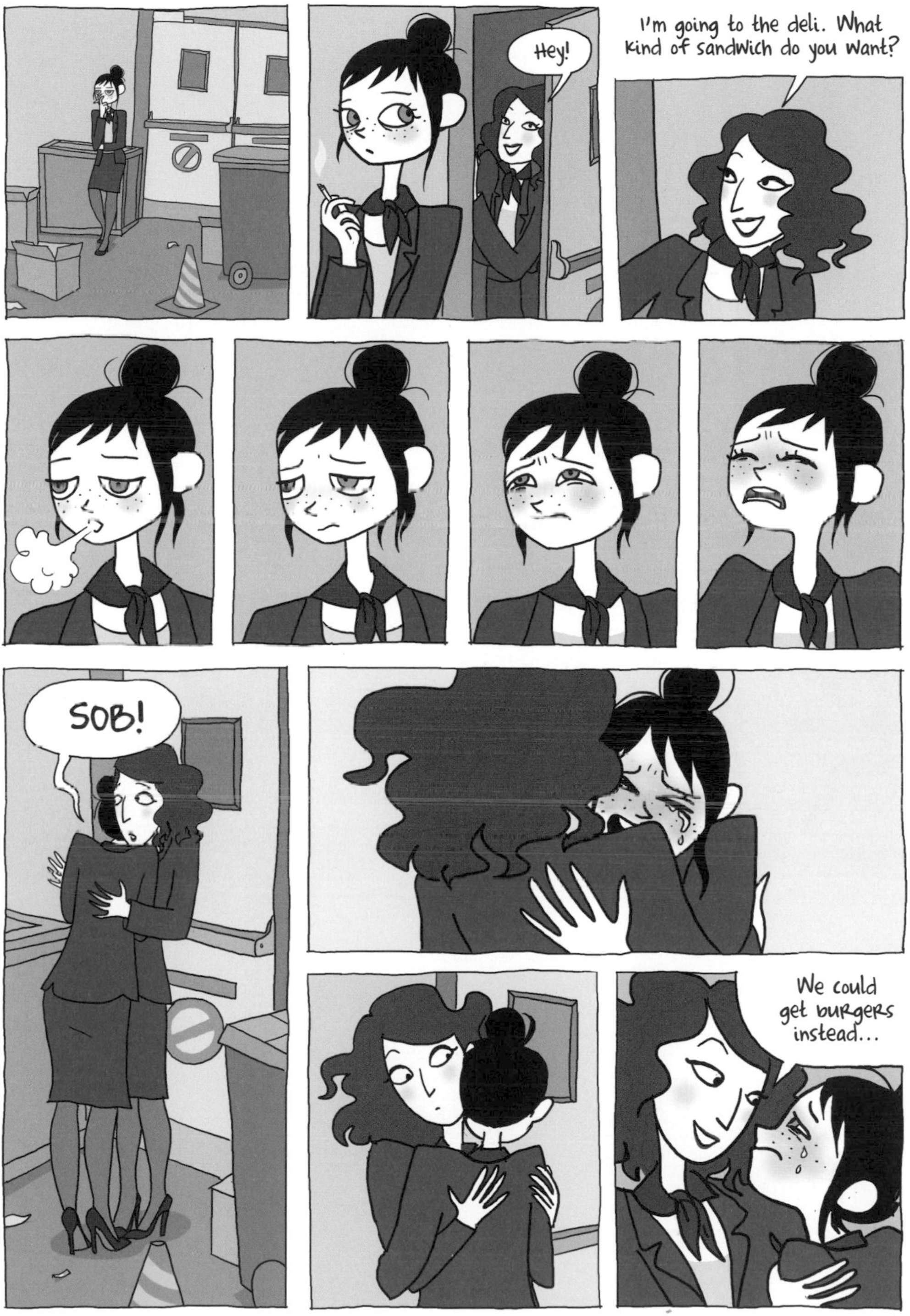
Hey!
I'm going to the deli. What kind of sandwich do you want?
SOB!
We could get burgers instead...

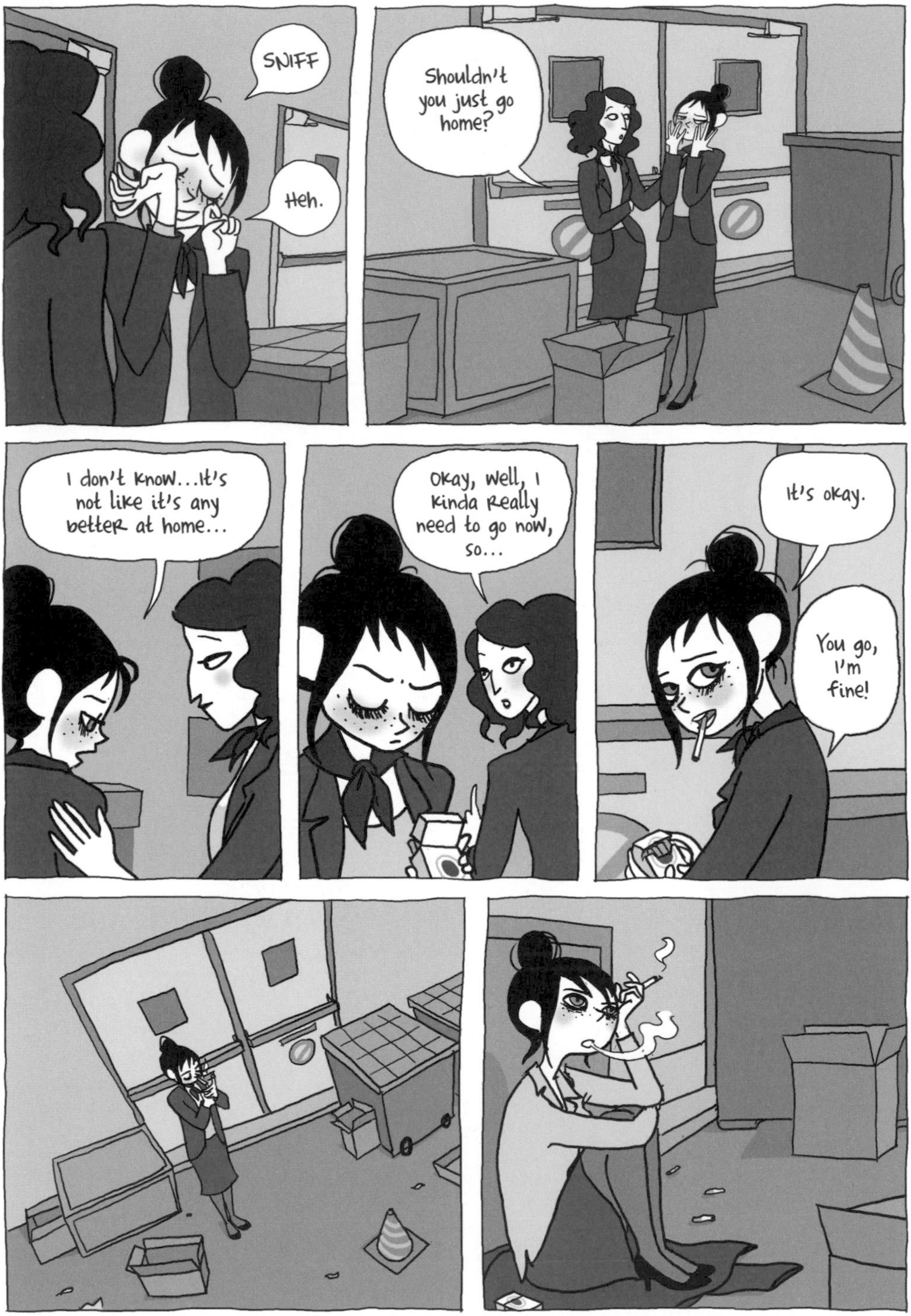
SNIFF
Heh.
Shouldn't you just go home?
I don't know...It's not like it's any better at home...
Okay, well, I kinda really need to go now, so...
It's okay.
You go, I'm fine!

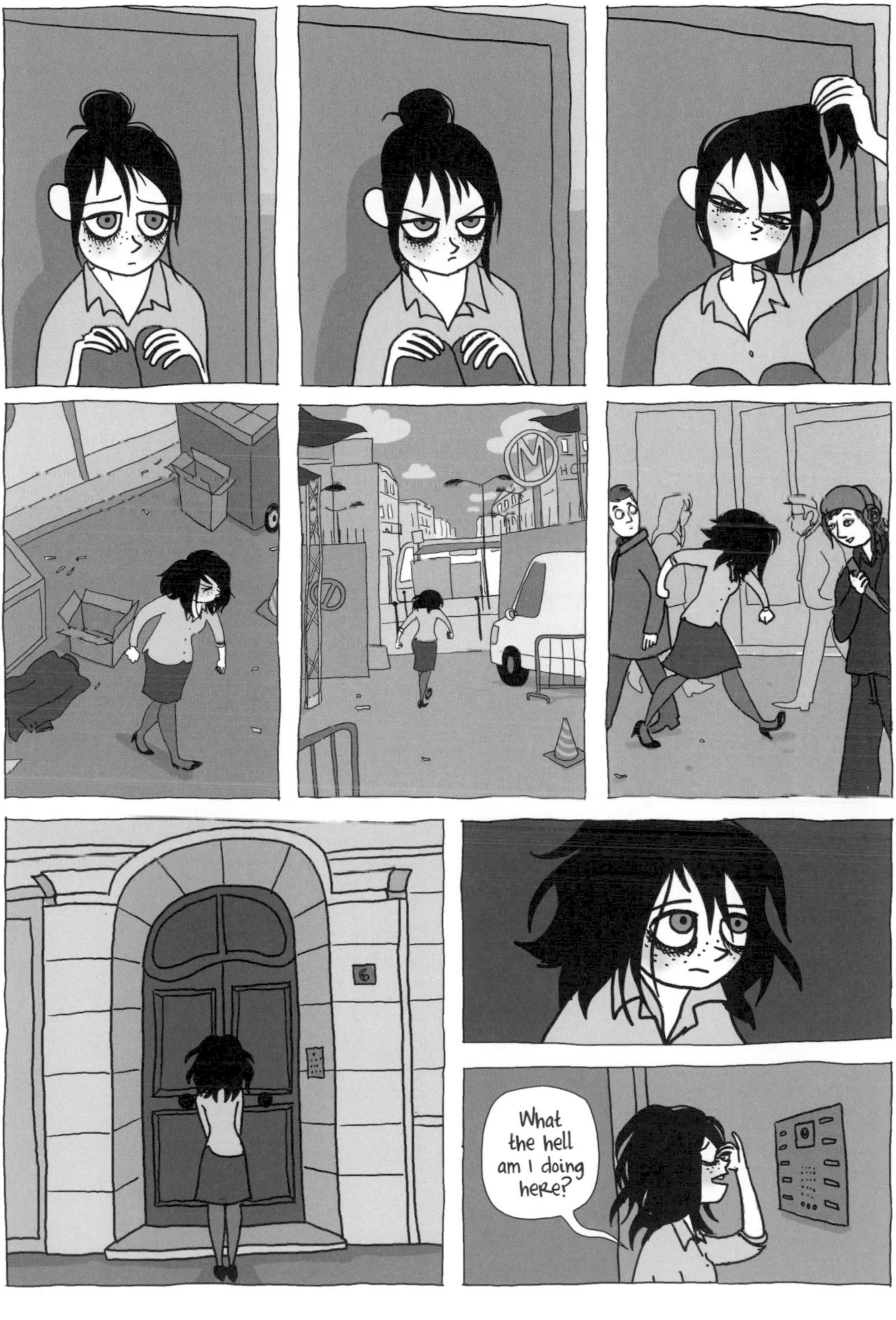
What the hell am I doing here?

BZZZZ

Come on, Run away before he answers...

...

Mister Rocher?

It's Zoe...I...I don't know if you Remember me...

Anybody home?

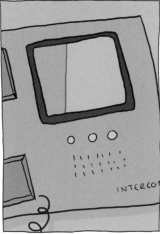

INTERCO

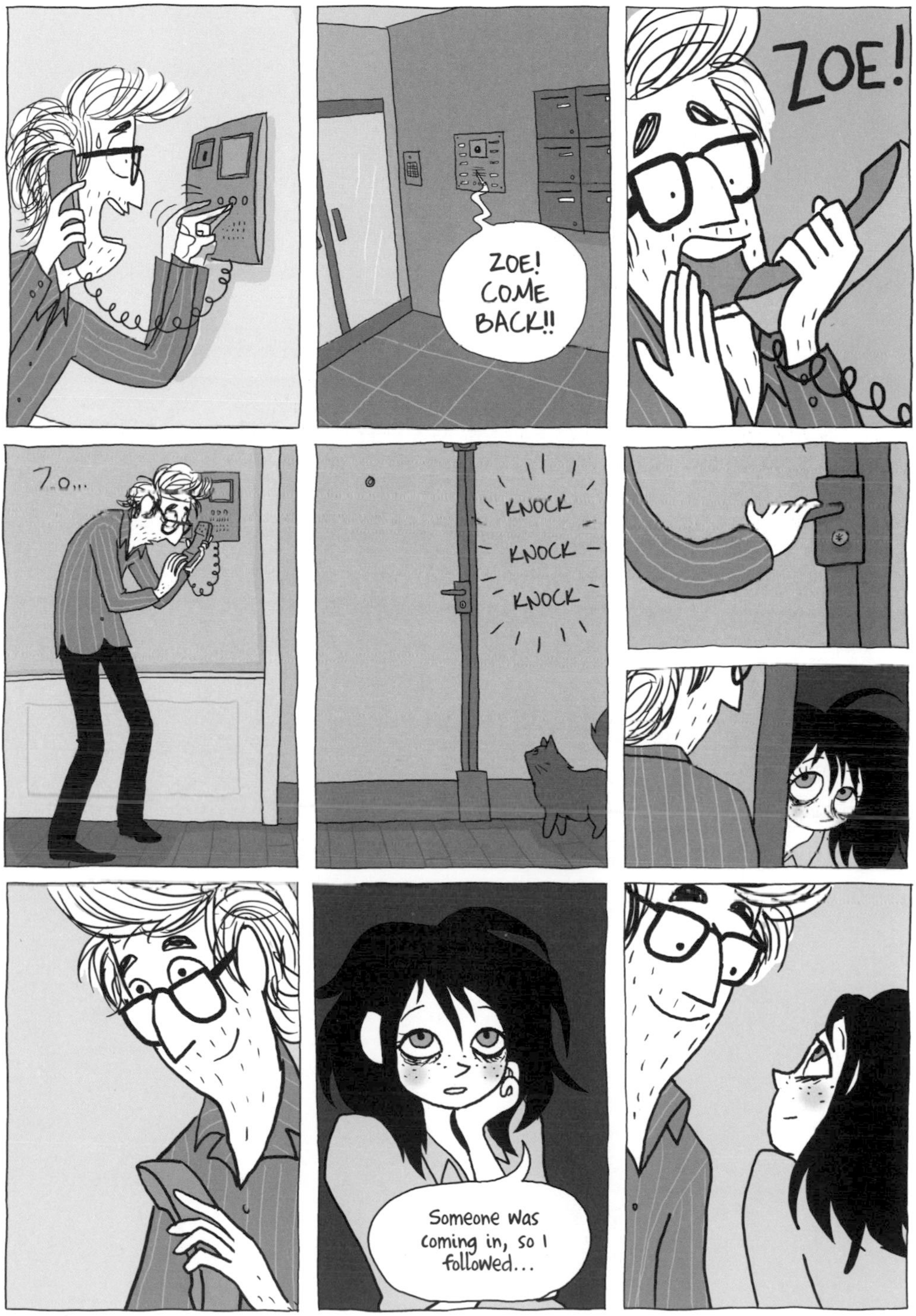
ZOE! COME BACK!!
ZOE!
Zo...
KNOCK
KNOCK
KNOCK
Someone was coming in, so I followed...

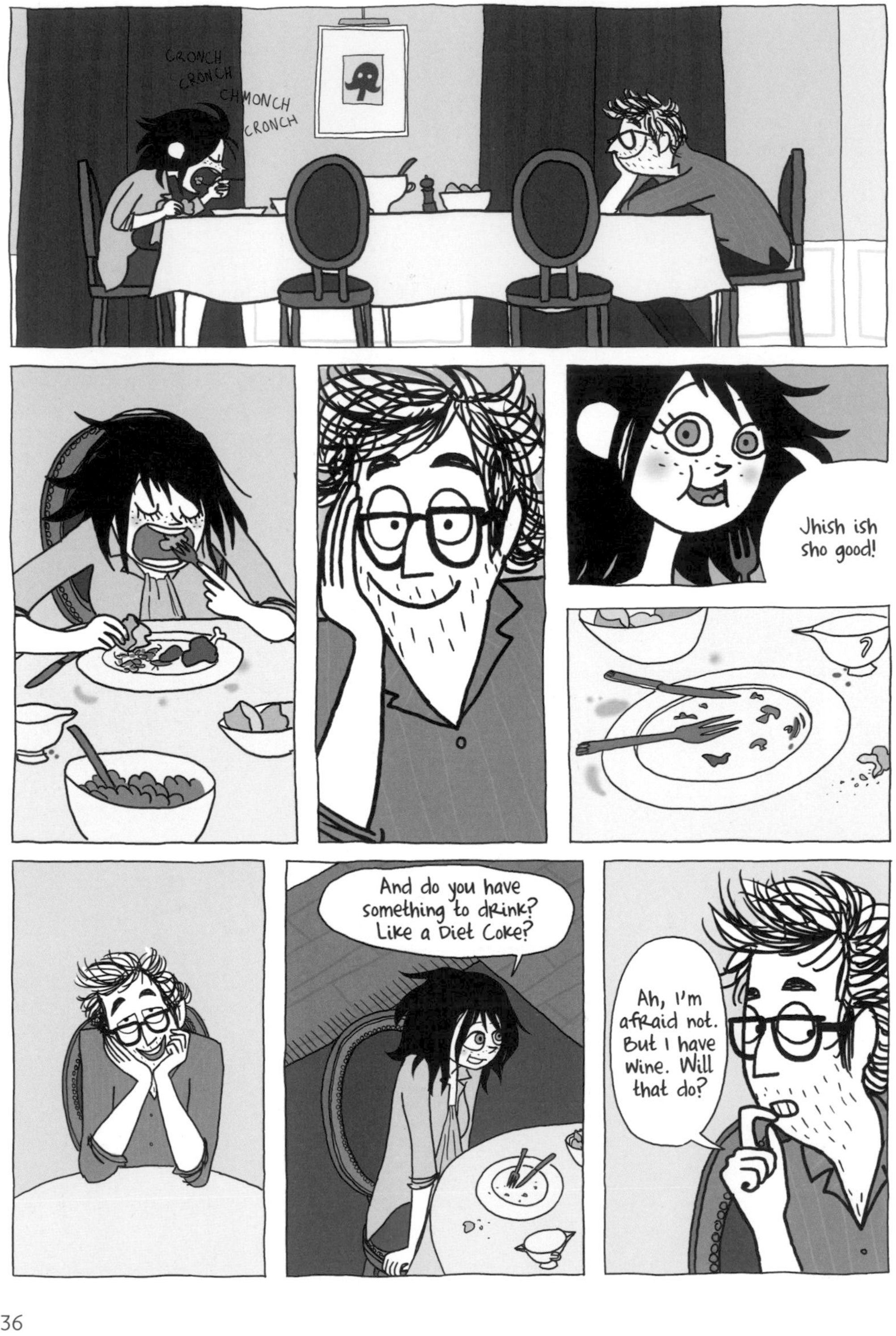
CRONCH
CRONCH
CHMONCH
CRONCH
Jhish ish sho good!
And do you have something to drink? Like a Diet Coke?
Ah, I'm afraid not. But I have wine. Will that do?

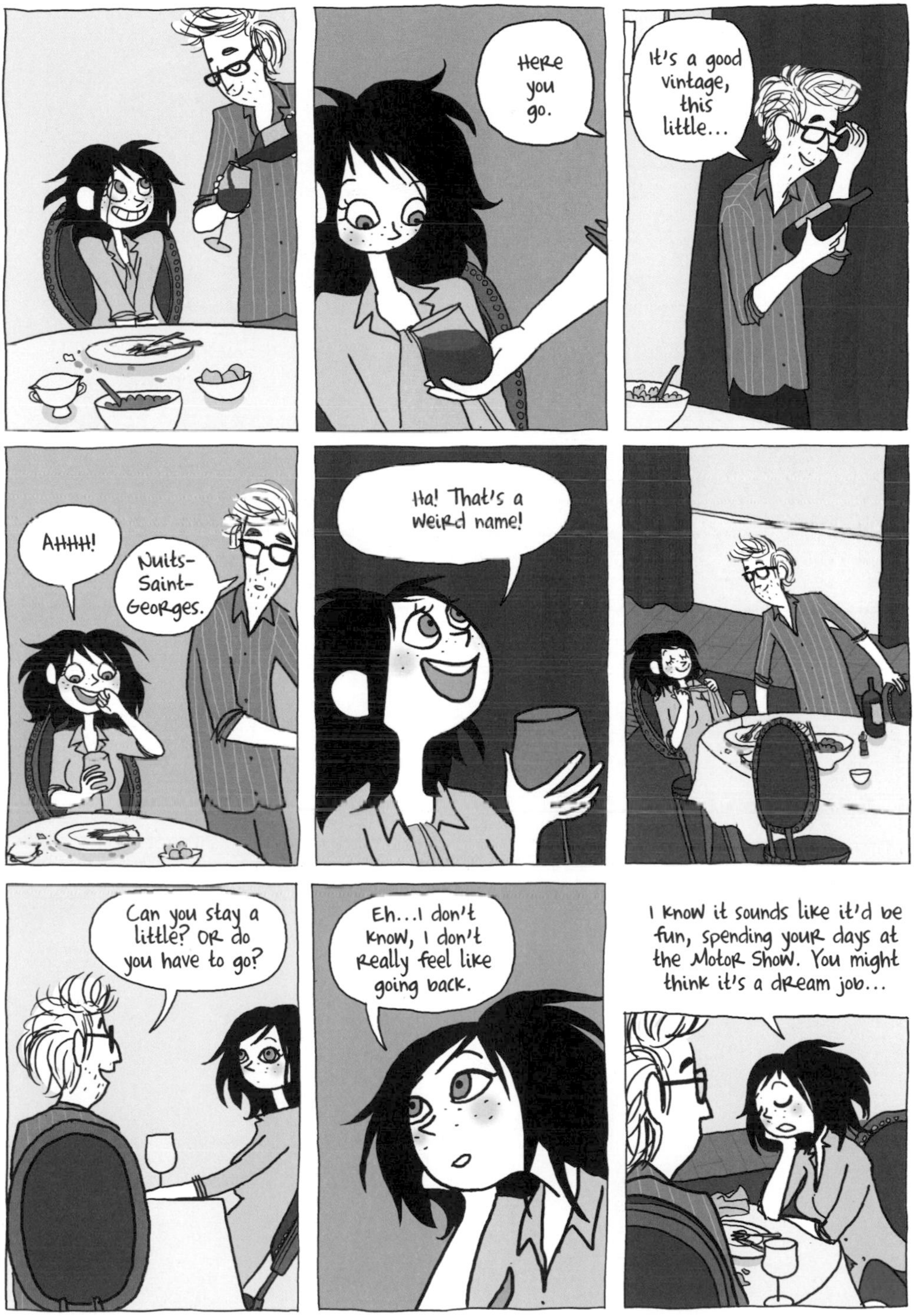
Here you go.
It's a good vintage, this little...
AHHH!
Nuits-Saint-Georges.
Ha! That's a weird name!
Can you stay a little? Or do you have to go?
Eh...I don't know, I don't really feel like going back.
I know it sounds like it'd be fun, spending your days at the Motor Show. You might think it's a dream job...

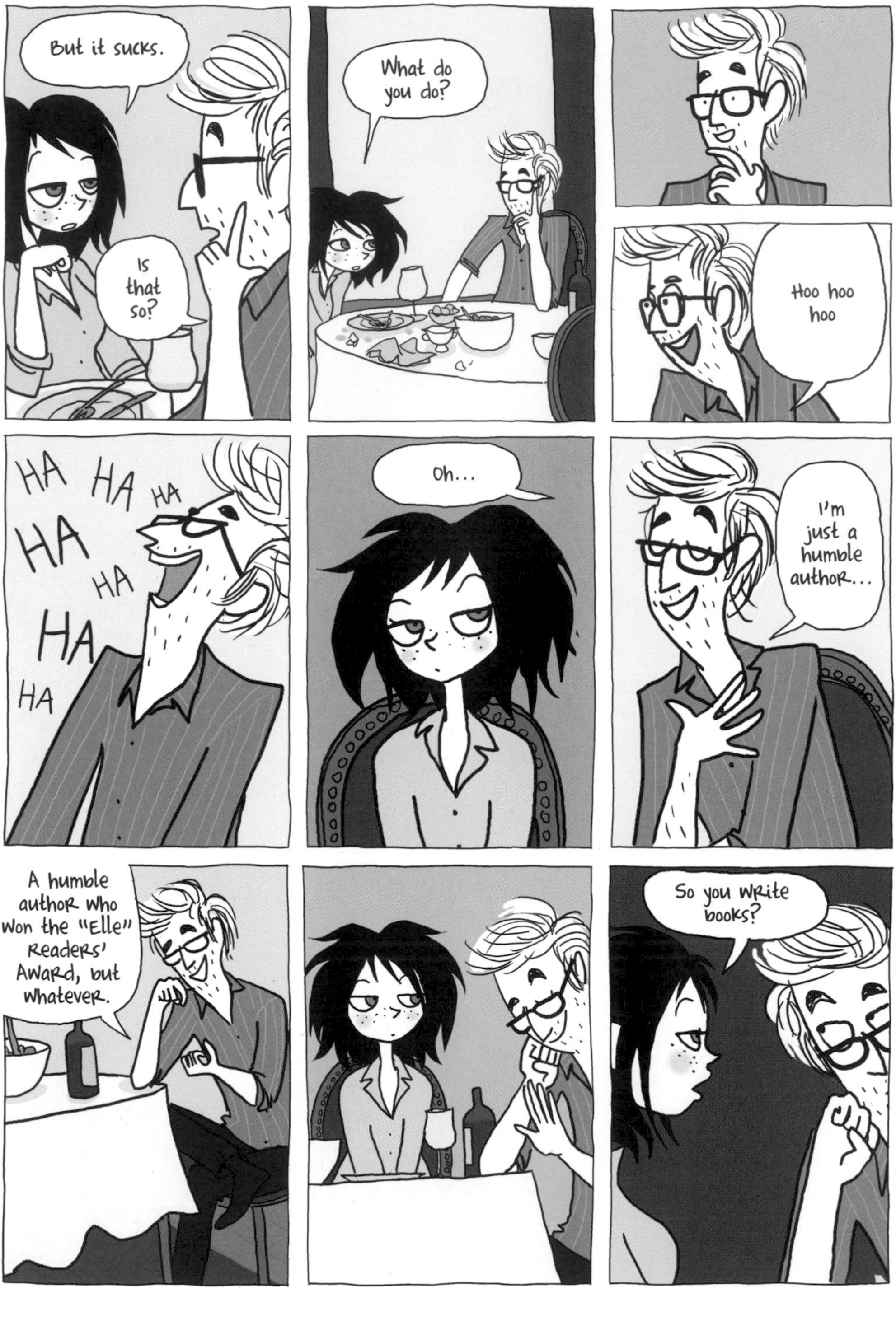

But it sucks.
Is that so?
What do you do?
Hoo hoo hoo
HA HA HA HA HA HA HA
Oh...
I'm just a humble author...
A humble author who won the "Elle" Readers' Award, but whatever.
So you write books?

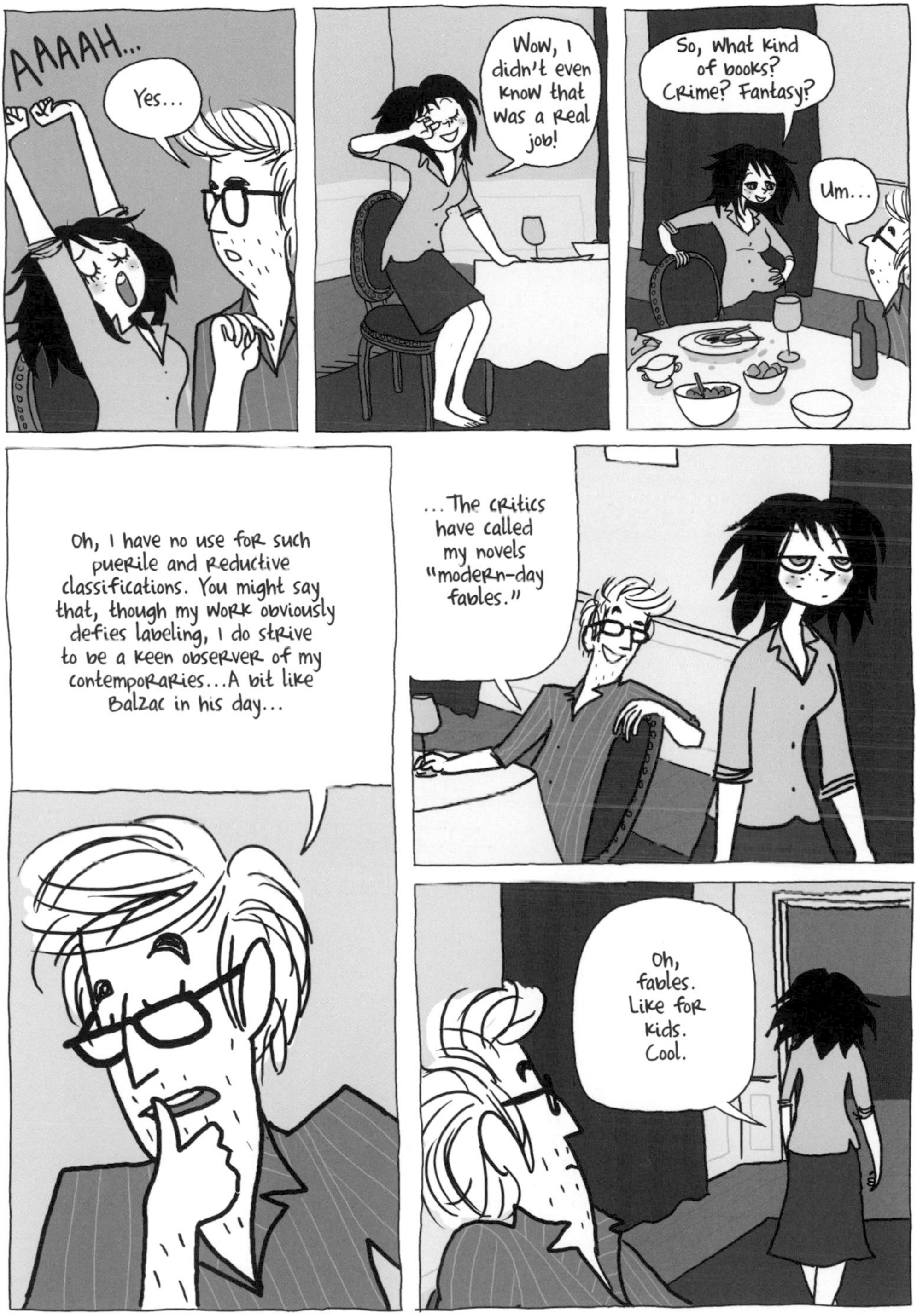

AAAAH...
Yes...
Wow, I didn't even know that was a real job!
So, what kind of books? Crime? Fantasy?
Um...
Oh, I have no use for such puerile and reductive classifications. You might say that, though my work obviously defies labeling, I do strive to be a keen observer of my contemporaries... A bit like Balzac in his day...
...The critics have called my novels "modern-day fables."
Oh, fables. Like for kids. Cool.

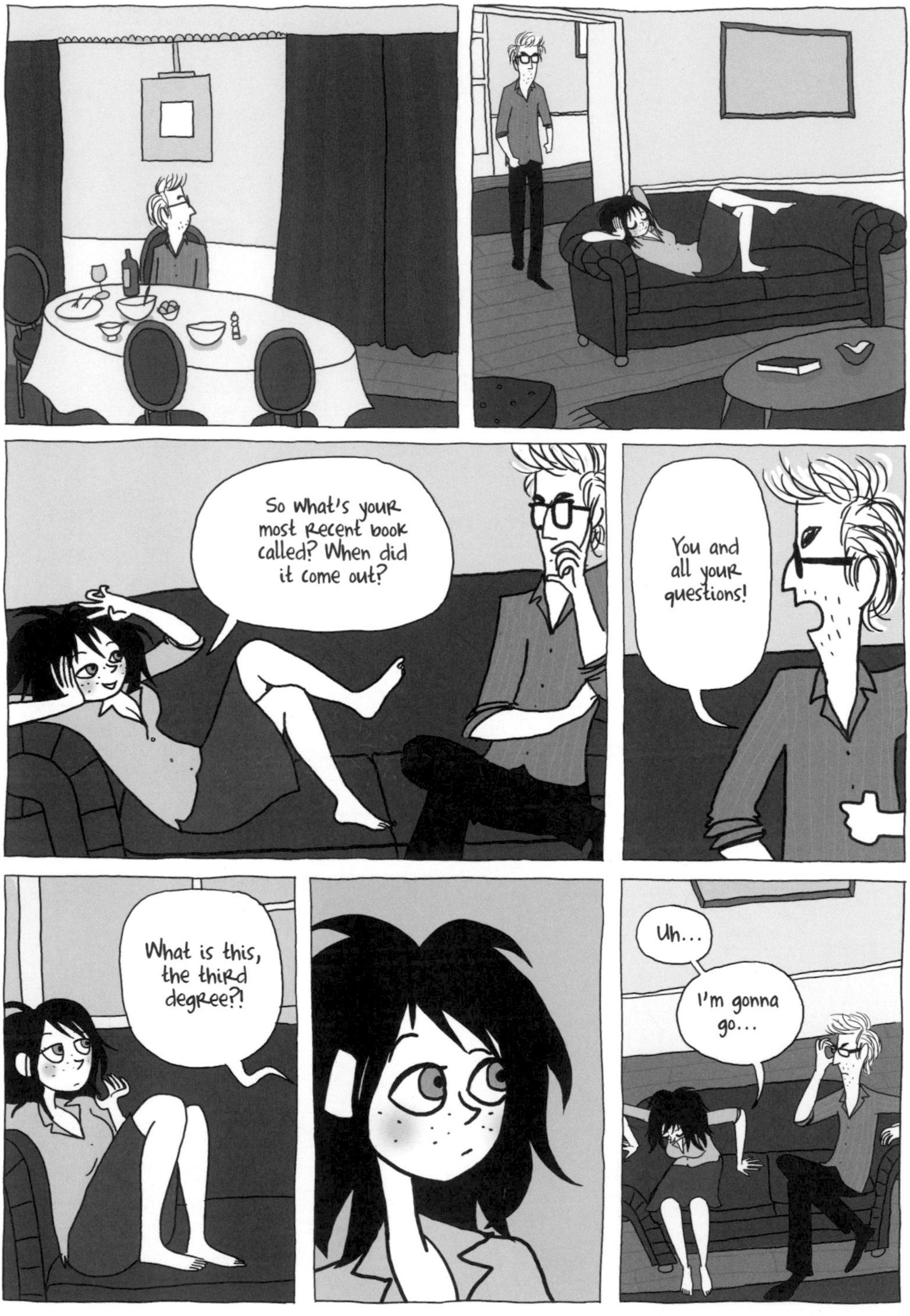

So what's your most recent book called? When did it come out?
You and all your questions!
What is this, the third degree?!
Uh...
I'm gonna go...

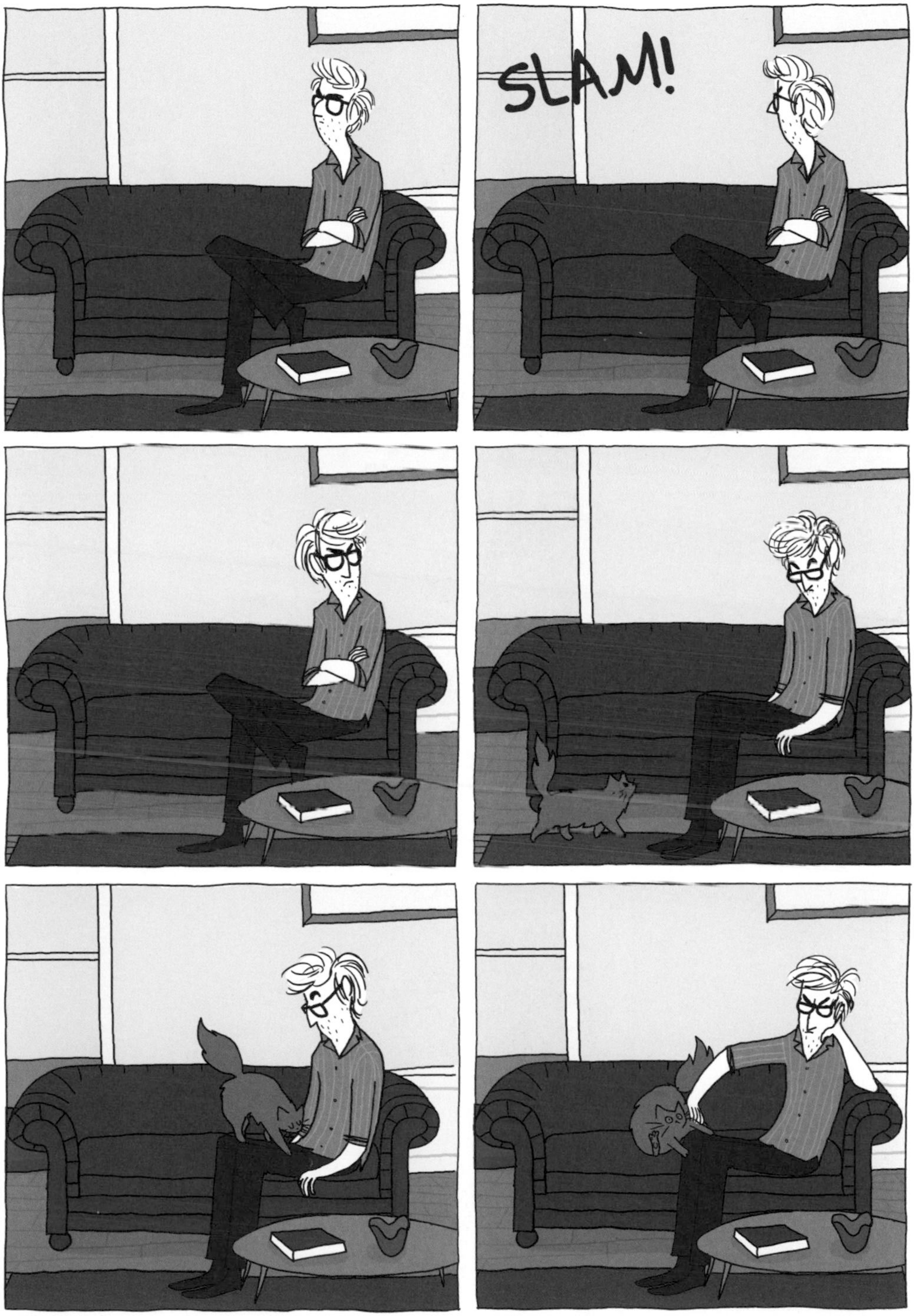
SLAM!

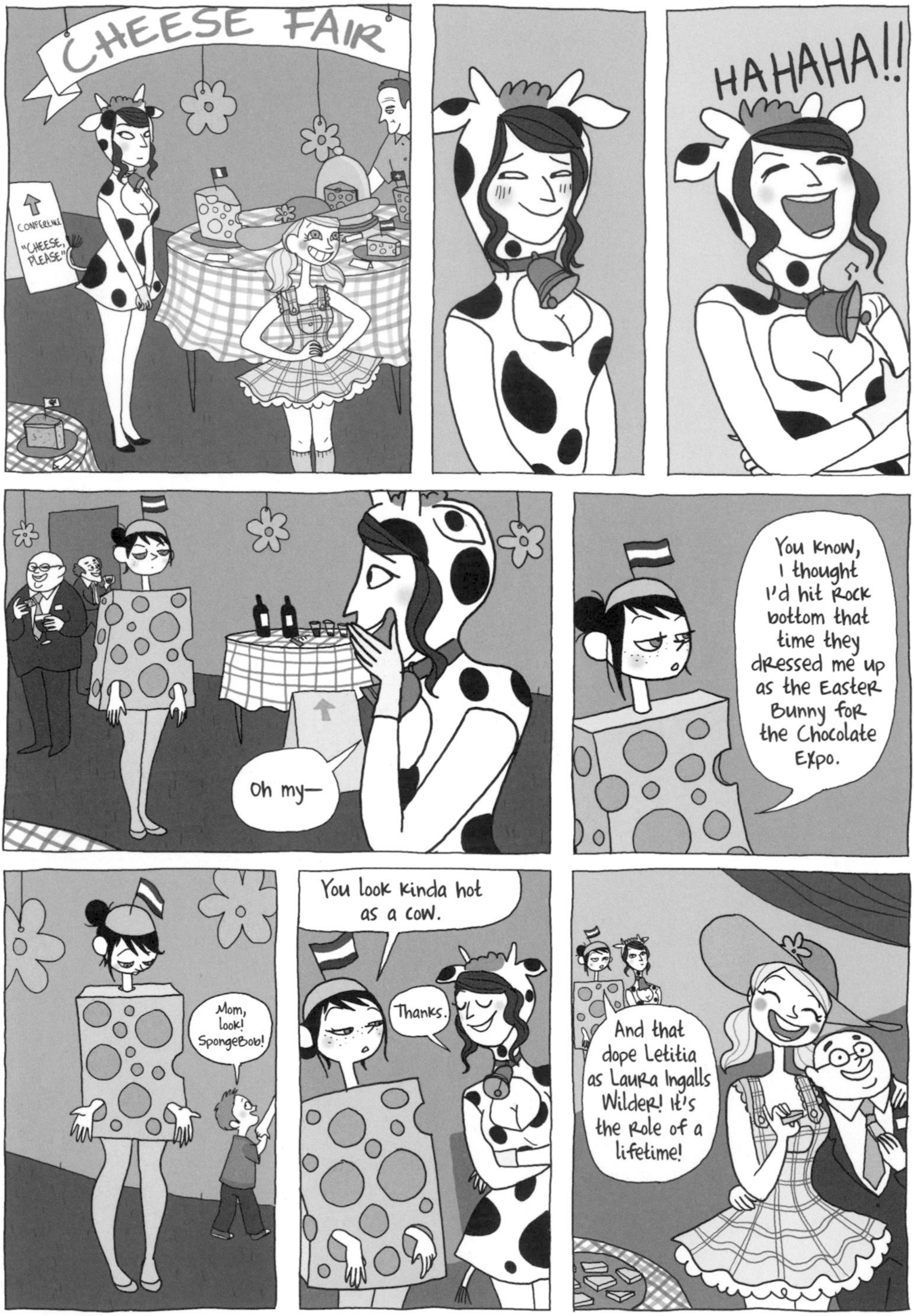
CHEESE FAIR
CONFERENCE "CHEESE, PLEASE"
HAHAHA!!
Oh my—
You know, I thought I'd hit rock bottom that time they dressed me up as the Easter Bunny for the Chocolate Expo.
Mom, look! SpongeBob!
You look kinda hot as a cow.
Thanks.
And that dope Letitia as Laura Ingalls Wilder! It's the role of a lifetime!

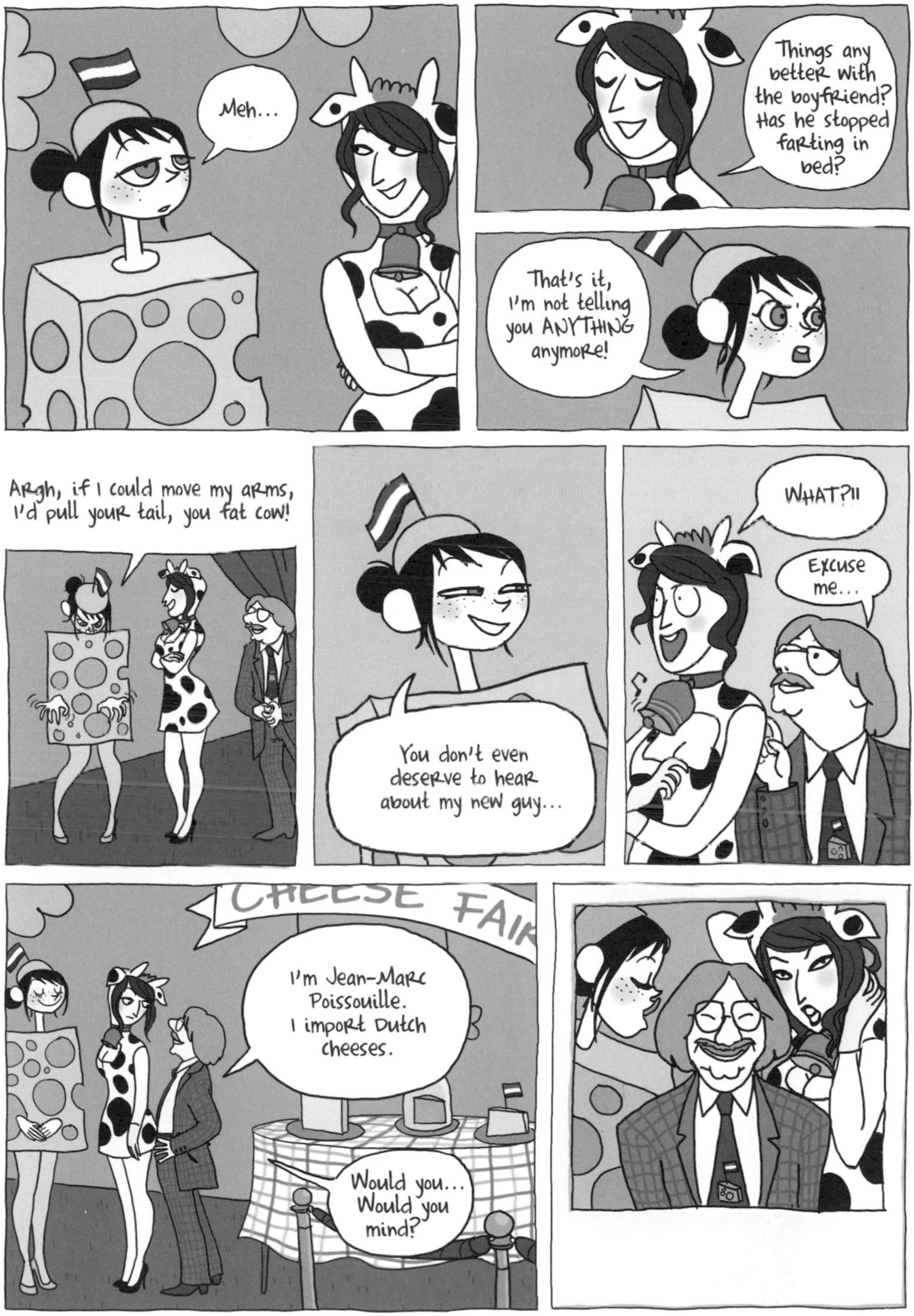

Meh...
Things any better with the boyfriend? Has he stopped farting in bed?
That's it, I'm not telling you ANYTHING anymore!
Argh, if I could move my arms, I'd pull your tail, you fat cow!
You don't even deserve to hear about my new guy...
WHAT?!!
Excuse me...
CHEESE FAIR
I'm Jean-Marc Poissouille. I import Dutch cheeses.
Would you... Would you mind?

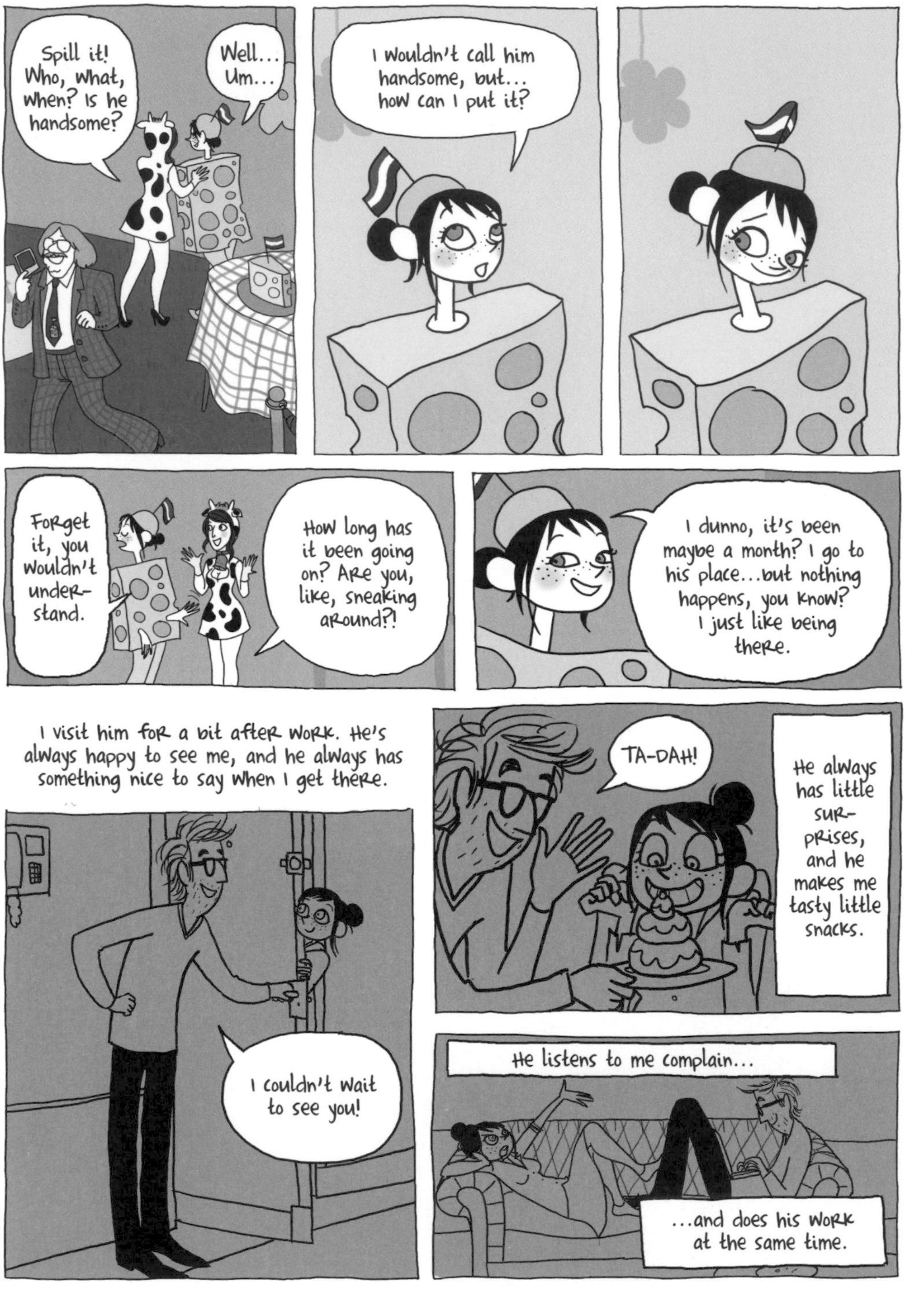
Spill it! Who, what, when? Is he handsome?
Well... Um...
I wouldn't call him handsome, but... how can I put it?
Forget it, you wouldn't under-stand.
How long has it been going on? Are you, like, sneaking around?!
I dunno, it's been maybe a month? I go to his place...but nothing happens, you know? I just like being there.
I visit him for a bit after work. He's always happy to see me, and he always has something nice to say when I get there.
I couldn't wait to see you!
TA-DAH!
He always has little sur-prises, and he makes me tasty little snacks.
He listens to me complain...
...and does his work at the same time.

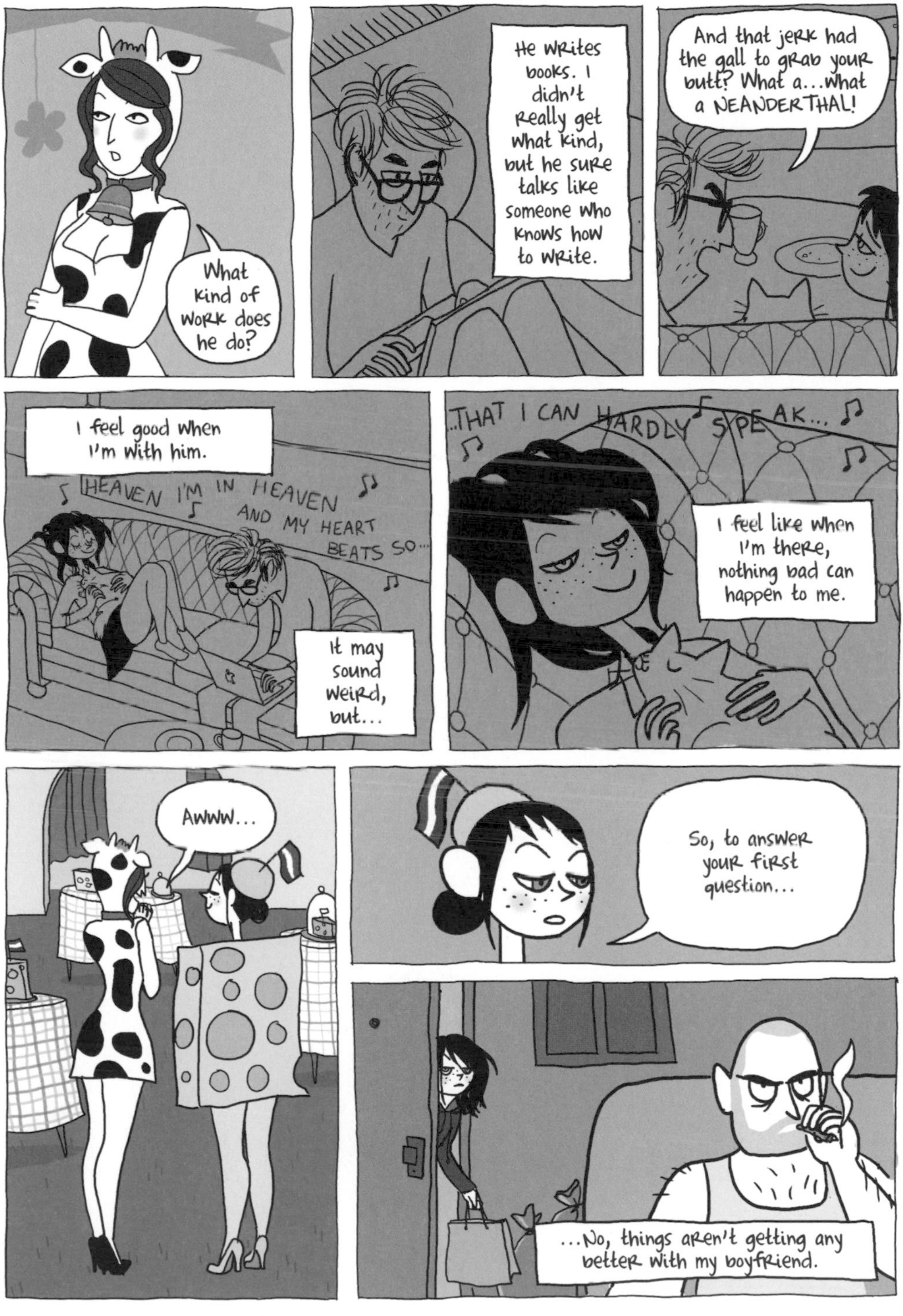
What kind of work does he do?
He writes books. I didn't really get what kind, but he sure talks like someone who knows how to write.
And that jerk had the gall to grab your butt? What a...what a NEANDERTHAL!
I feel good when I'm with him.
HEAVEN I'M IN HEAVEN AND MY HEART BEATS SO...
It may sound weird, but...
..THAT I CAN HARDLY SPEAK...
I feel like when I'm there, nothing bad can happen to me.
AWWW...
So, to answer your first question...
...No, things aren't getting any better with my boyfriend.

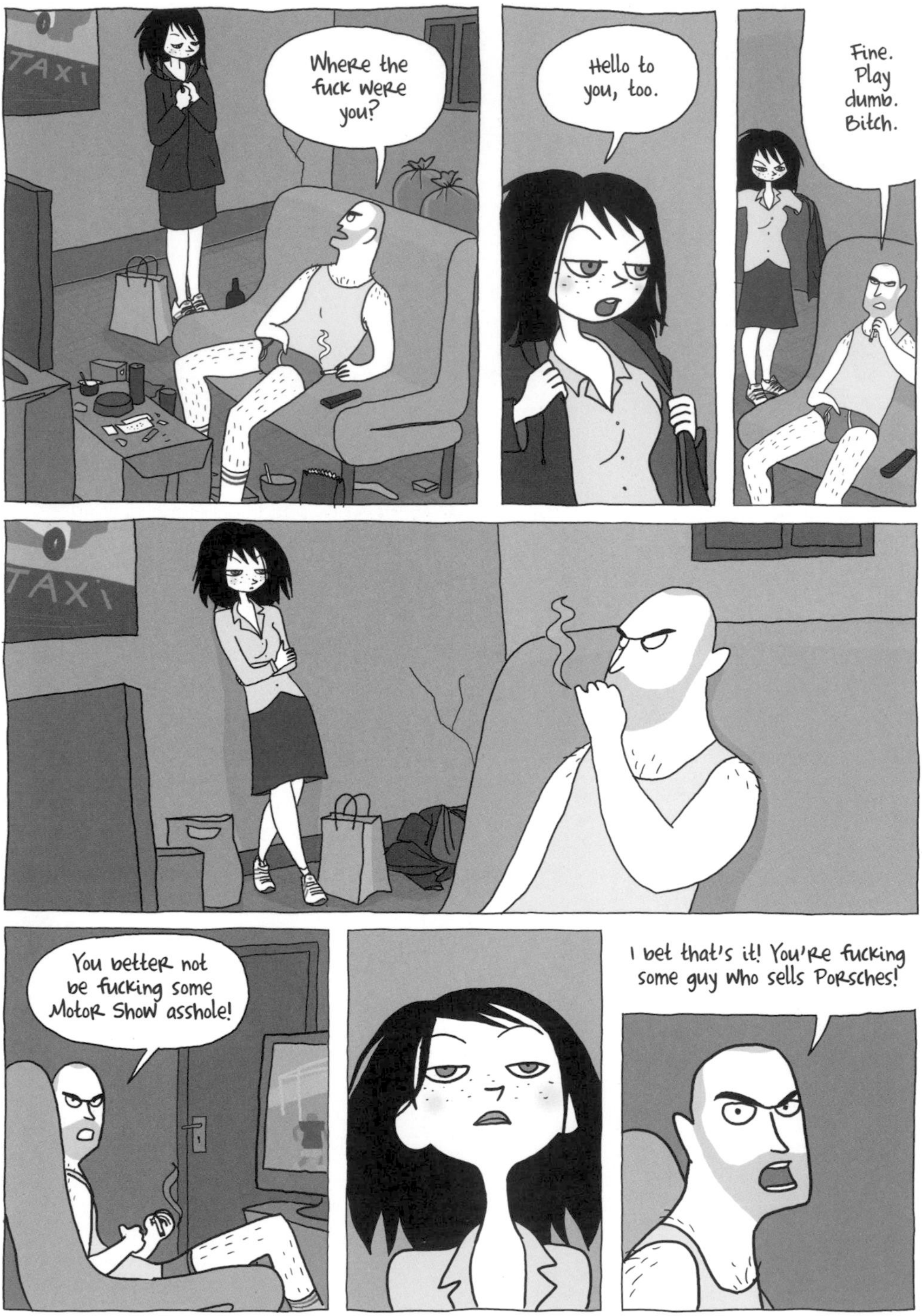
Where the fuck were you?
Hello to you, too.
Fine. Play dumb. Bitch.
TAXi
You better not be fucking some Motor Show asshole!
I bet that's it! You're fucking some guy who sells Porsches!

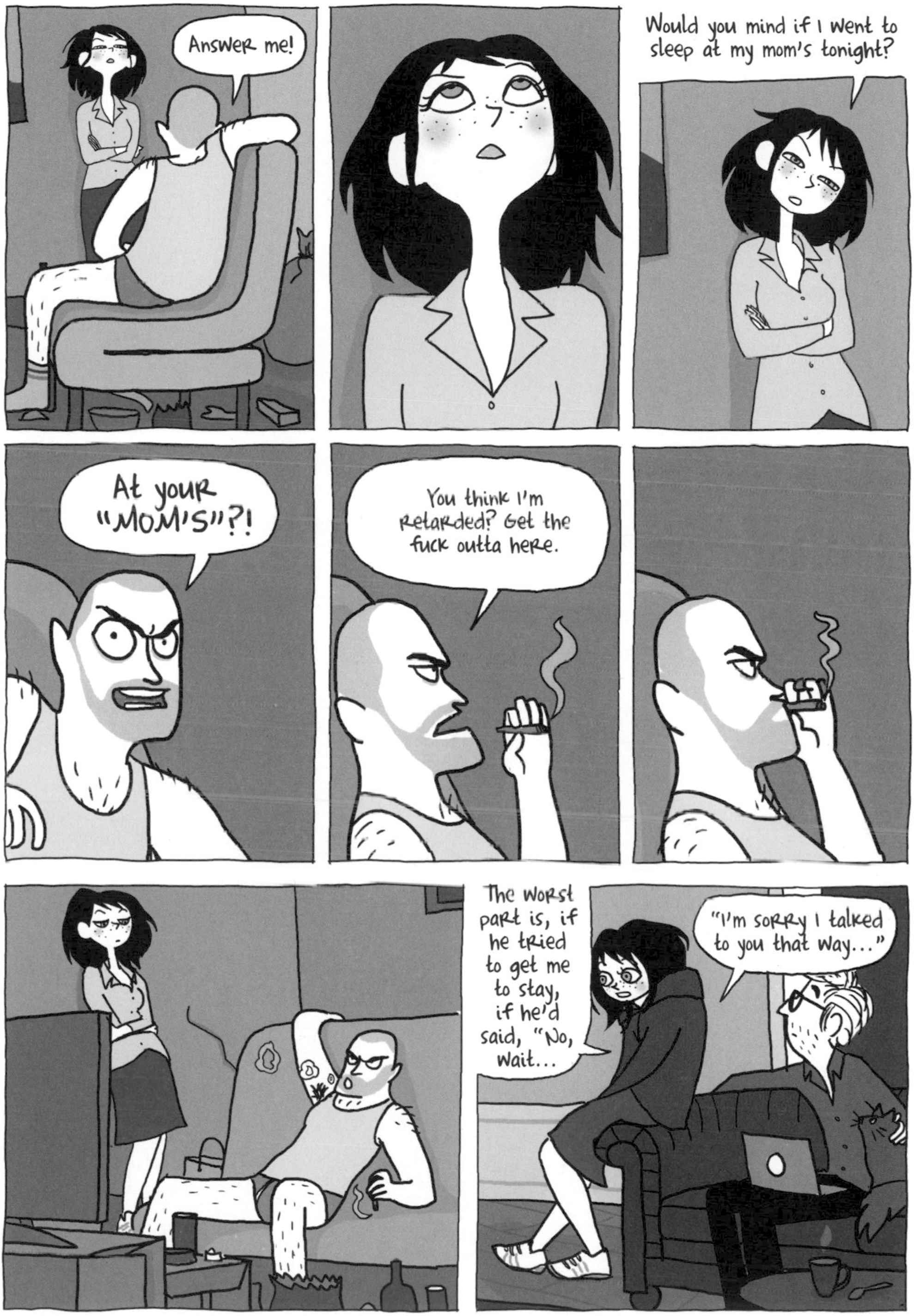
Answer me!
Would you mind if I went to sleep at my mom's tonight?
At your "MOM'S"?!
You think I'm retarded? Get the fuck outta here.
The worst part is, if he tried to get me to stay, if he'd said, "No, wait...
"I'm sorry I talked to you that way..."

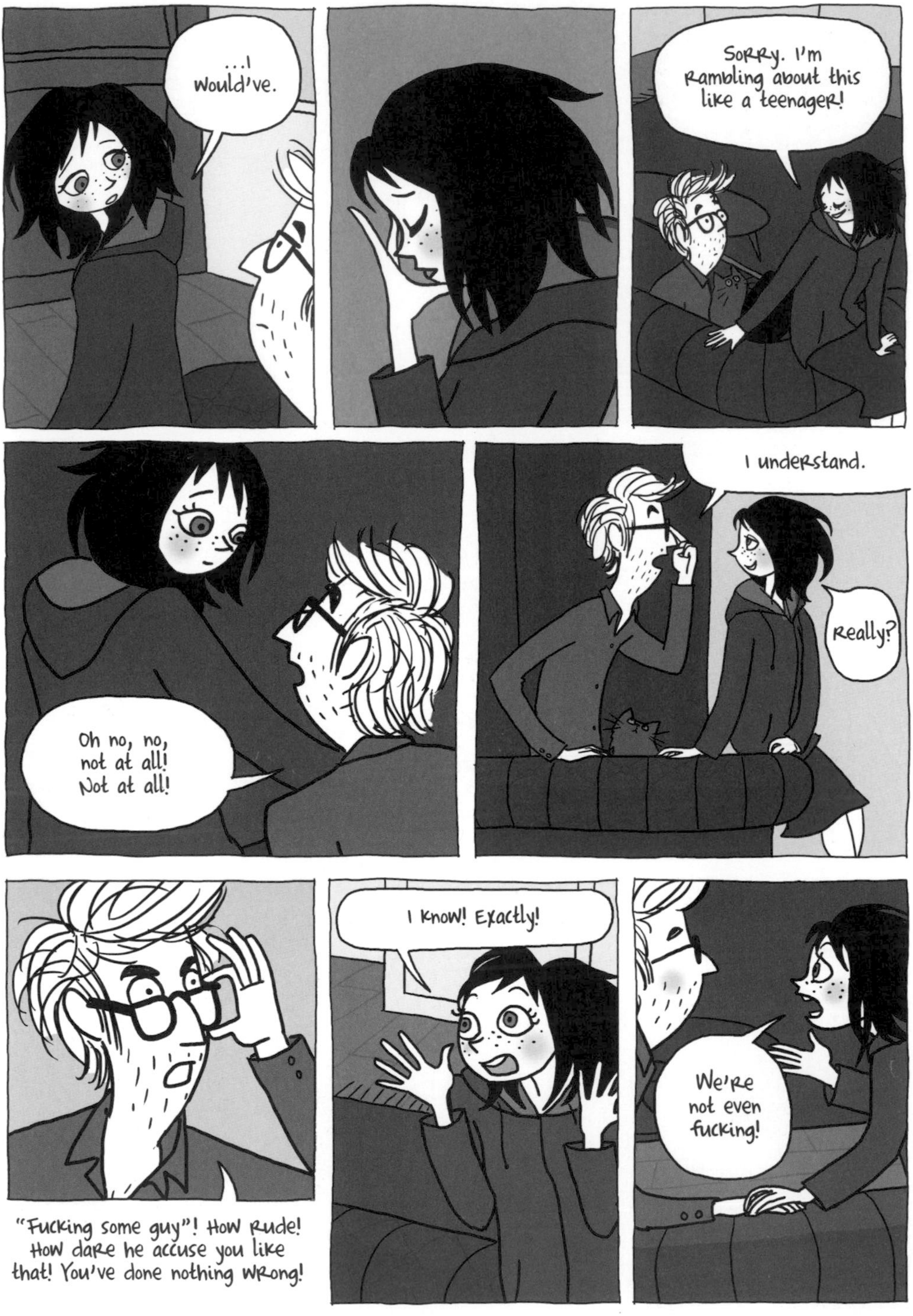

...I would've.
Sorry. I'm rambling about this like a teenager!
Oh no, no, not at all! Not at all!
I understand.
Really?
"Fucking some guy"! How rude! How dare he accuse you like that! You've done nothing wrong!
I know! Exactly!
We're not even fucking!

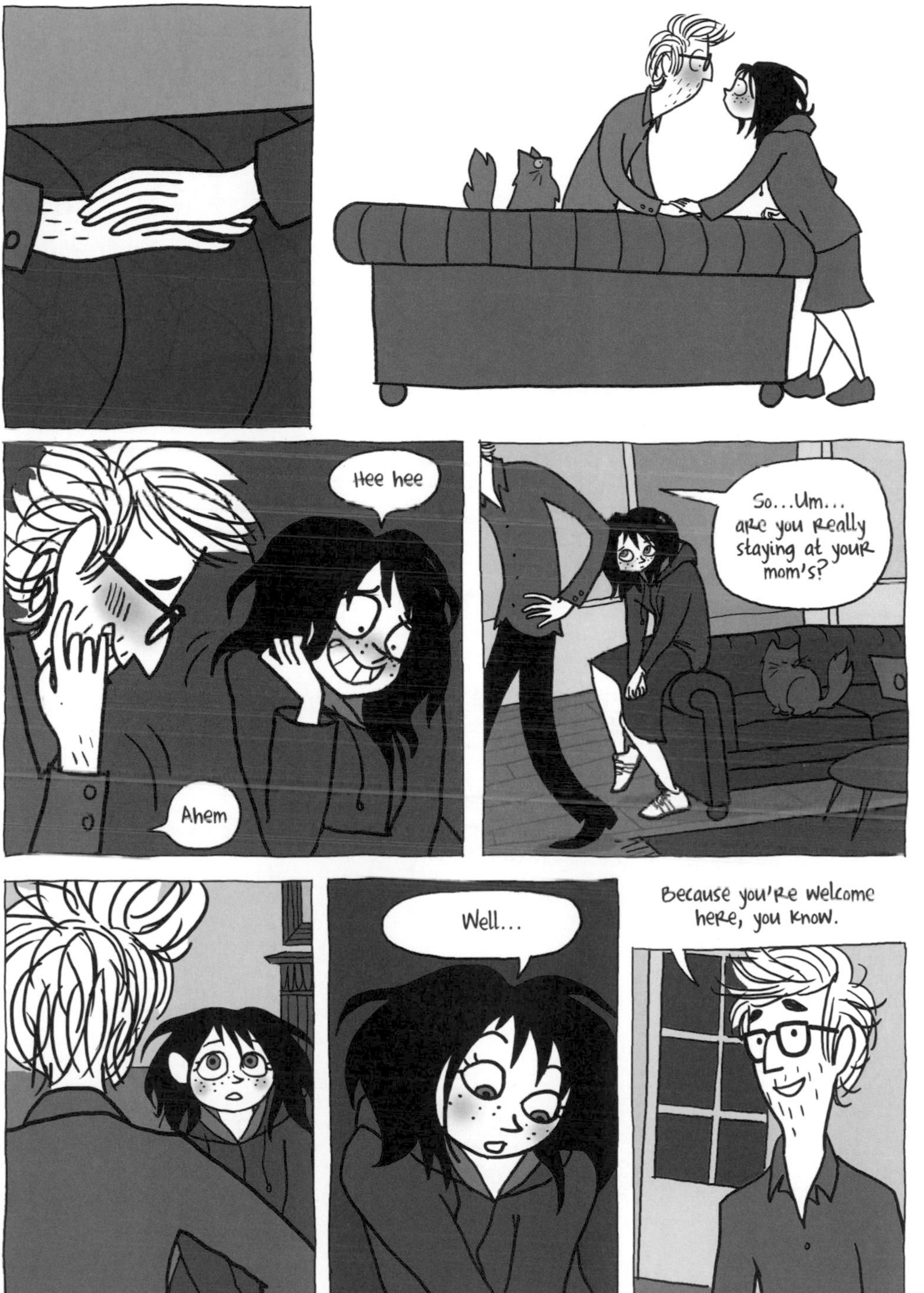
Hee hee
Ahem
So...Um... are you really staying at your mom's?
Well...
Because you're welcome here, you know.

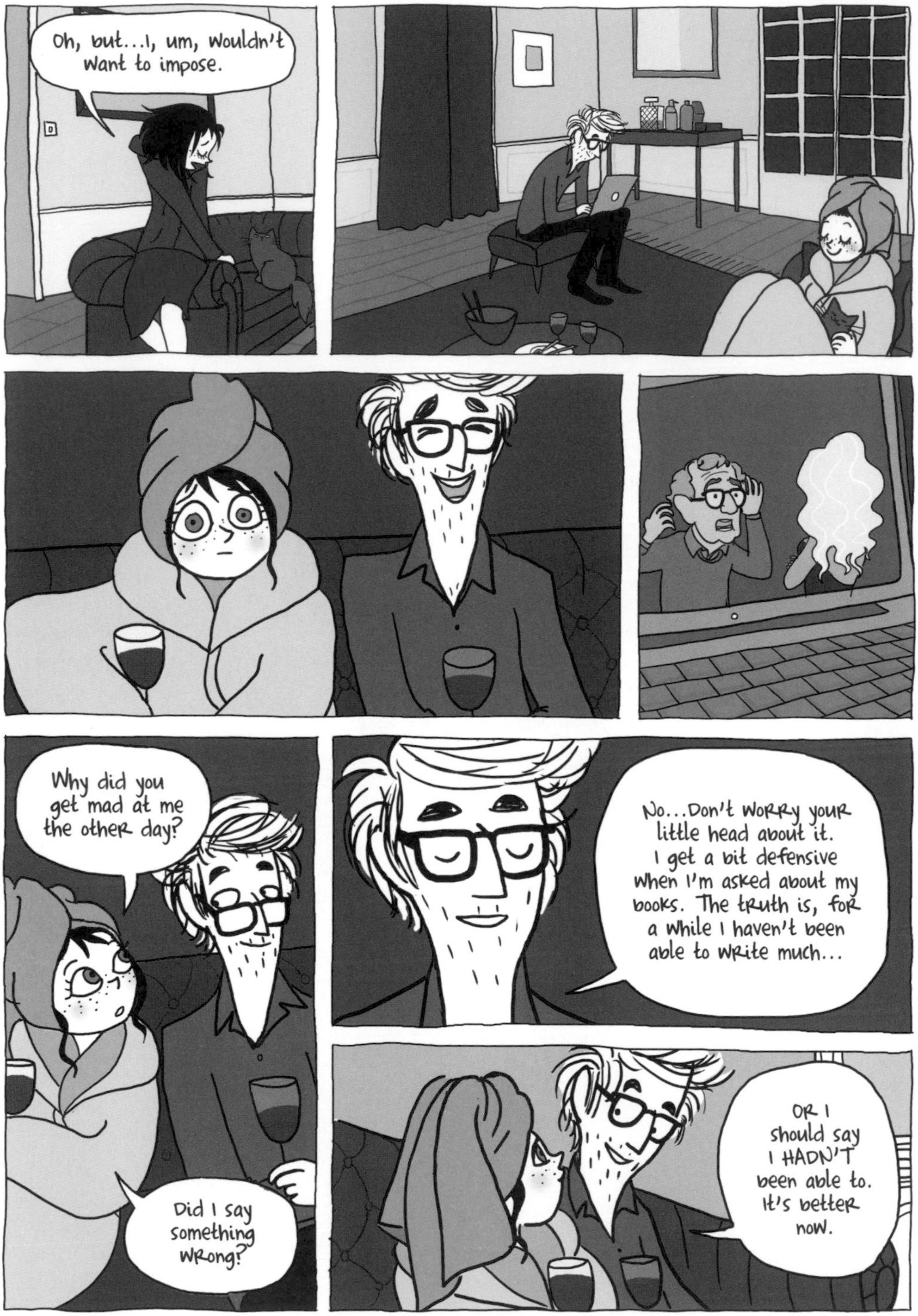
Oh, but...I, um, wouldn't want to impose.
Why did you get mad at me the other day?
Did I say something wrong?
No...Don't worry your little head about it. I get a bit defensive when I'm asked about my books. The truth is, for a while I haven't been able to write much...
Or I should say I HADN'T been able to. It's better now.

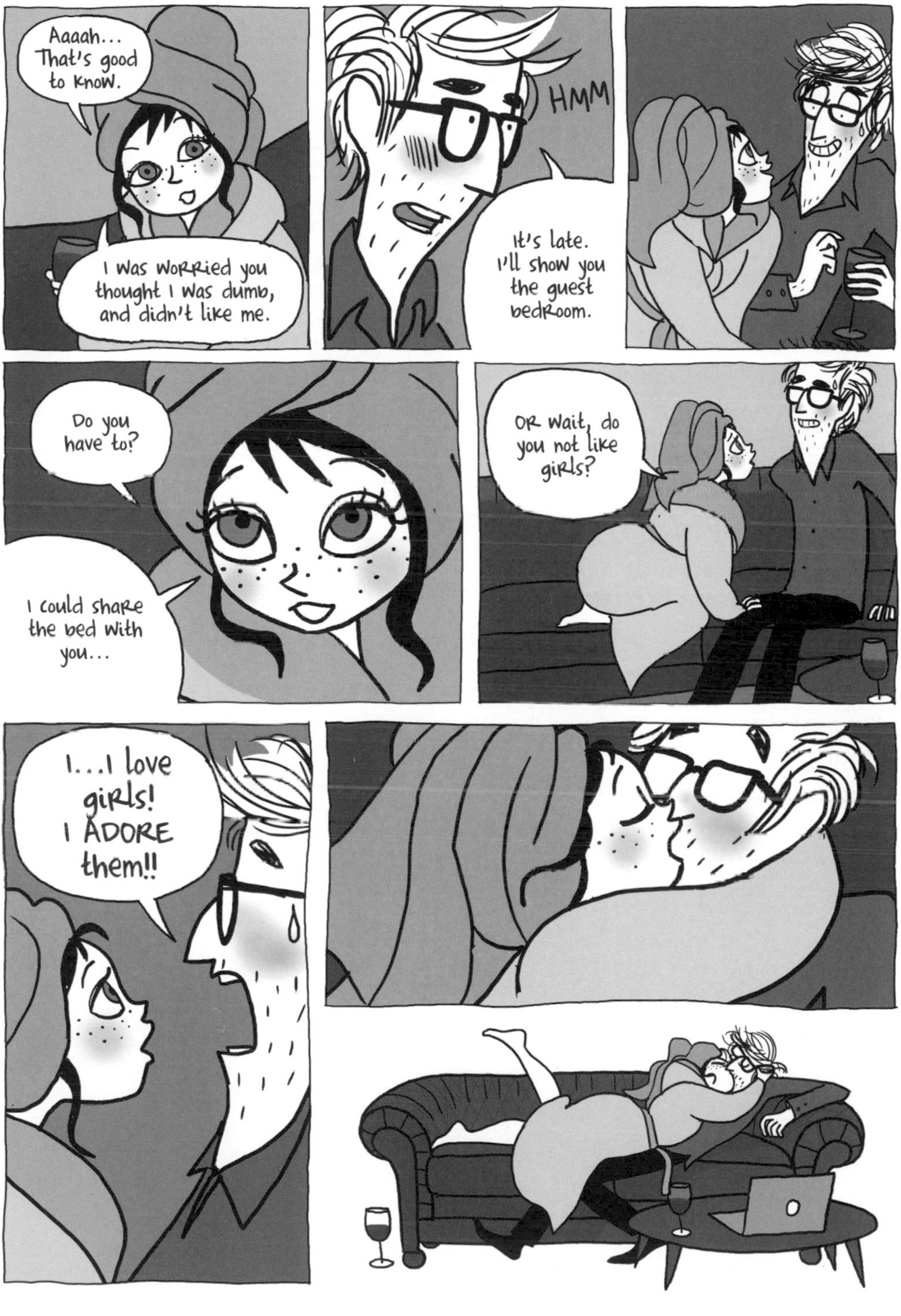
Aaaah... That's good to know.
I was worried you thought I was dumb, and didn't like me.
HMM
It's late. I'll show you the guest bedroom.
Do you have to?
I could share the bed with you...
Or wait, do you not like girls?
I...I love girls! I ADORE them!!

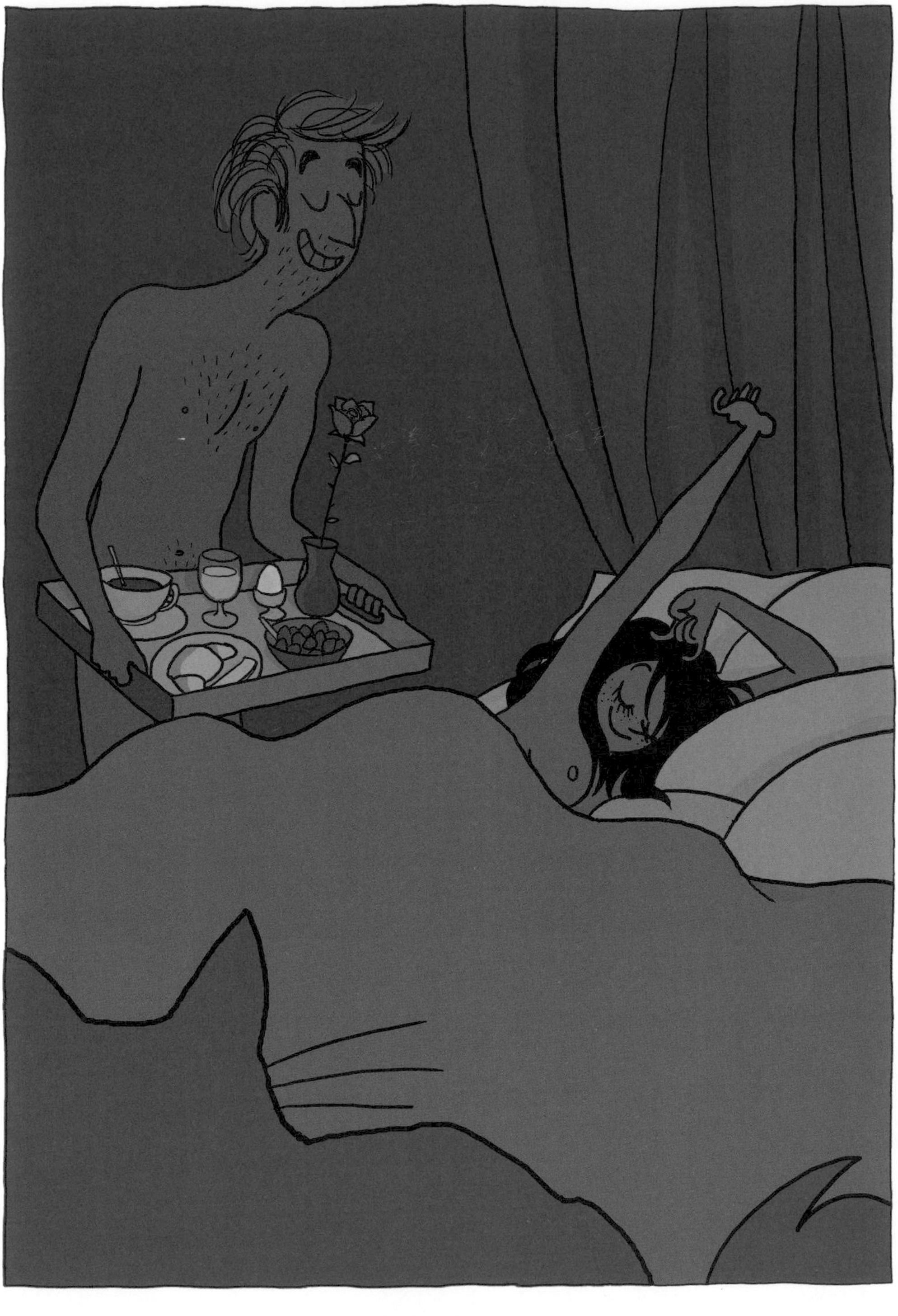

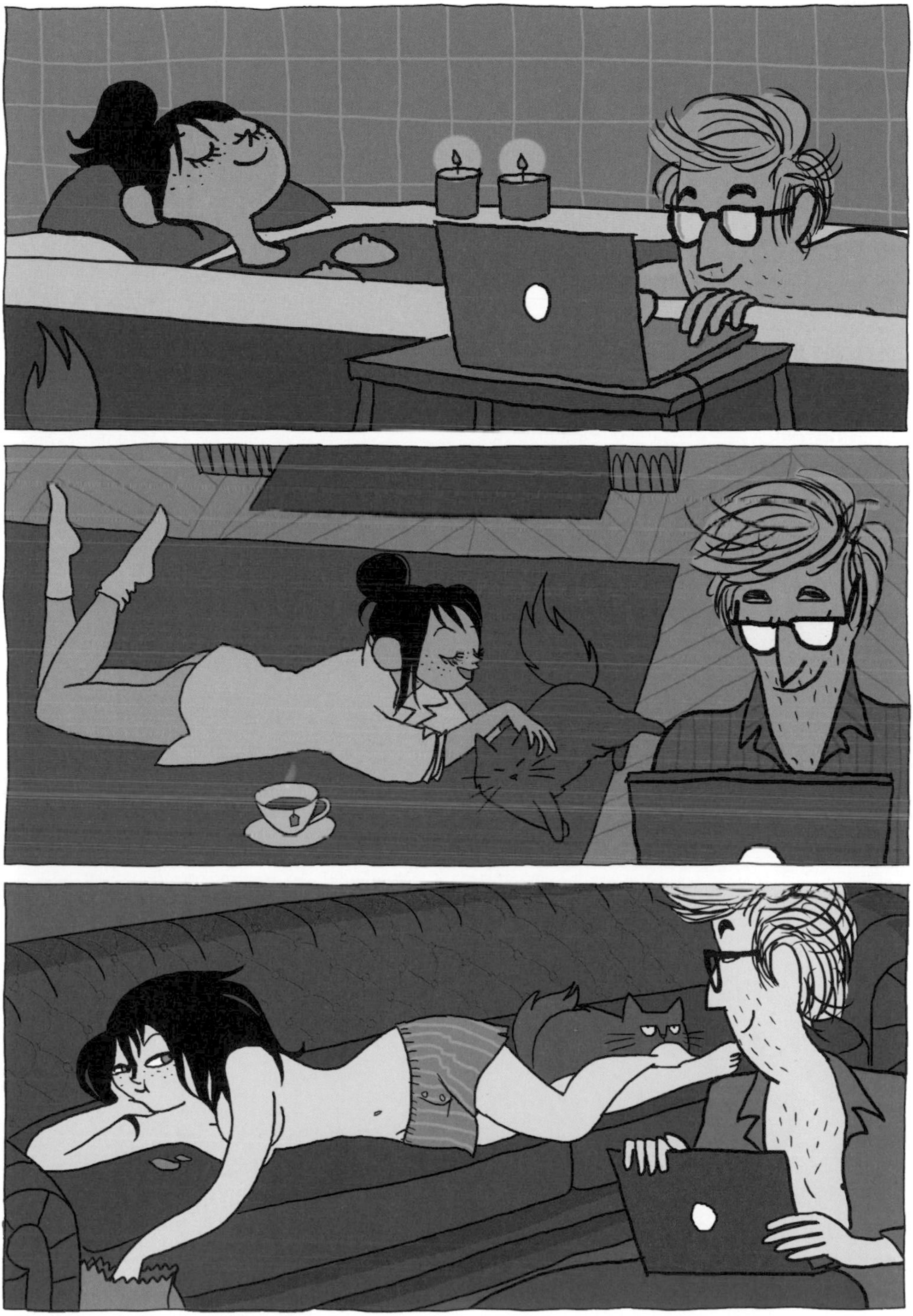

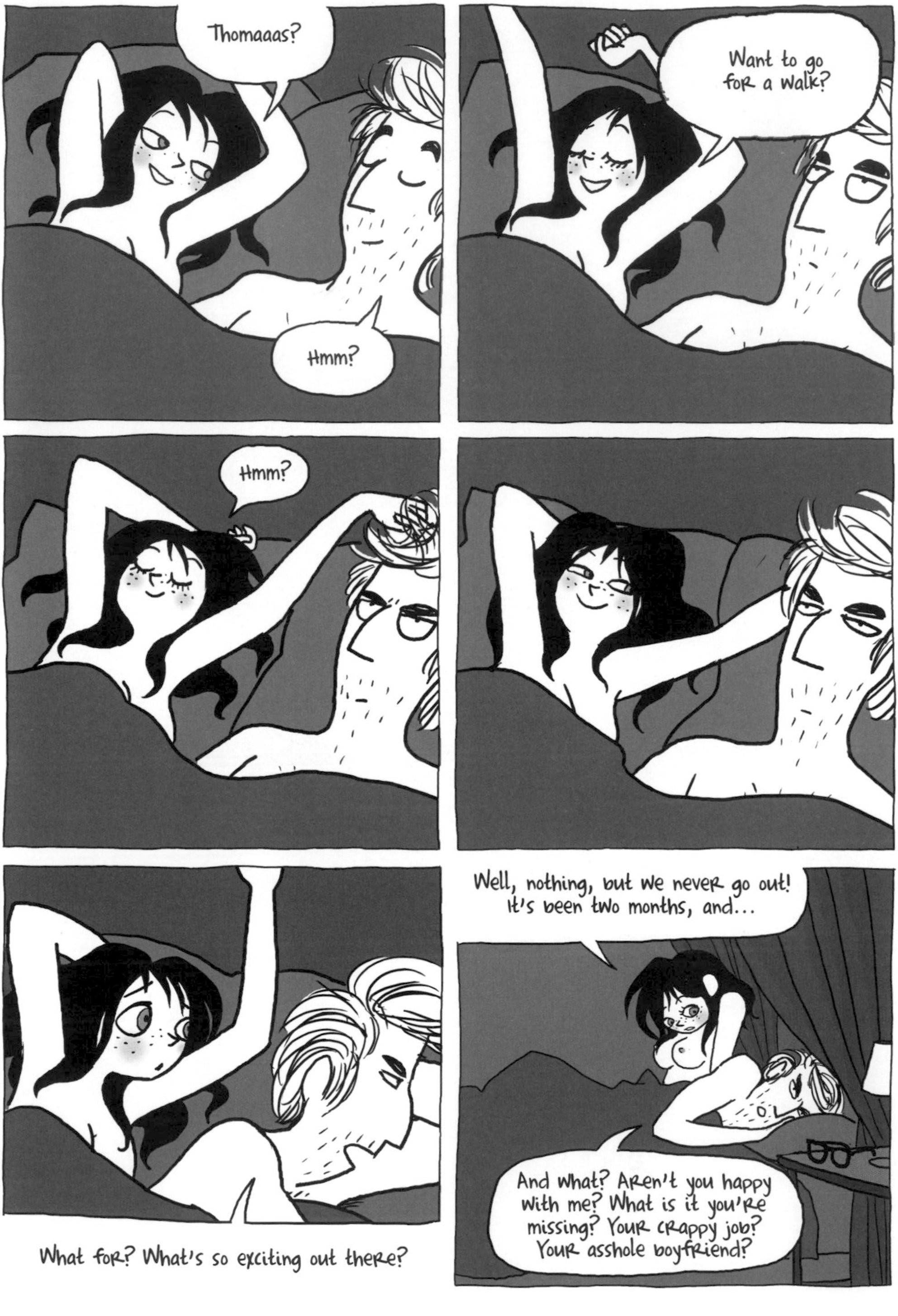
Thomaaas?
Hmm?
Want to go for a walk?
Hmm?
What for? What's so exciting out there?
Well, nothing, but we never go out! It's been two months, and...
And what? Aren't you happy with me? What is it you're missing? Your crappy job? Your asshole boyfriend?

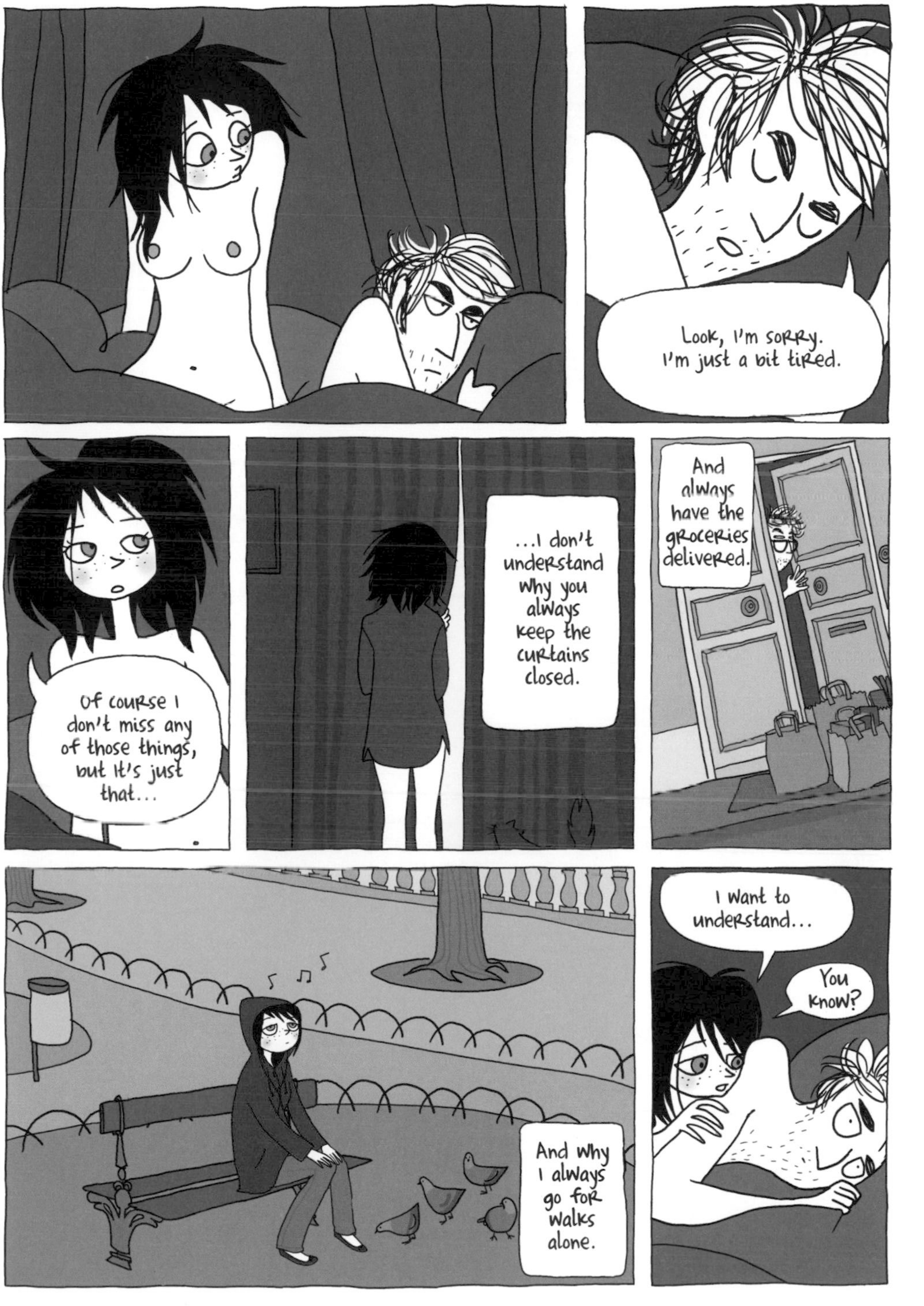
Look, I'm sorry. I'm just a bit tired.
Of course I don't miss any of those things, but it's just that...
...I don't understand why you always keep the curtains closed.
And always have the groceries delivered.
And why I always go for walks alone.
I want to understand...
You know?

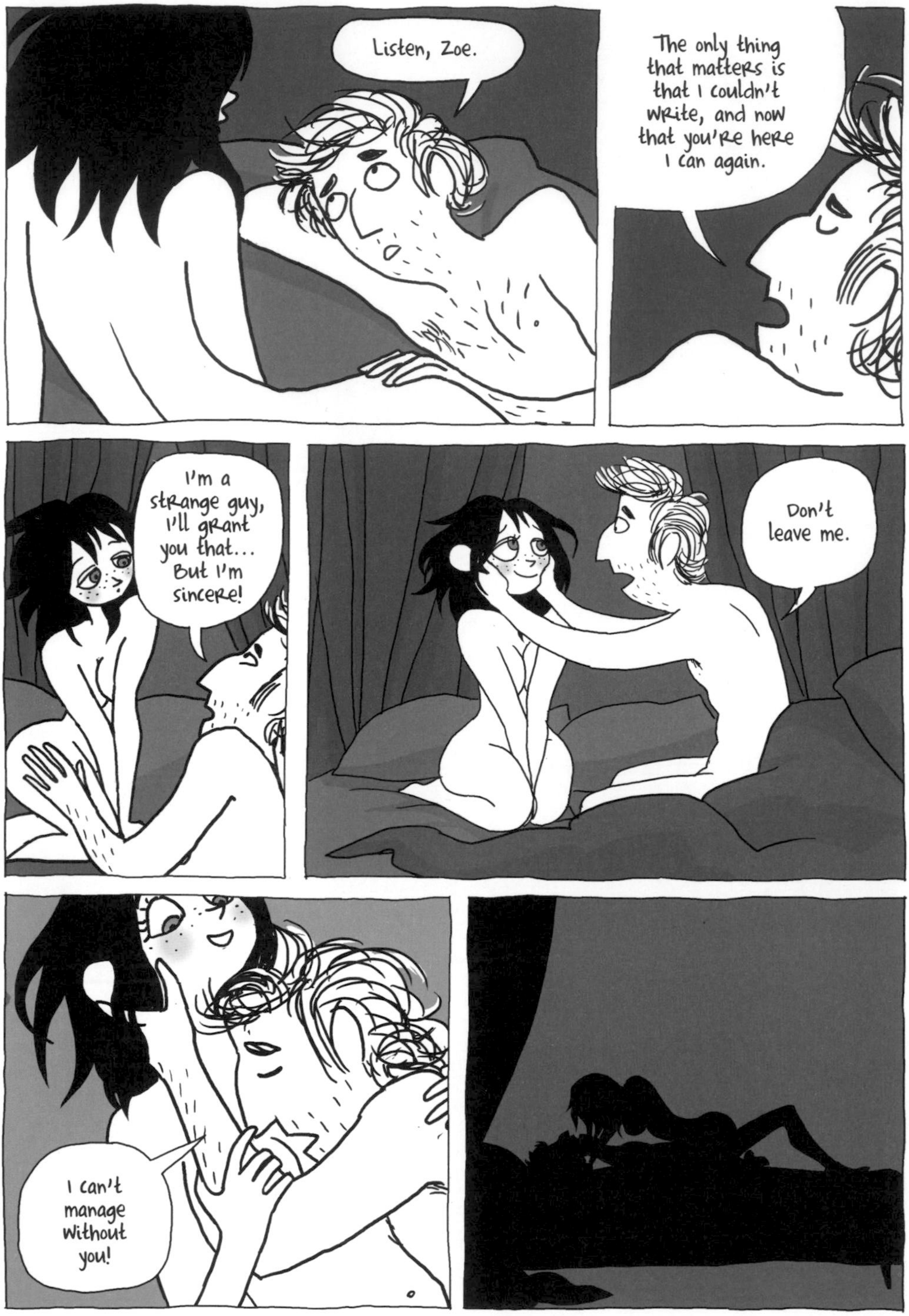
Listen, Zoe.
The only thing that matters is that I couldn't write, and now that you're here I can again.
I'm a strange guy, I'll grant you that... But I'm sincere!
Don't leave me.
I can't manage without you!

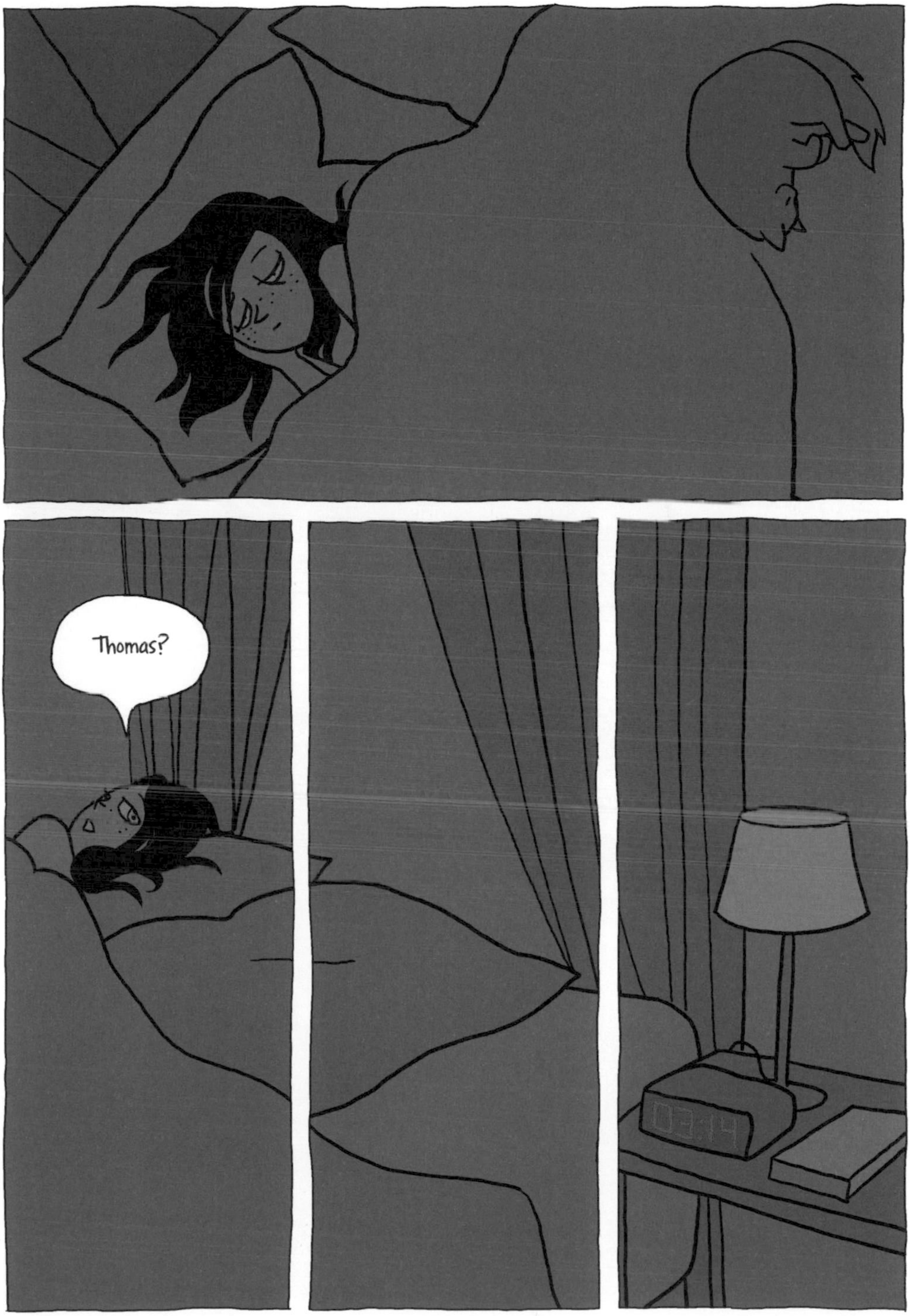
Thomas?

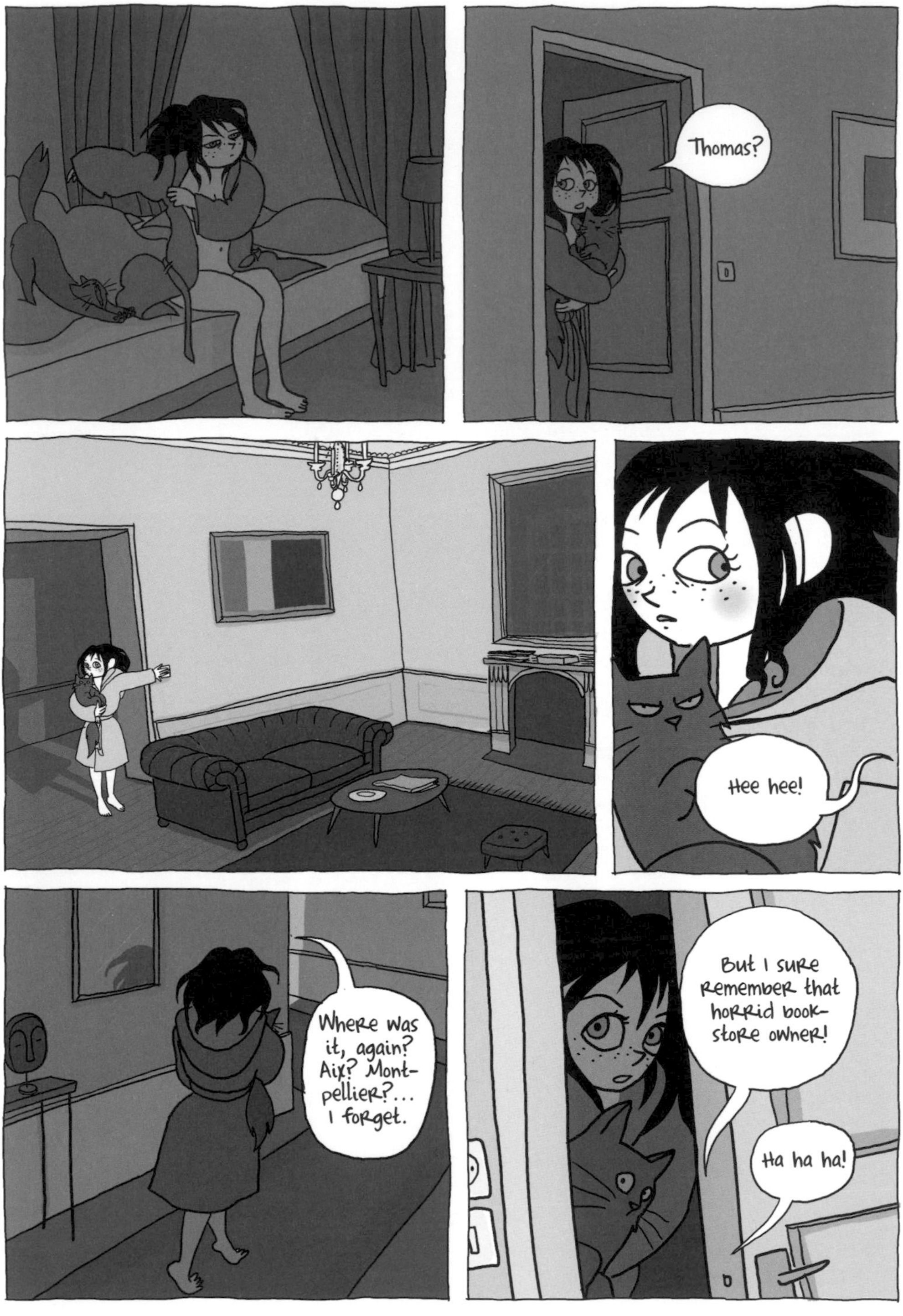
Thomas?
Hee hee!
Where was it, again? Aix? Montpellier?... I forget.
But I sure remember that horrid bookstore owner!
Ha ha ha!

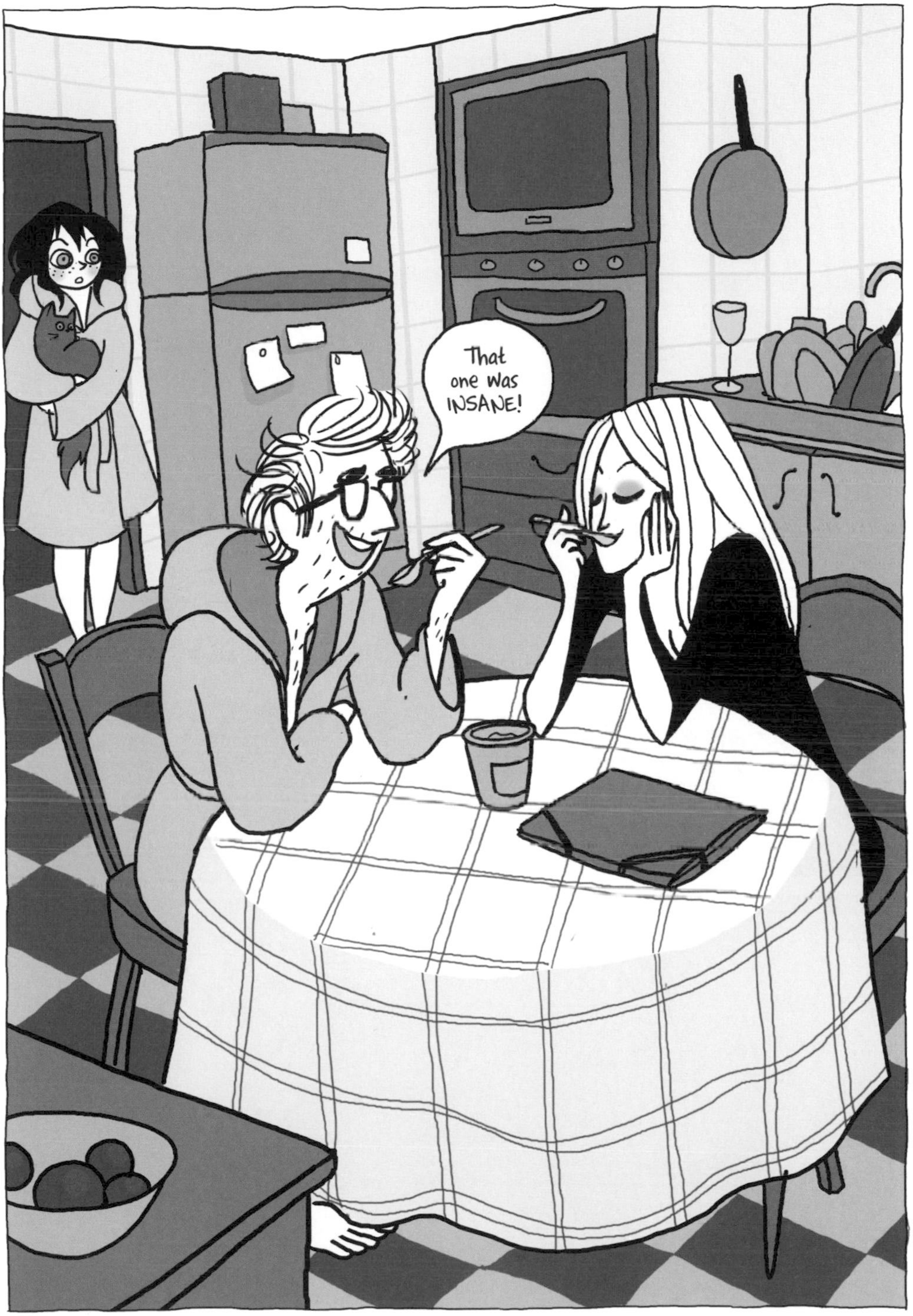
That one was INSANE!

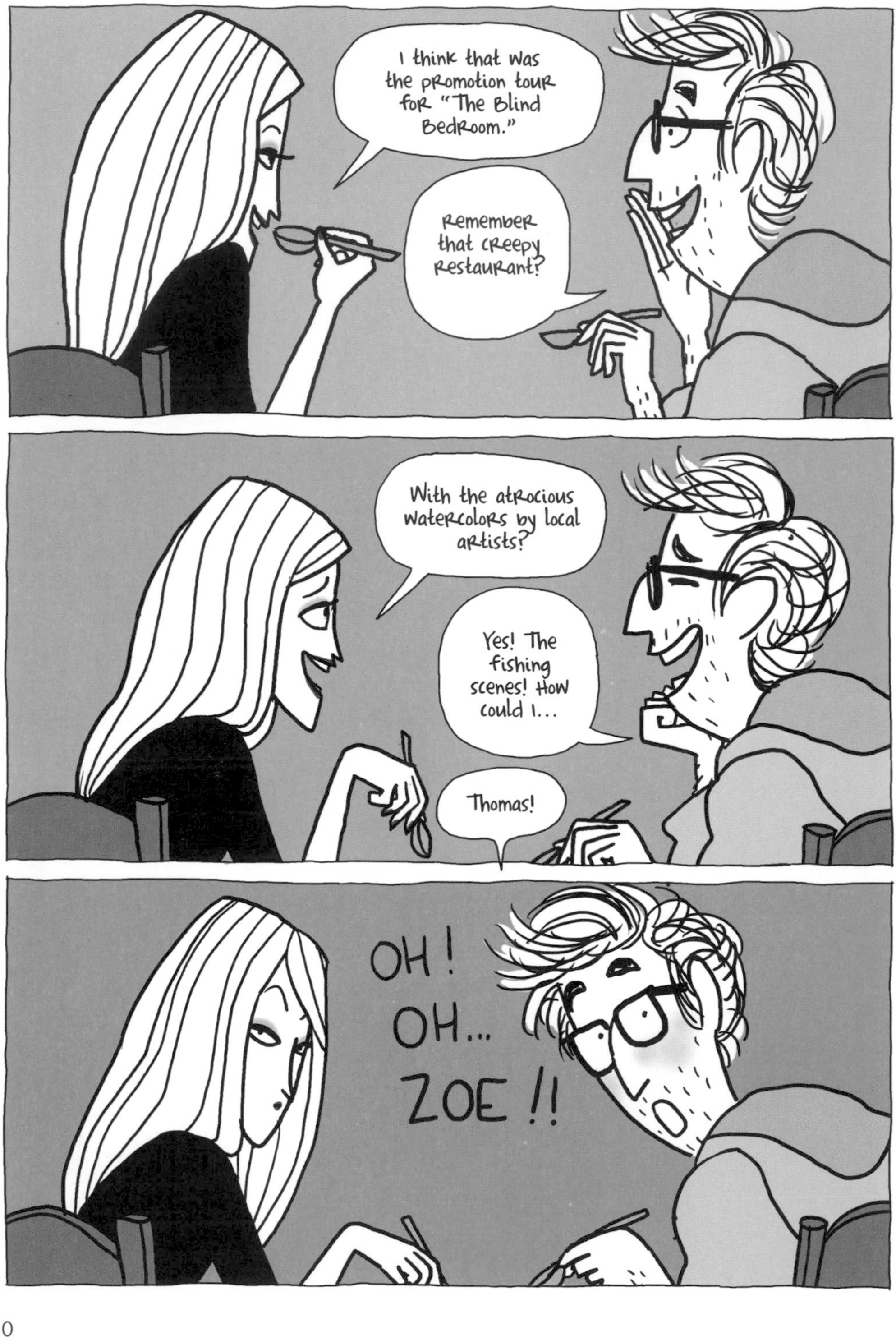
I think that was the promotion tour for "The Blind Bedroom."
Remember that creepy restaurant?
With the atrocious watercolors by local artists?
Yes! The fishing scenes! How could I...
Thomas!
OH!
OH...
ZOE!!

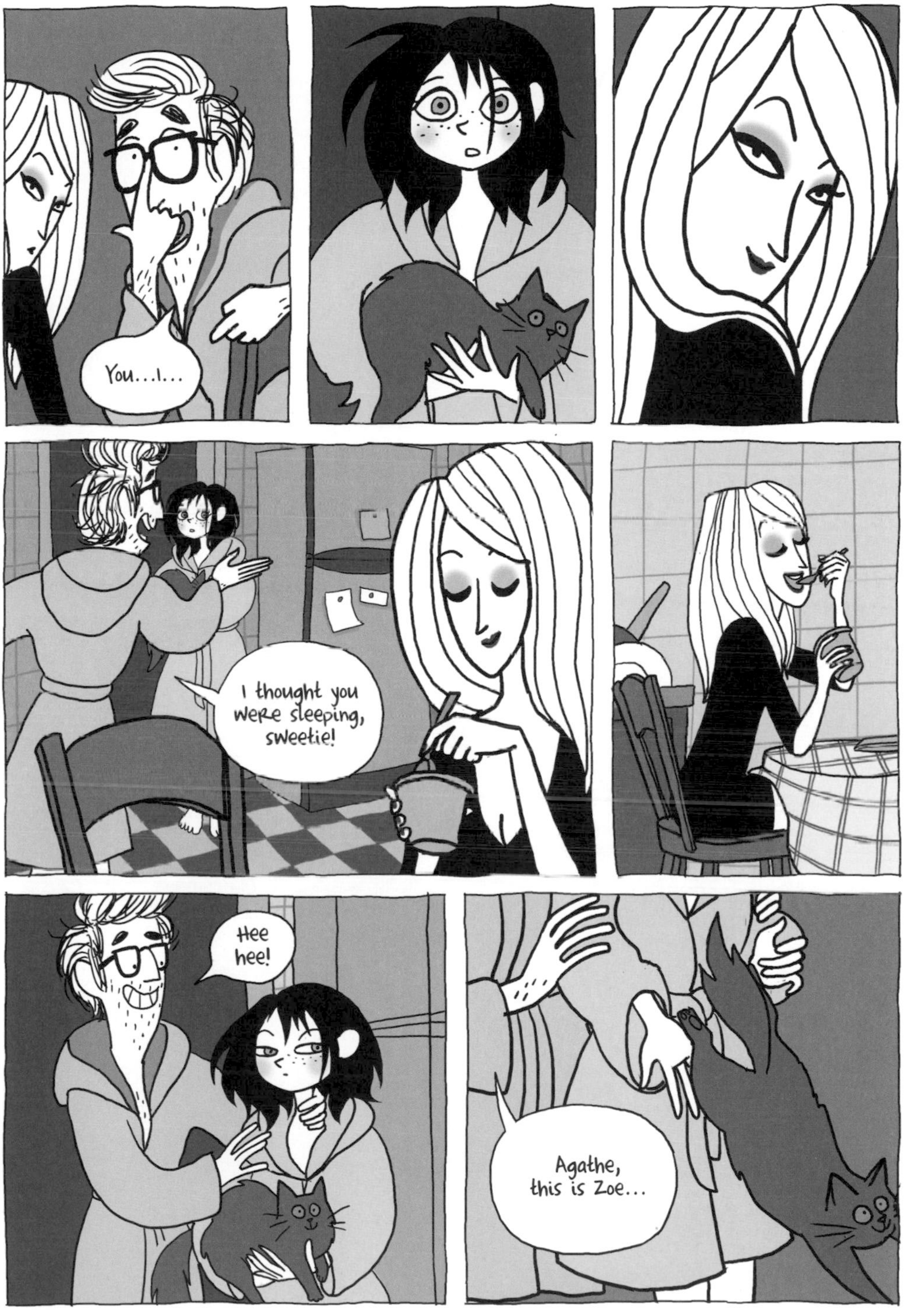
You... I...
I thought you were sleeping, sweetie!
Hee hee!
Agathe, this is Zoe...

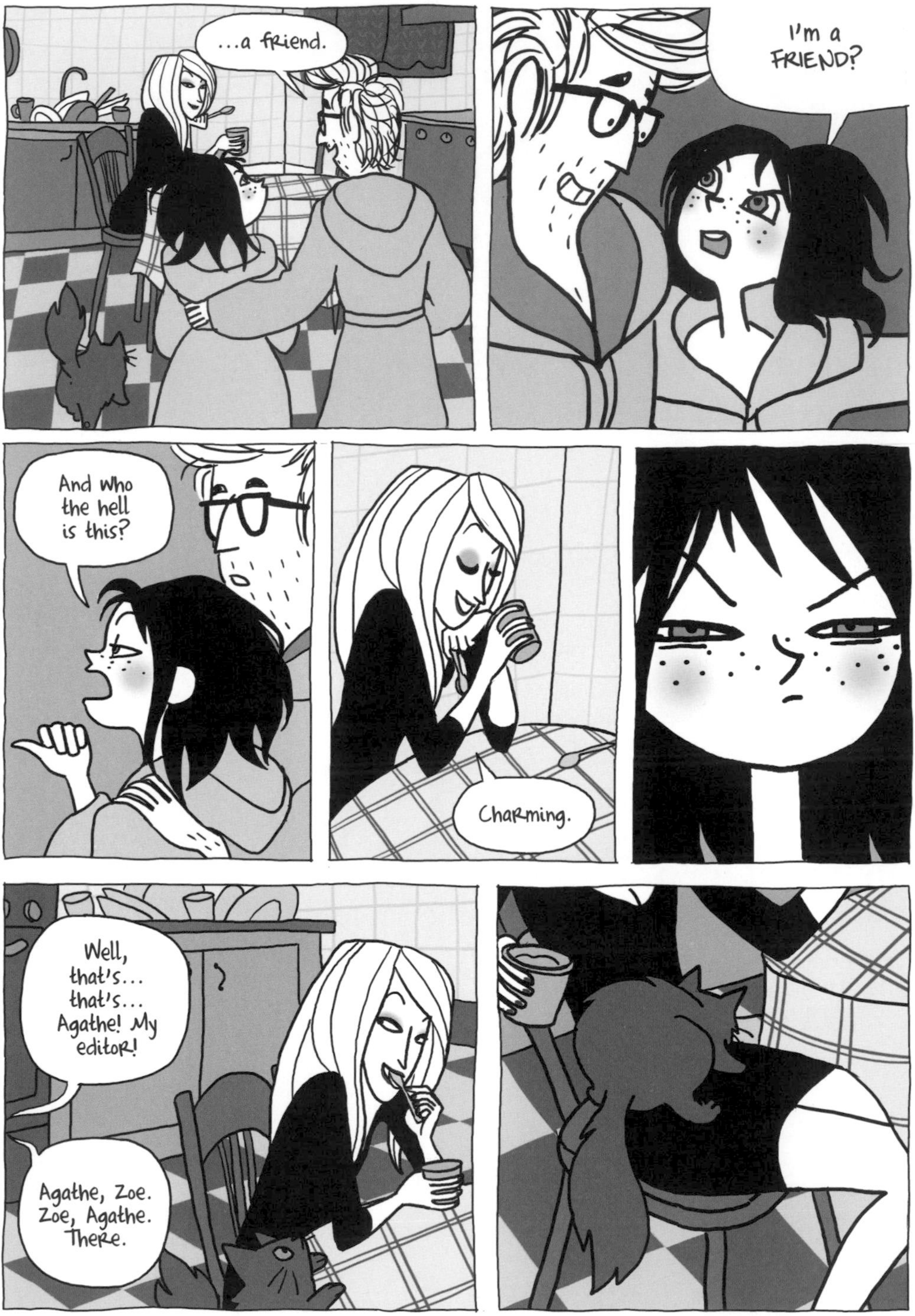
...a friend.
I'm a FRIEND?
And who the hell is this?
Charming.
Well, that's... that's... Agathe! My editor!
Agathe, Zoe. Zoe, Agathe. There.

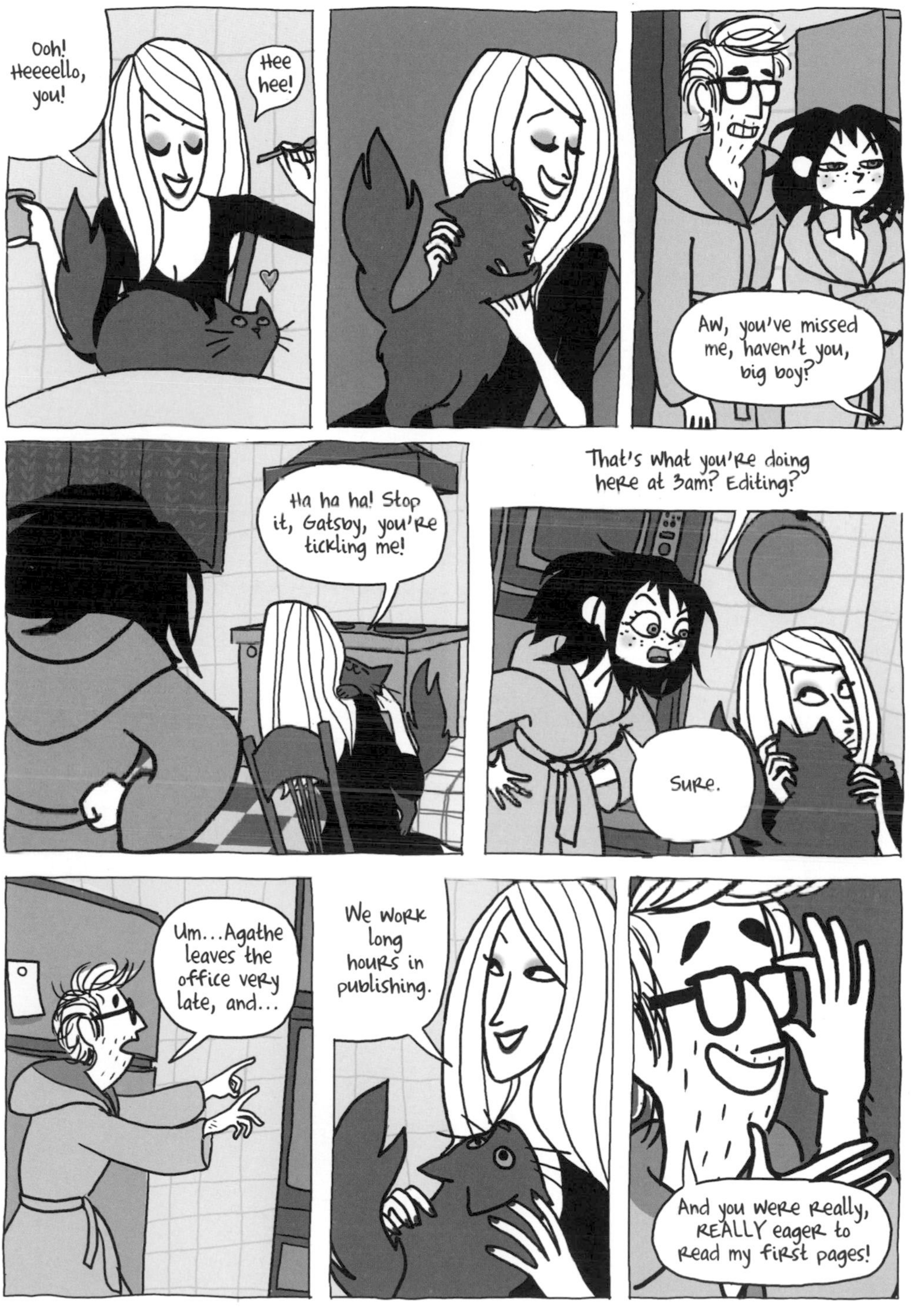
Ooh! Heeeello, you!
Hee hee!
Aw, you've missed me, haven't you, big boy?
Ha ha ha! Stop it, Gatsby, you're tickling me!
That's what you're doing here at 3am? Editing?
Sure.
Um...Agathe leaves the office very late, and...
We work long hours in publishing.
And you were really, REALLY eager to read my first pages!

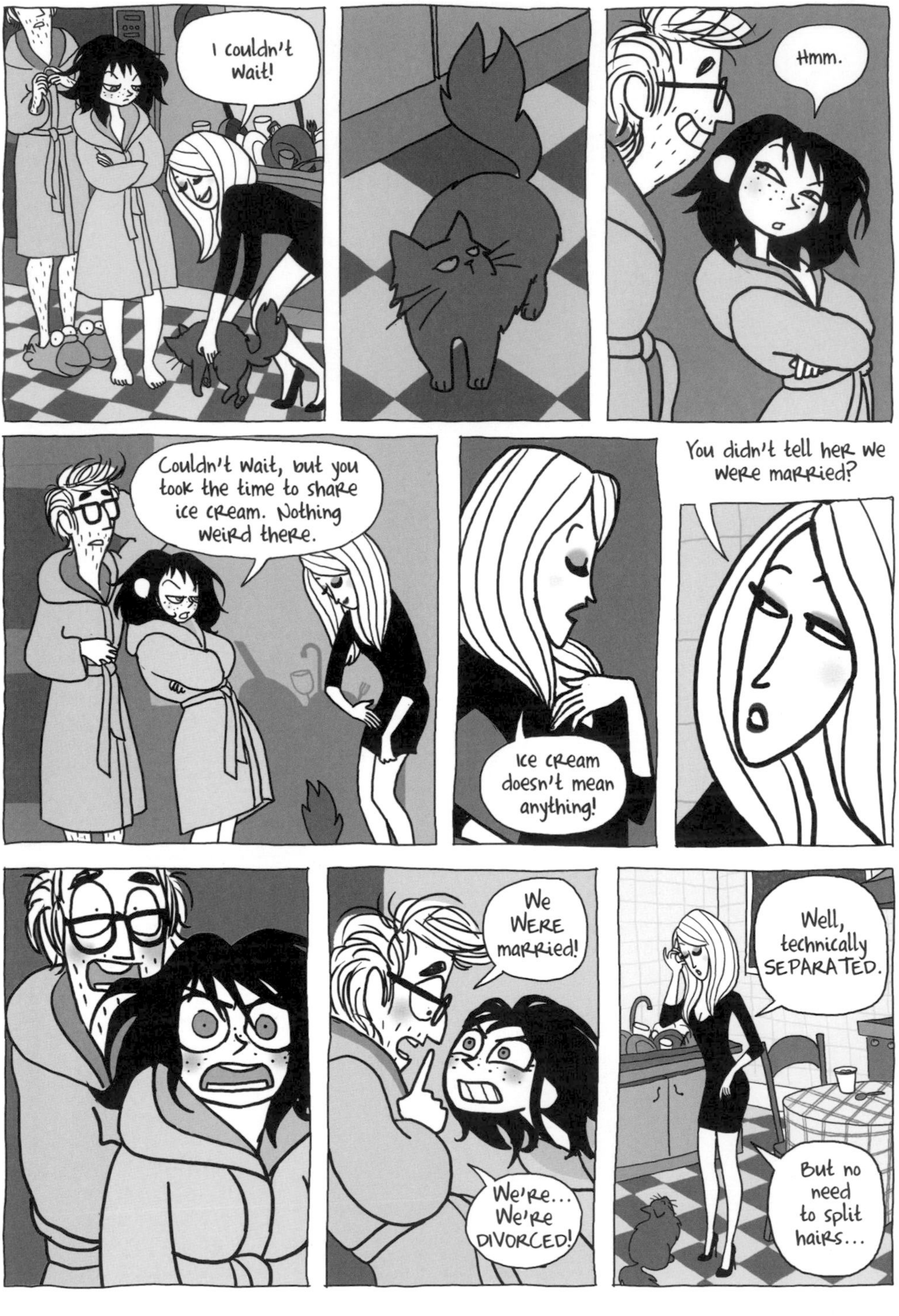
I couldn't wait!
Hmm.
Couldn't wait, but you took the time to share ice cream. Nothing weird there.
Ice cream doesn't mean anything!
You didn't tell her we were married?
We WERE married!
We're... We're DIVORCED!
Well, technically SEPARATED.
But no need to split hairs...

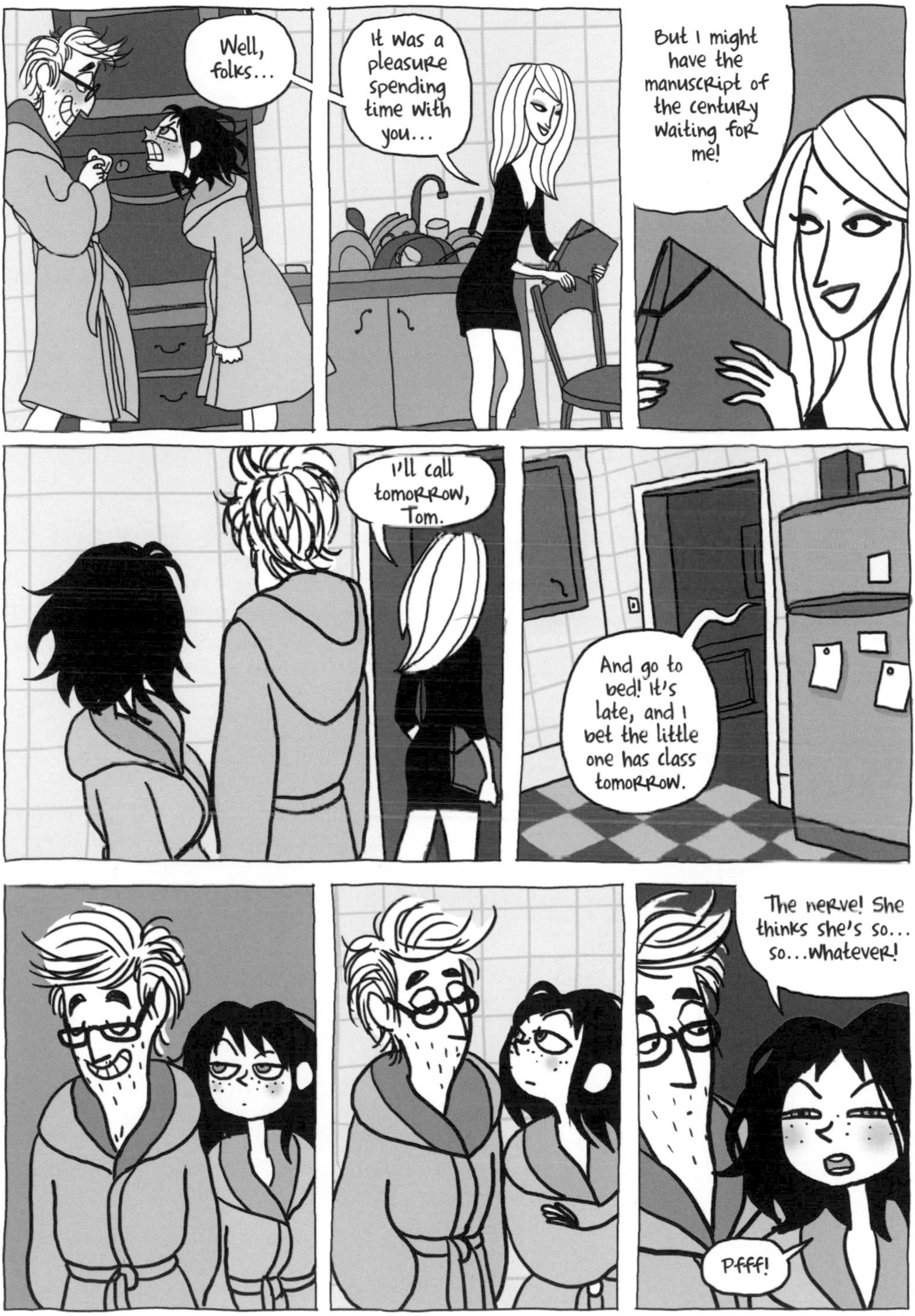
Well, folks...
It was a pleasure spending time with you...
But I might have the manuscript of the century waiting for me!
I'll call tomorrow, Tom.
And go to bed! It's late, and I bet the little one has class tomorrow.
The nerve! She thinks she's so... so... whatever!
Pfff!

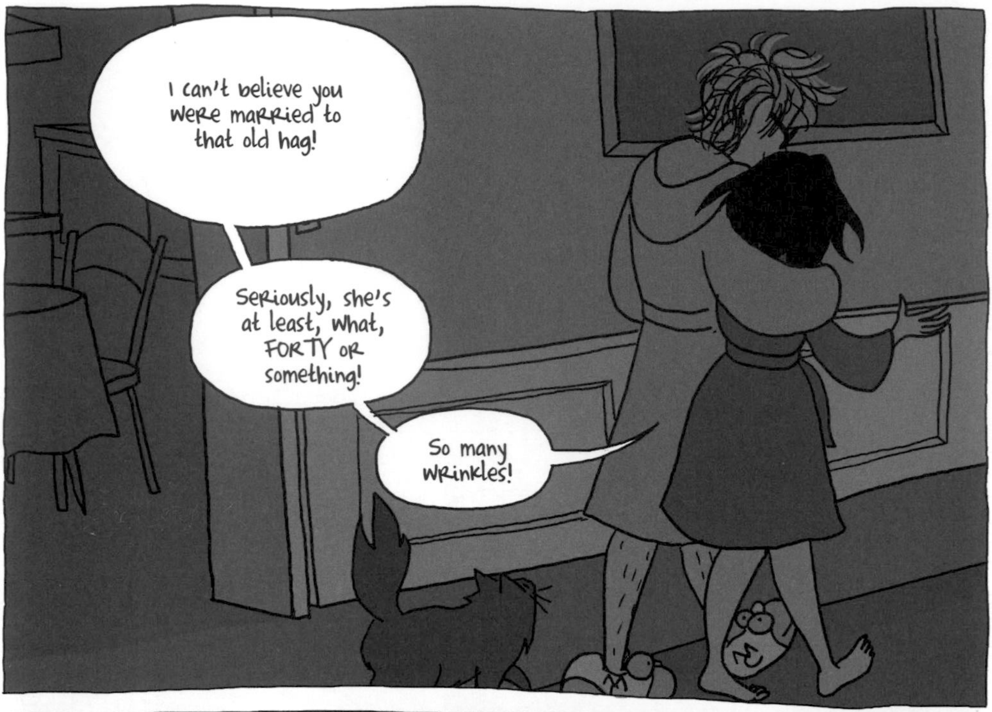
I can't believe you were married to that old hag!
Seriously, she's at least, what, FORTY or something!
So many wrinkles!

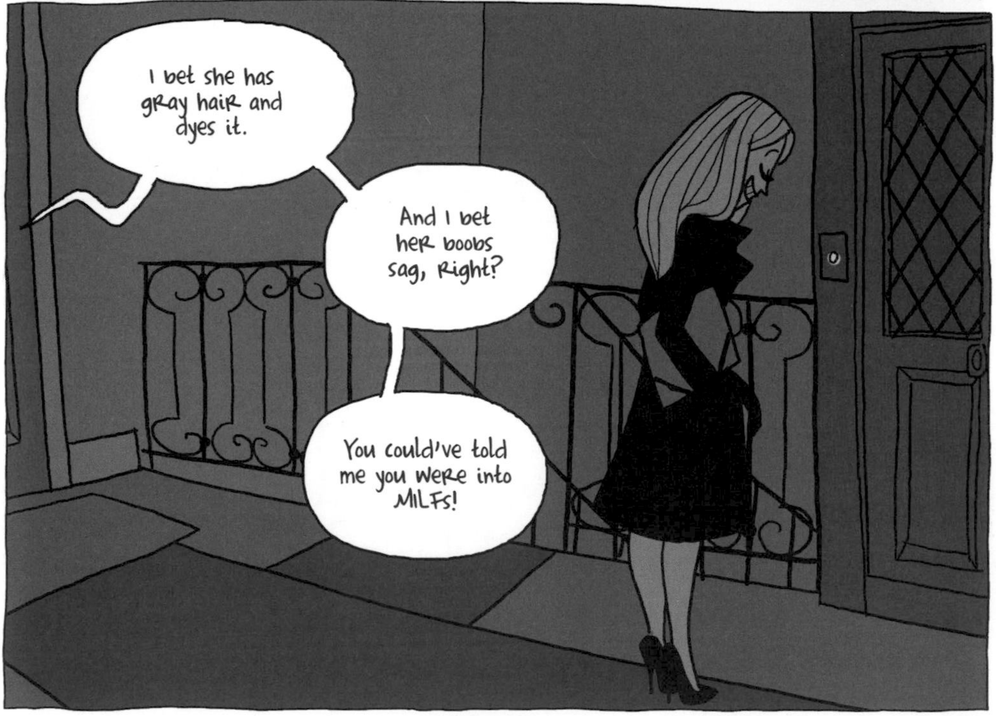
I bet she has gray hair and dyes it.
And I bet her boobs sag, right?
You could've told me you were into MILFs!

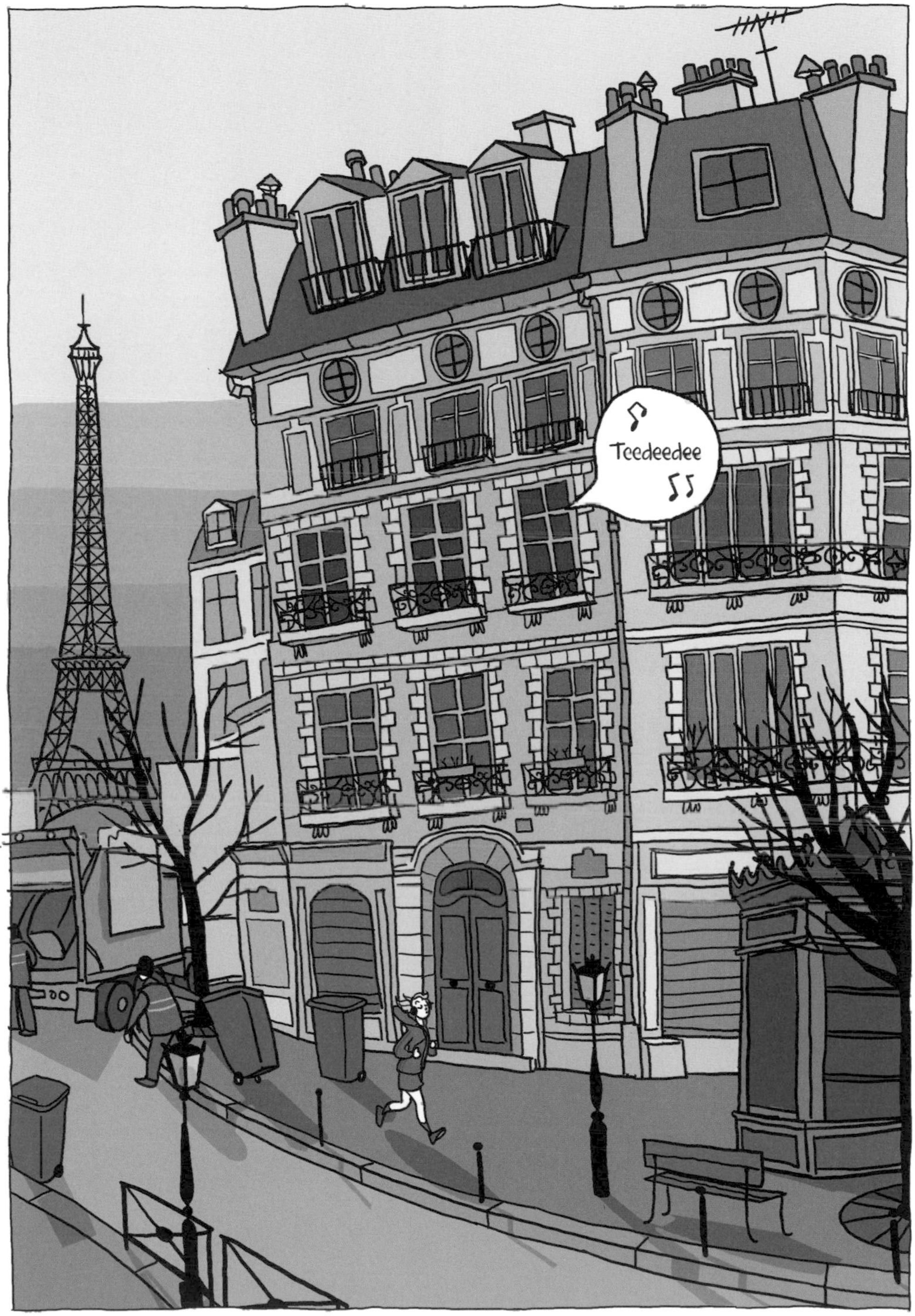
Teedeedee

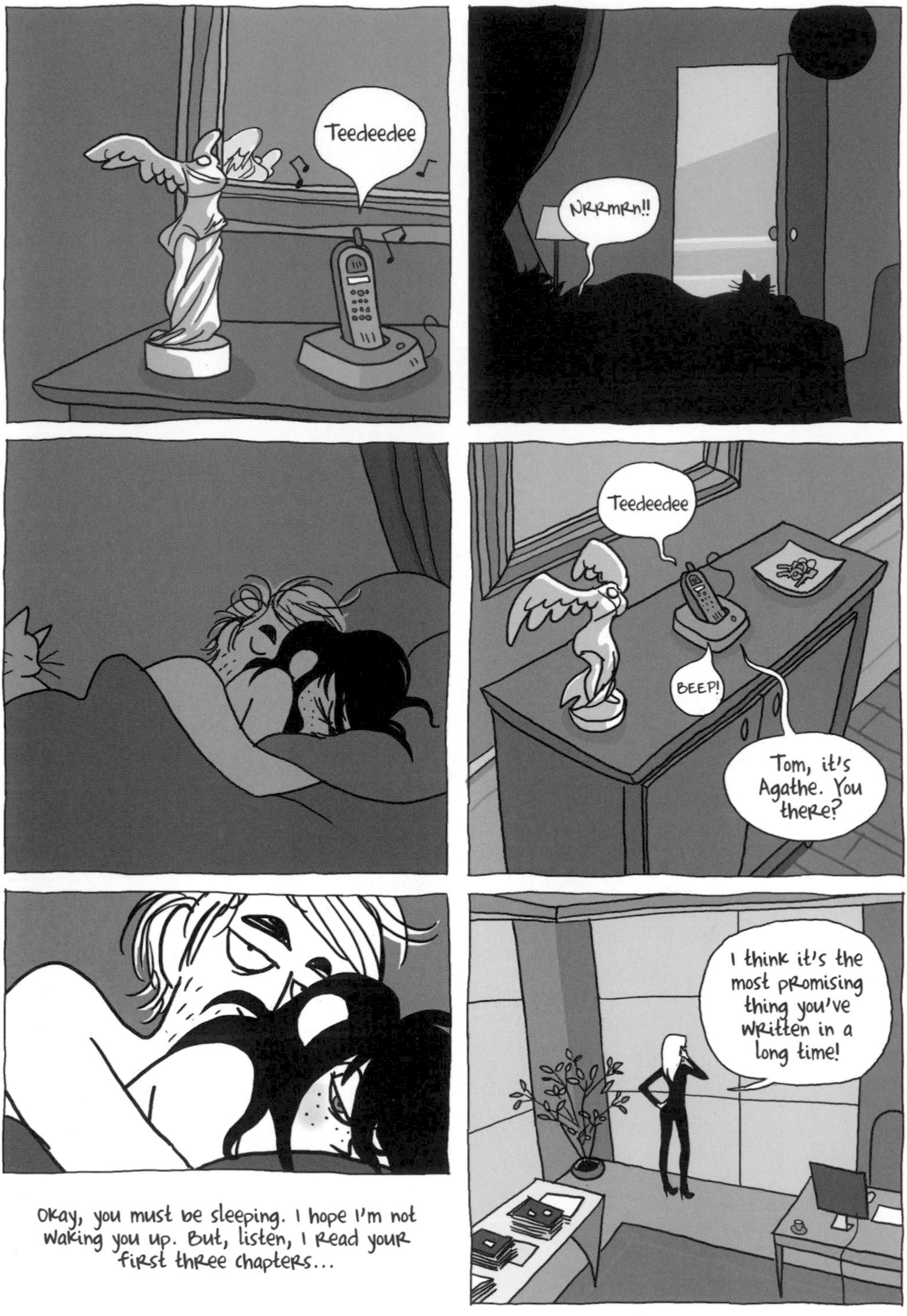

Teedeedee
NRRMRN!!
Teedeedee
BEEP!
Tom, it's Agathe. You there?
Okay, you must be sleeping. I hope I'm not waking you up. But, listen, I read your first three chapters...
I think it's the most promising thing you've written in a long time!

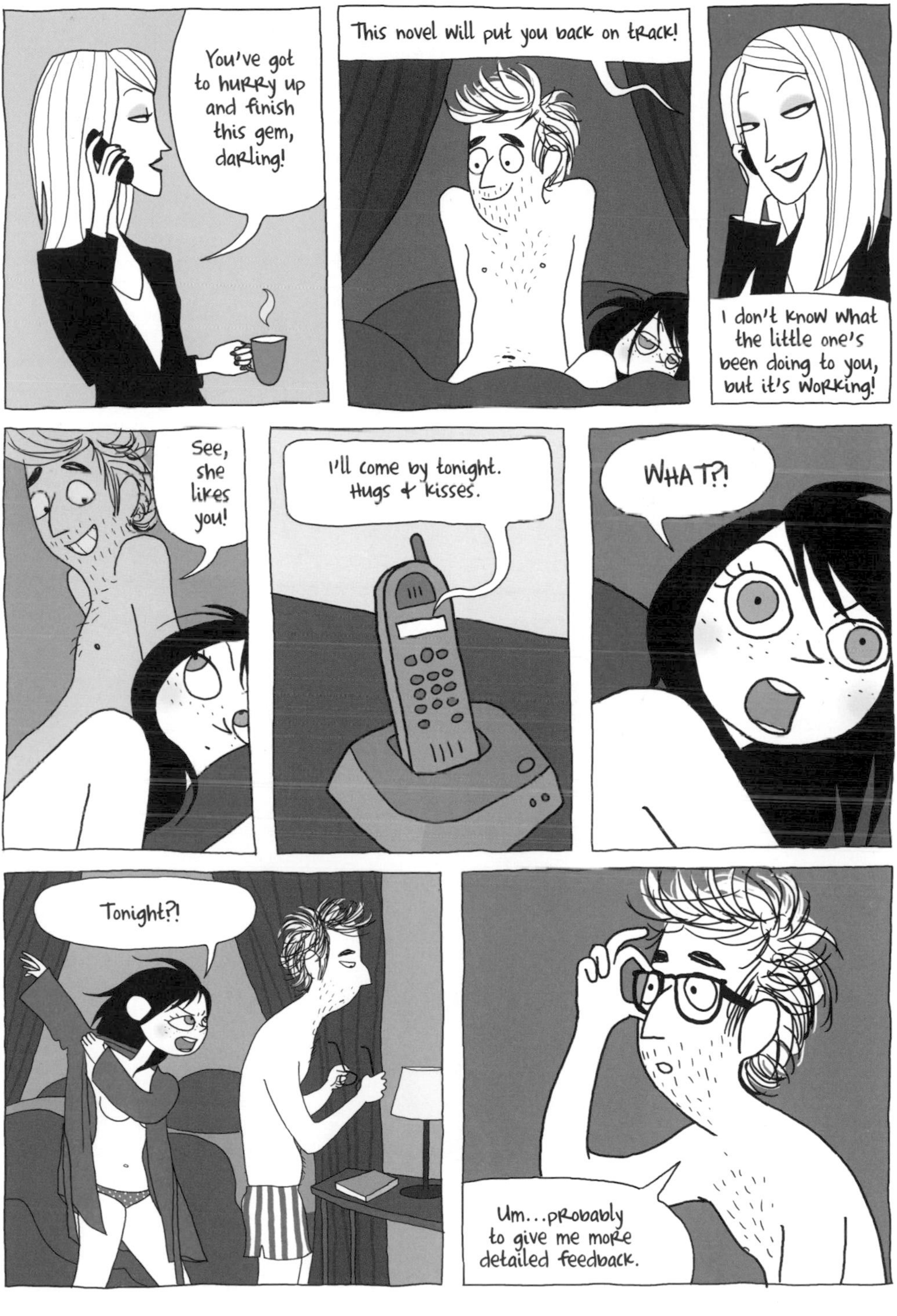
You've got to hurry up and finish this gem, darling!
This novel will put you back on track!
I don't know what the little one's been doing to you, but it's working!
See, she likes you!
I'll come by tonight. Hugs & kisses.
WHAT?!
Tonight?!
Um...probably to give me more detailed feedback.

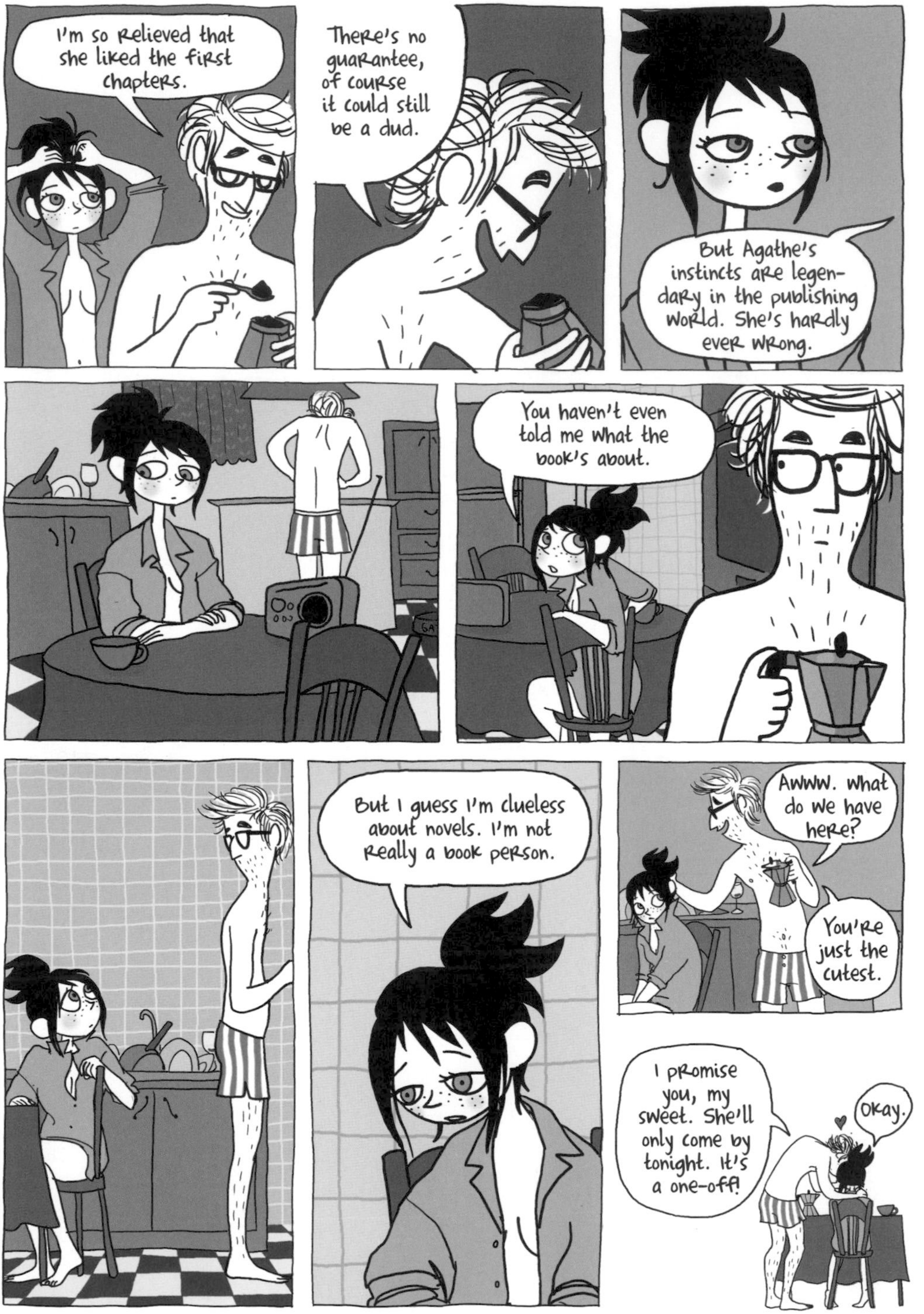
I'm so relieved that she liked the first chapters.
There's no guarantee, of course it could still be a dud.
But Agathe's instincts are legendary in the publishing world. She's hardly ever wrong.
You haven't even told me what the book's about.
But I guess I'm clueless about novels. I'm not really a book person.
Awww. What do we have here?
You're just the cutest.
I promise you, my sweet. She'll only come by tonight. It's a one-off!
Okay.

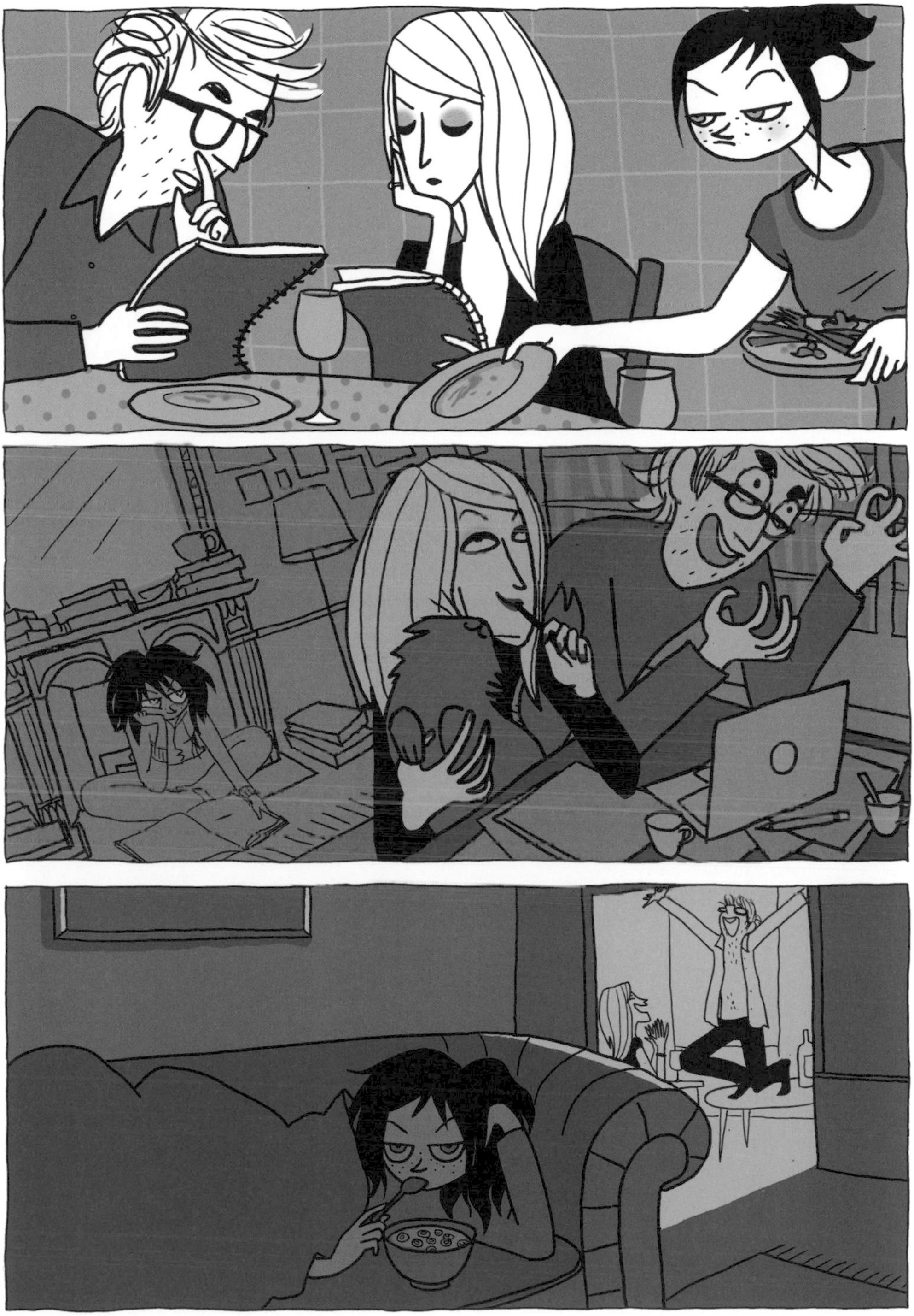

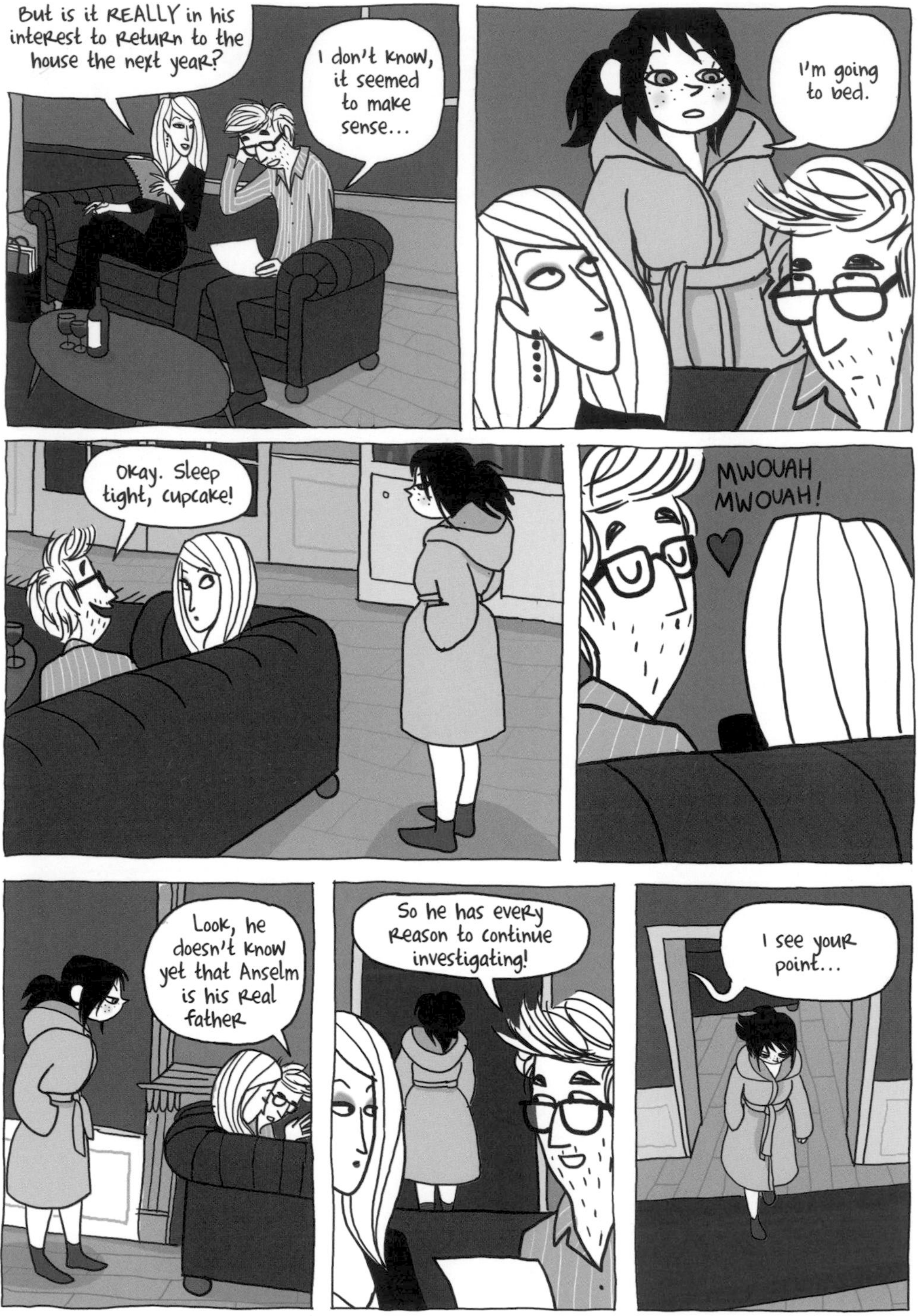
But is it REALLY in his interest to return to the house the next year?
I don't know, it seemed to make sense...
I'm going to bed.
Okay. Sleep tight, cupcake!
MWOUAH MWOUAH!
Look, he doesn't know yet that Anselm is his real father
So he has every reason to continue investigating!
I see your point...

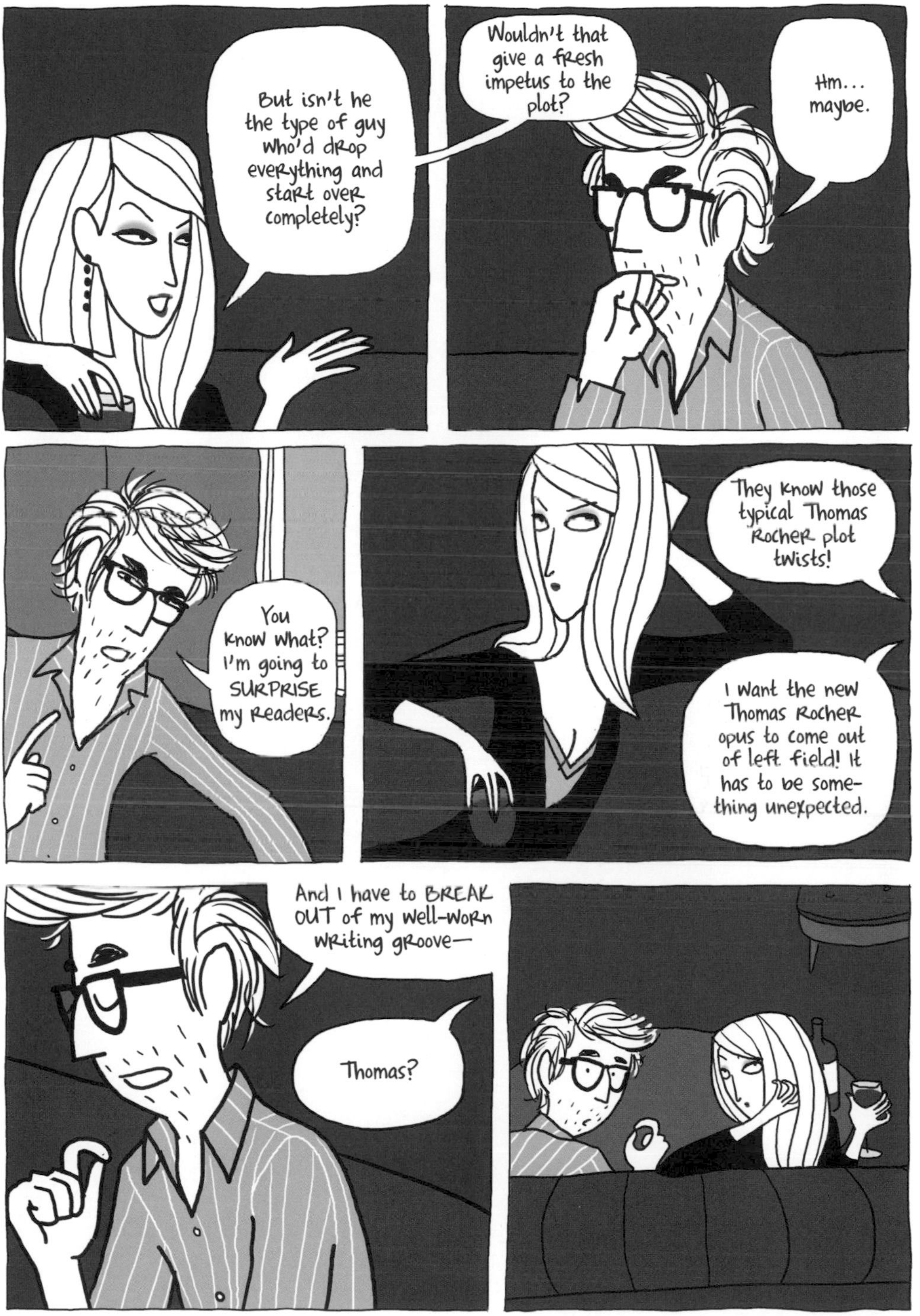
But isn't he the type of guy who'd drop everything and start over completely?
Wouldn't that give a fresh impetus to the plot?
Hm... maybe.
You know what? I'm going to SURPRISE my readers.
They know those typical Thomas Rocher plot twists!
I want the new Thomas Rocher opus to come out of left field! It has to be something unexpected.
And I have to BREAK OUT of my well-worn writing groove—
Thomas?

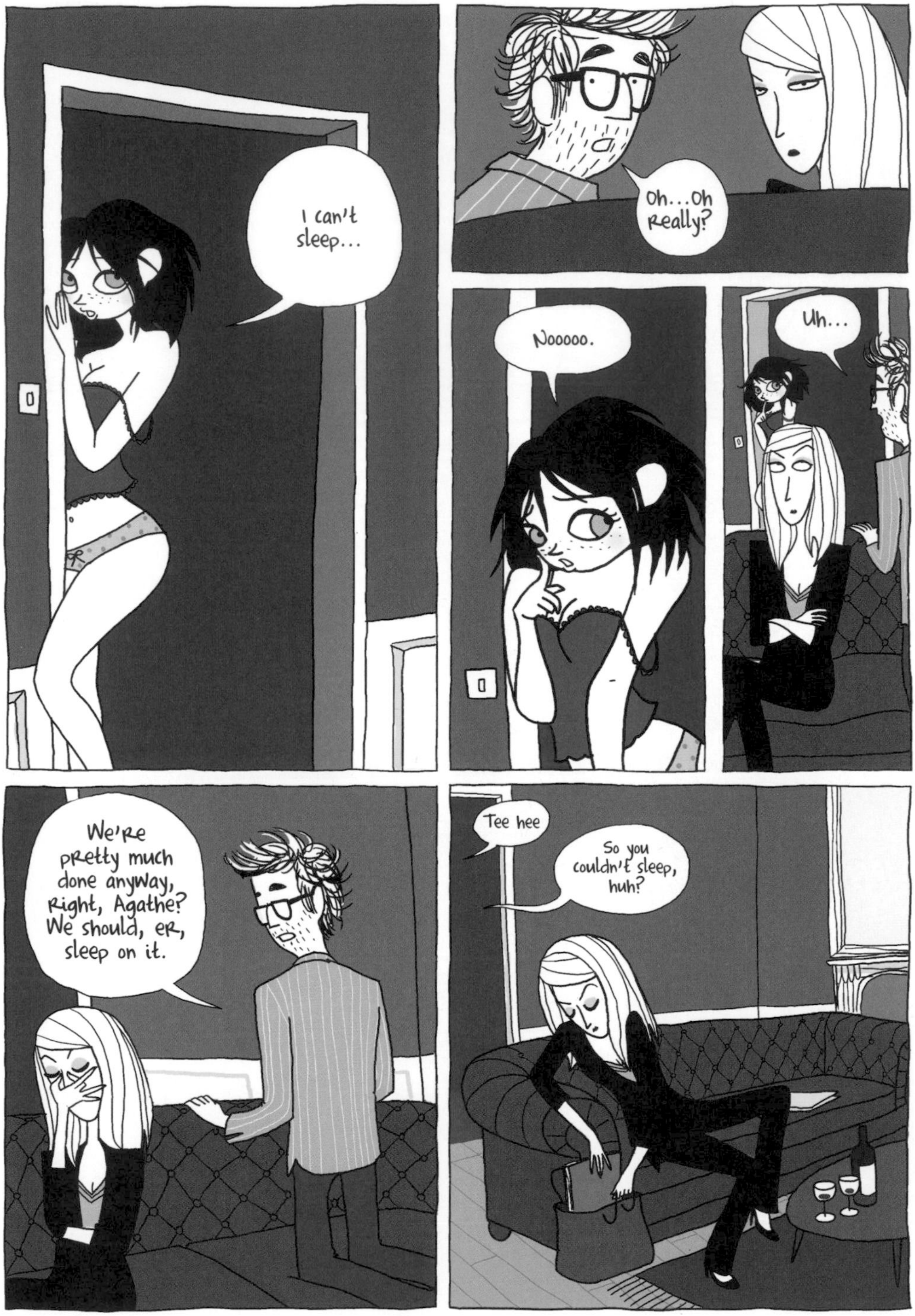
I can't sleep...
Oh...Oh really?
Nooooo.
Uh...
We're pretty much done anyway, right, Agathe? We should, er, sleep on it.
Tee hee
So you couldn't sleep, huh?

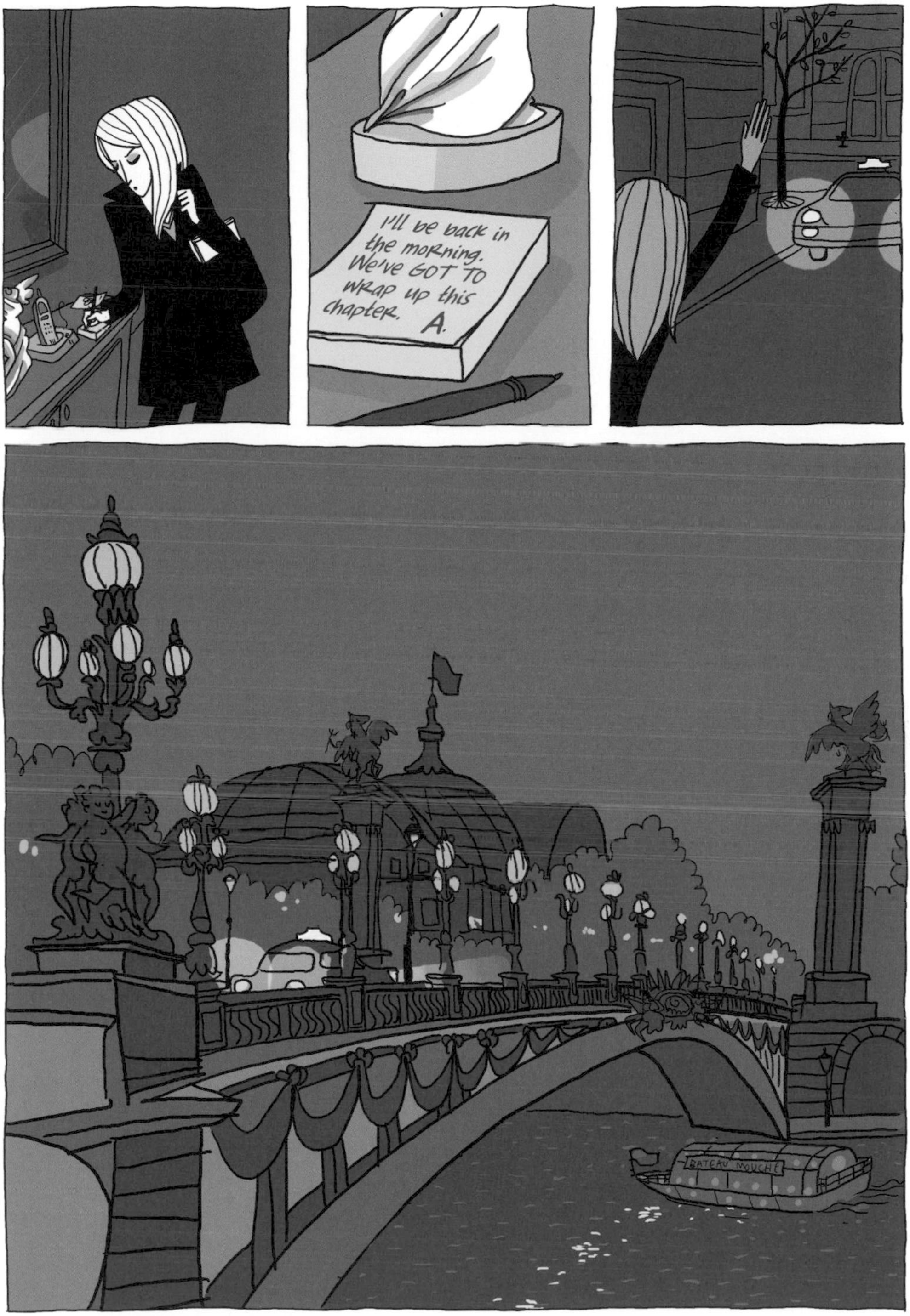
I'll be back in the morning. We've GOT TO wrap up this chapter. A.
BATEAU MOUCHE

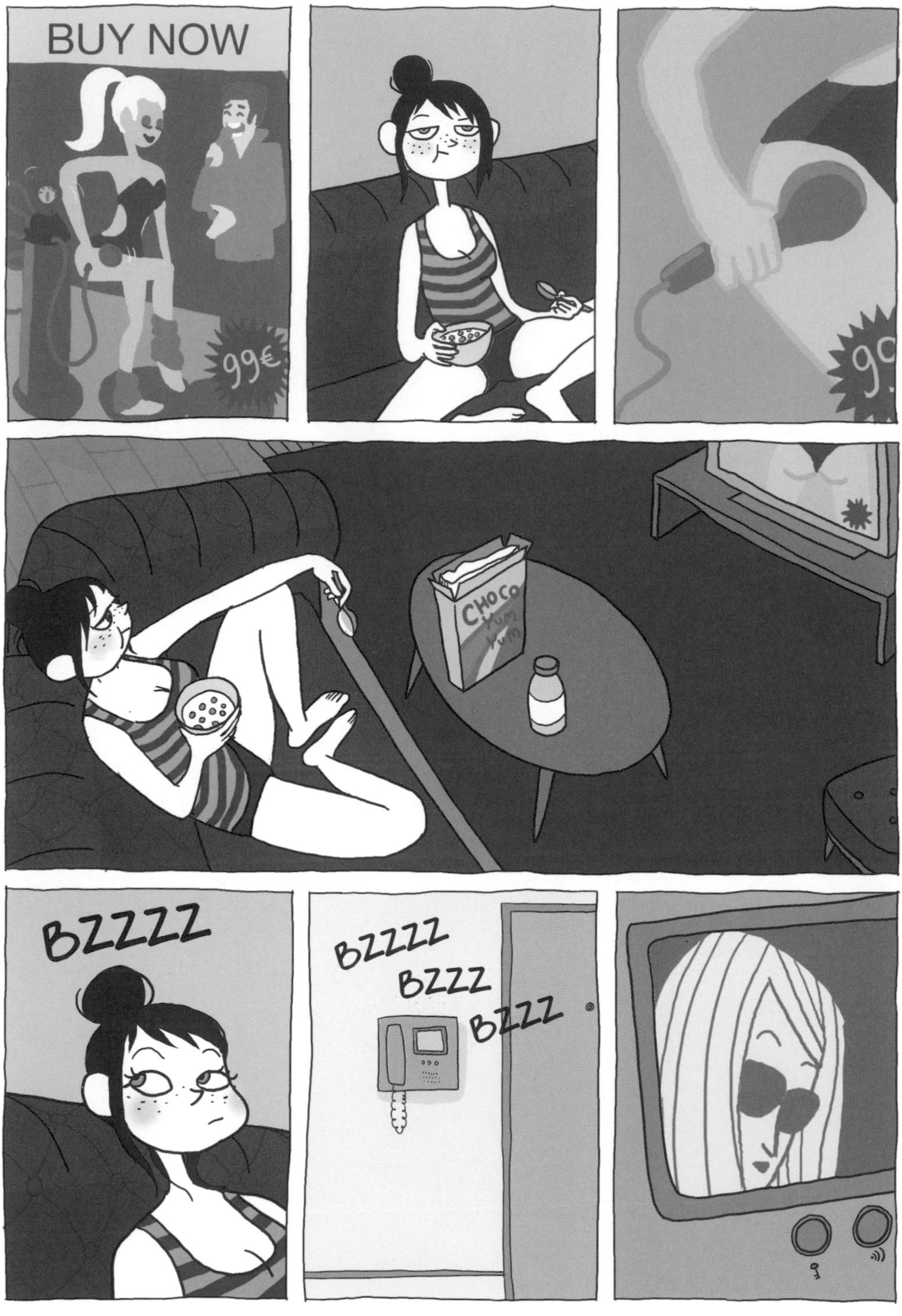
BUY NOW
99€
CHOCO
Yum
Yum
BZZZZ
BZZZZ
BZZZ
BZZZ

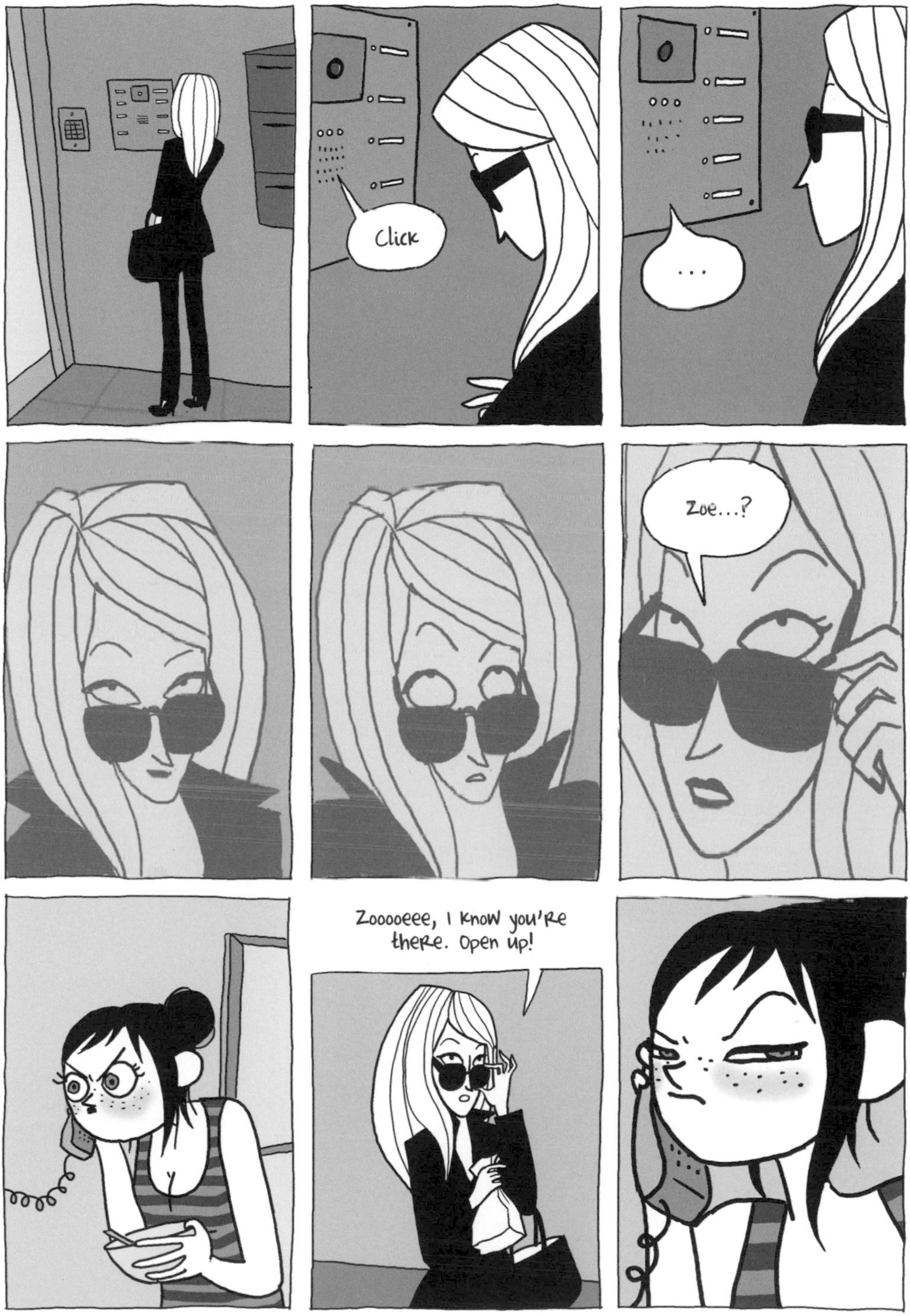
Click
...
Zoe...?
Zoooooeee, I know you're there. Open up!

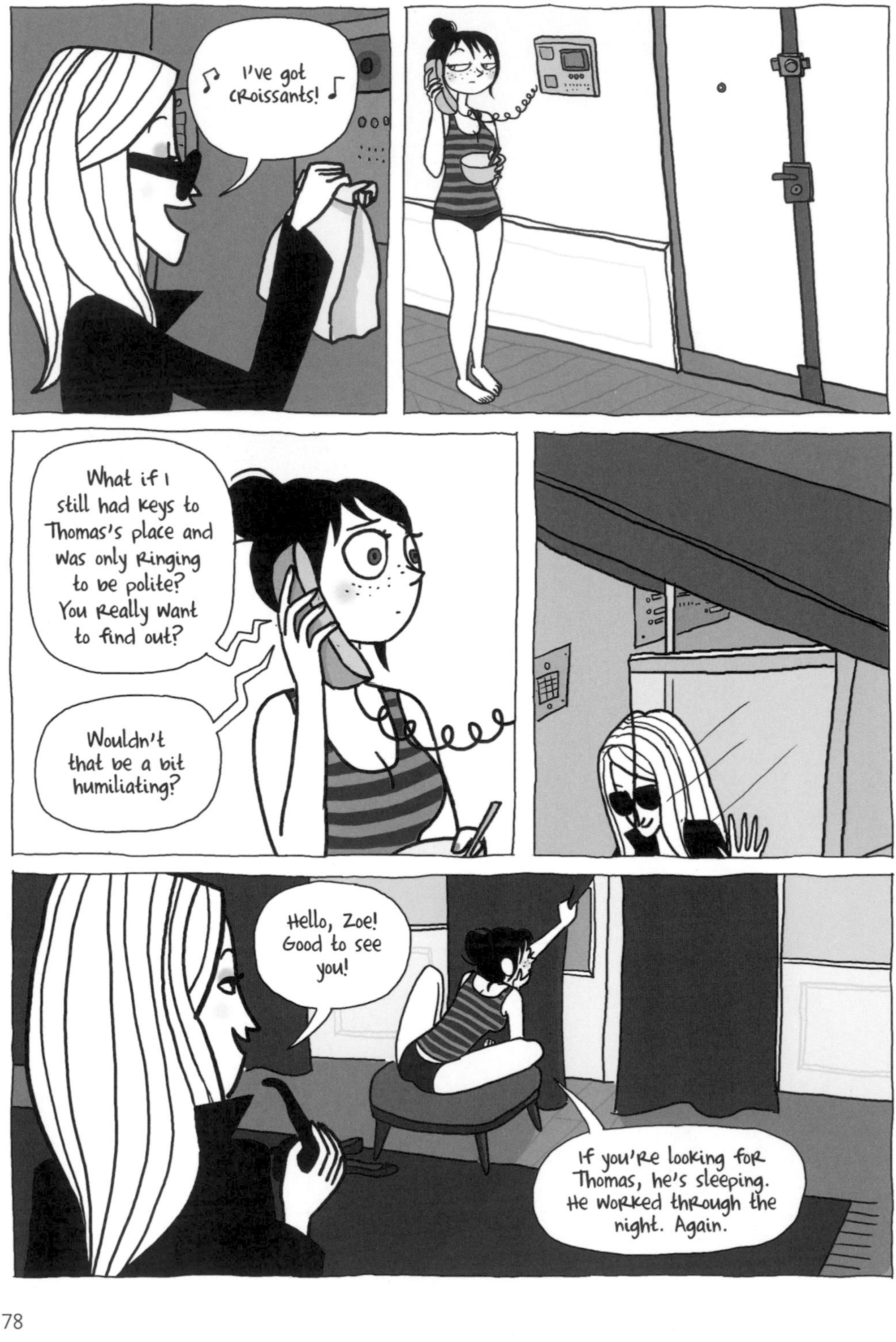
I've got croissants!
What if I still had keys to Thomas's place and was only ringing to be polite? You really want to find out?
Wouldn't that be a bit humiliating?
Hello, Zoe! Good to see you!
If you're looking for Thomas, he's sleeping. He worked through the night. Again.

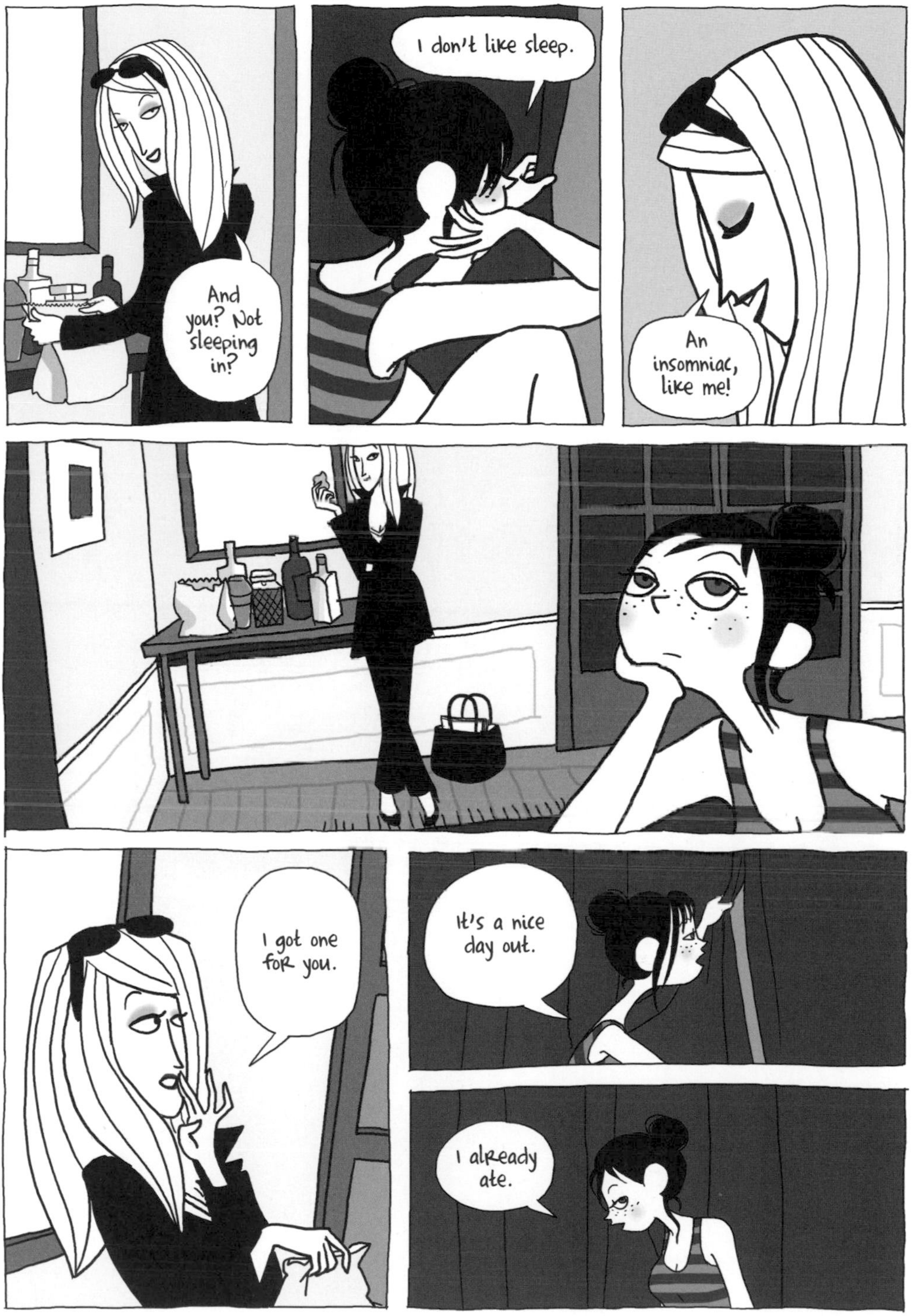
And you? Not sleeping in?
I don't like sleep.
An insomniac, like me!
I got one for you.
It's a nice day out.
I already ate.

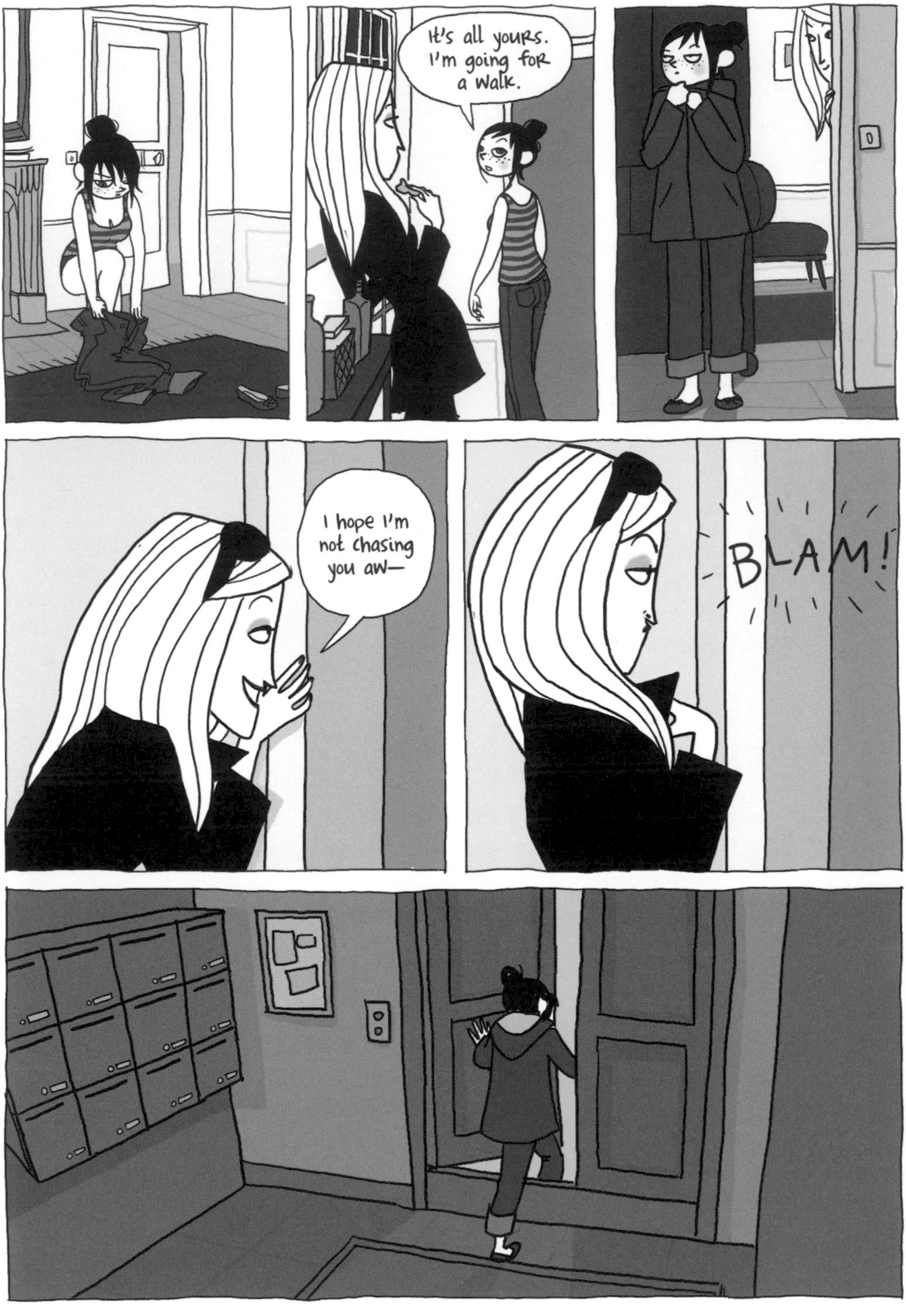
It's all yours. I'm going for a walk.
I hope I'm not chasing you aw—
BLAM!

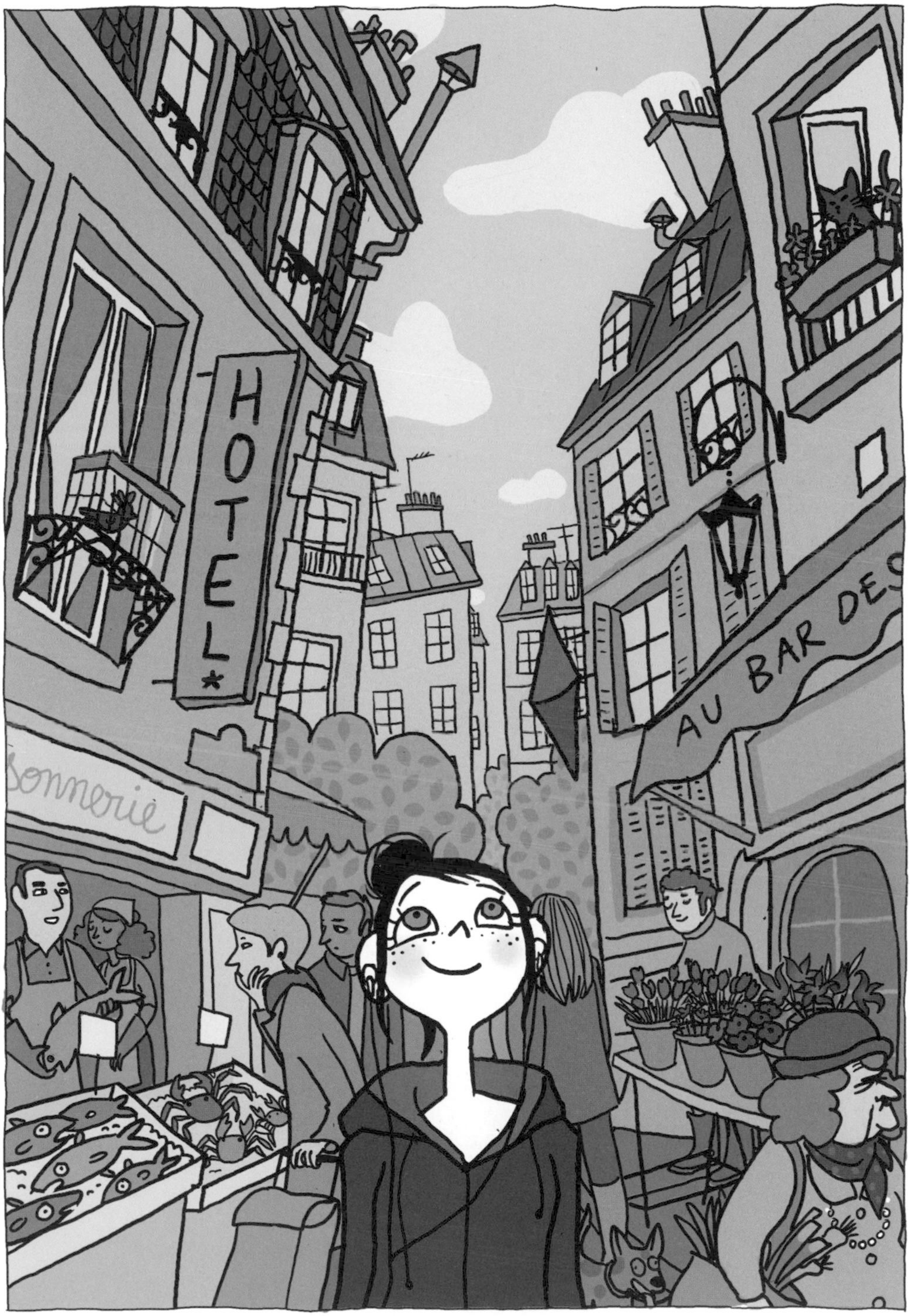
HOTEL*
AU BAR DES
onnerie

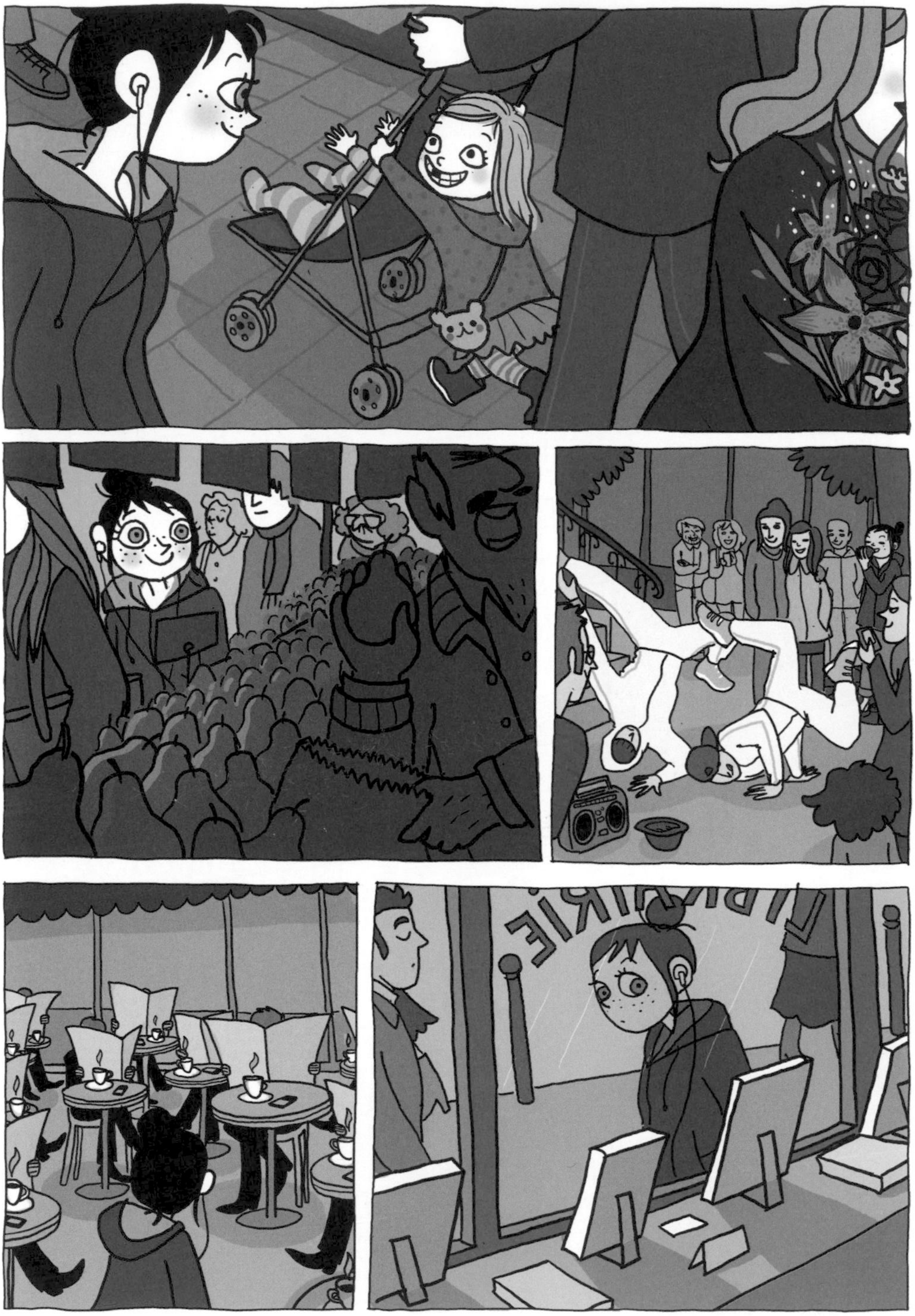

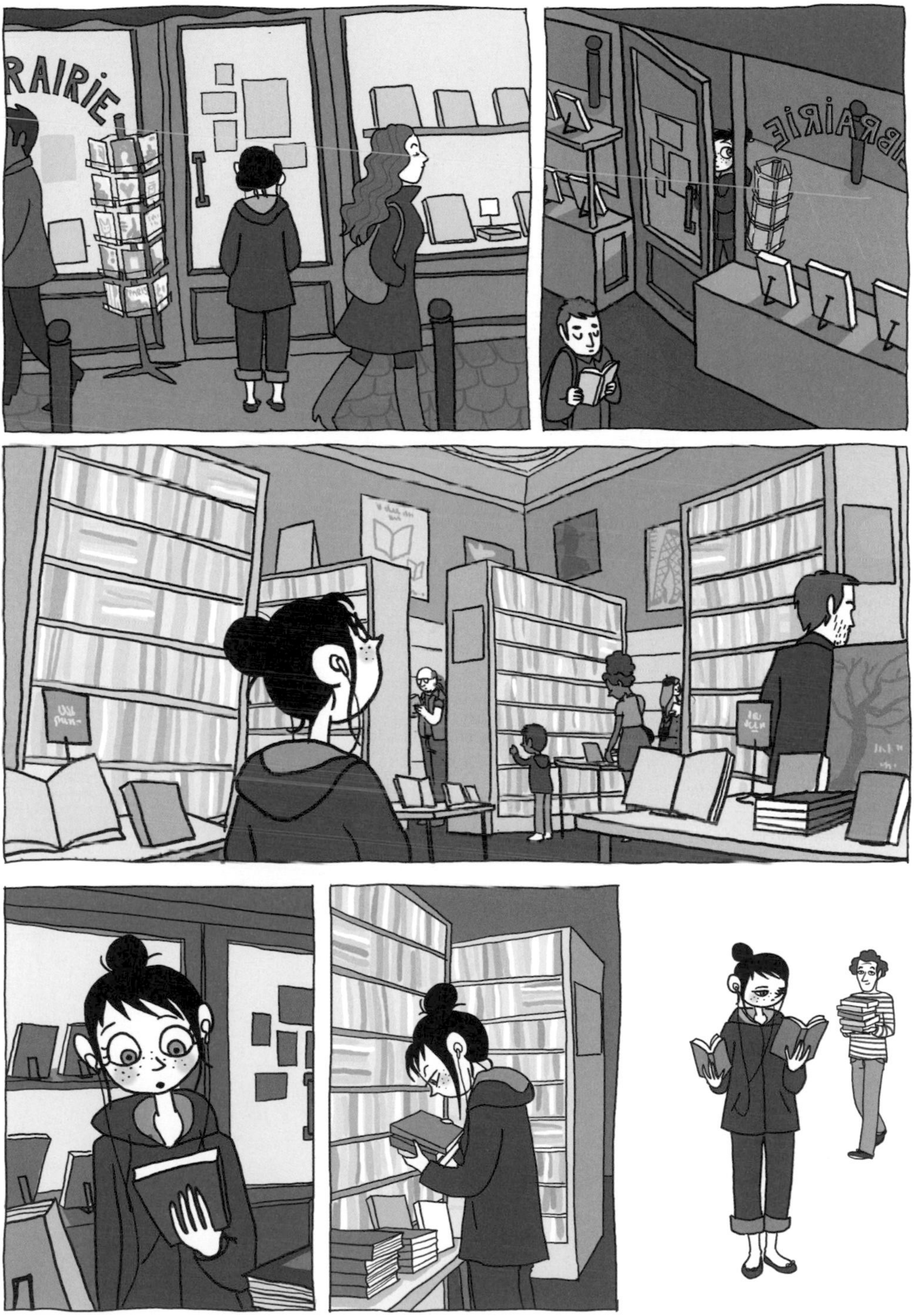
RAIRIE

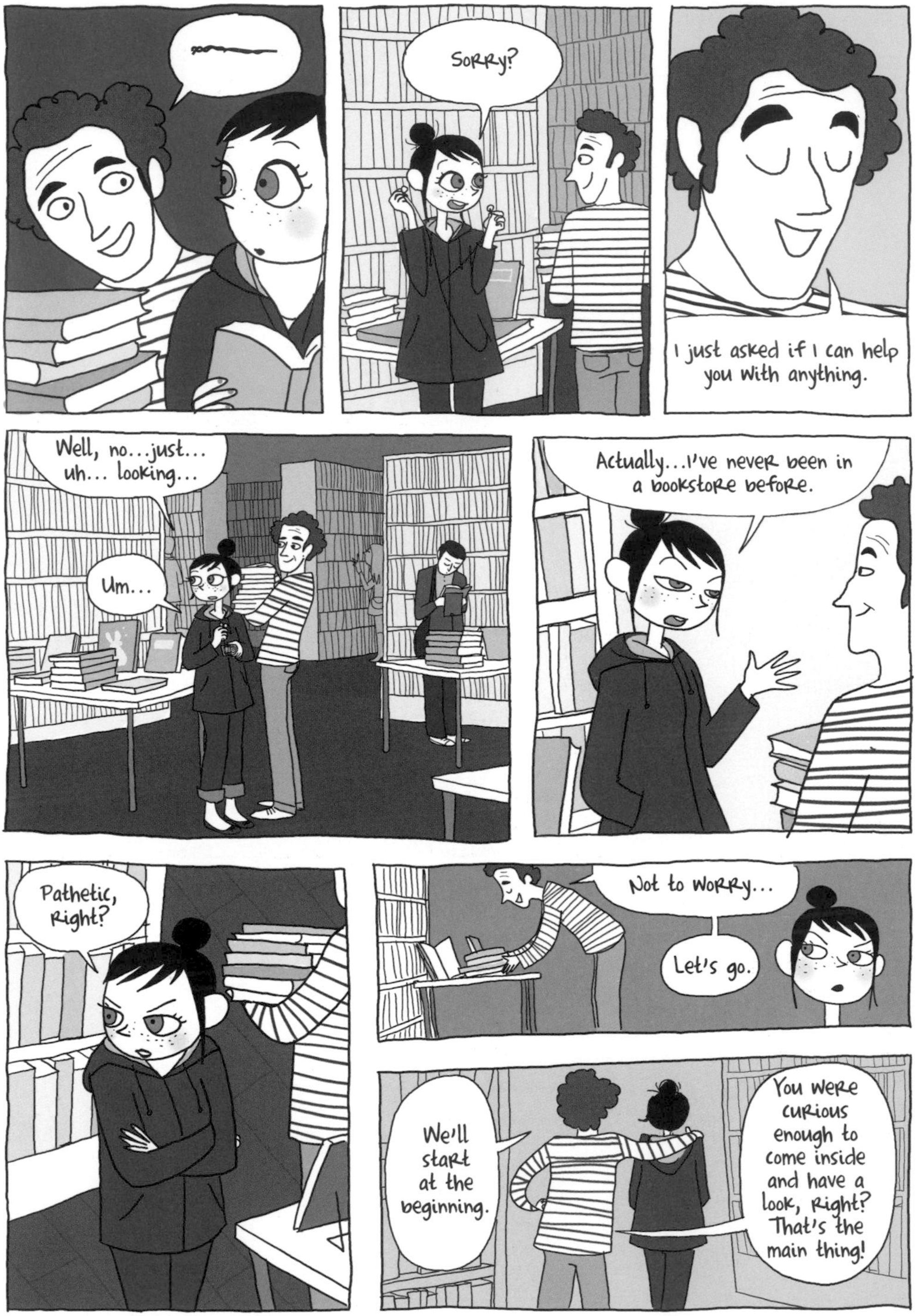
Sorry?
I just asked if I can help you with anything.
Well, no...just... uh... looking...
Um...
Actually...I've never been in a bookstore before.
Pathetic, right?
Not to worry...
Let's go.
We'll start at the beginning.
You were curious enough to come inside and have a look, right? That's the main thing!

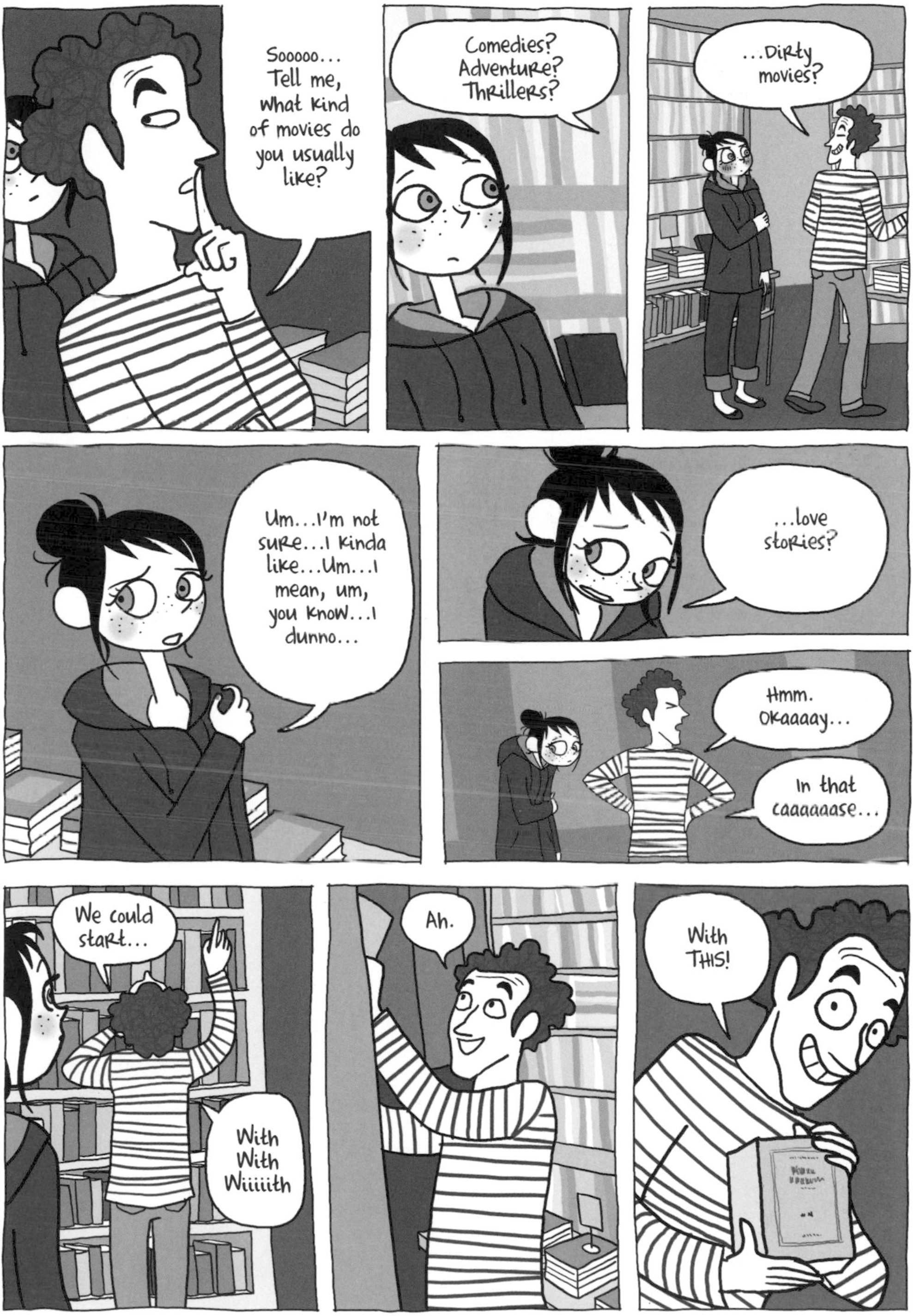
Sooooo... Tell me, what kind of movies do you usually like?
Comedies? Adventure? Thrillers?
...Dirty movies?
Um...I'm not sure...I kinda like...Um...I mean, um, you know...I dunno...
...love stories?
Hmm. Okaaaay...
In that caaaaaase...
We could start...
With With Wiiiiith
Ah.
With THIS!

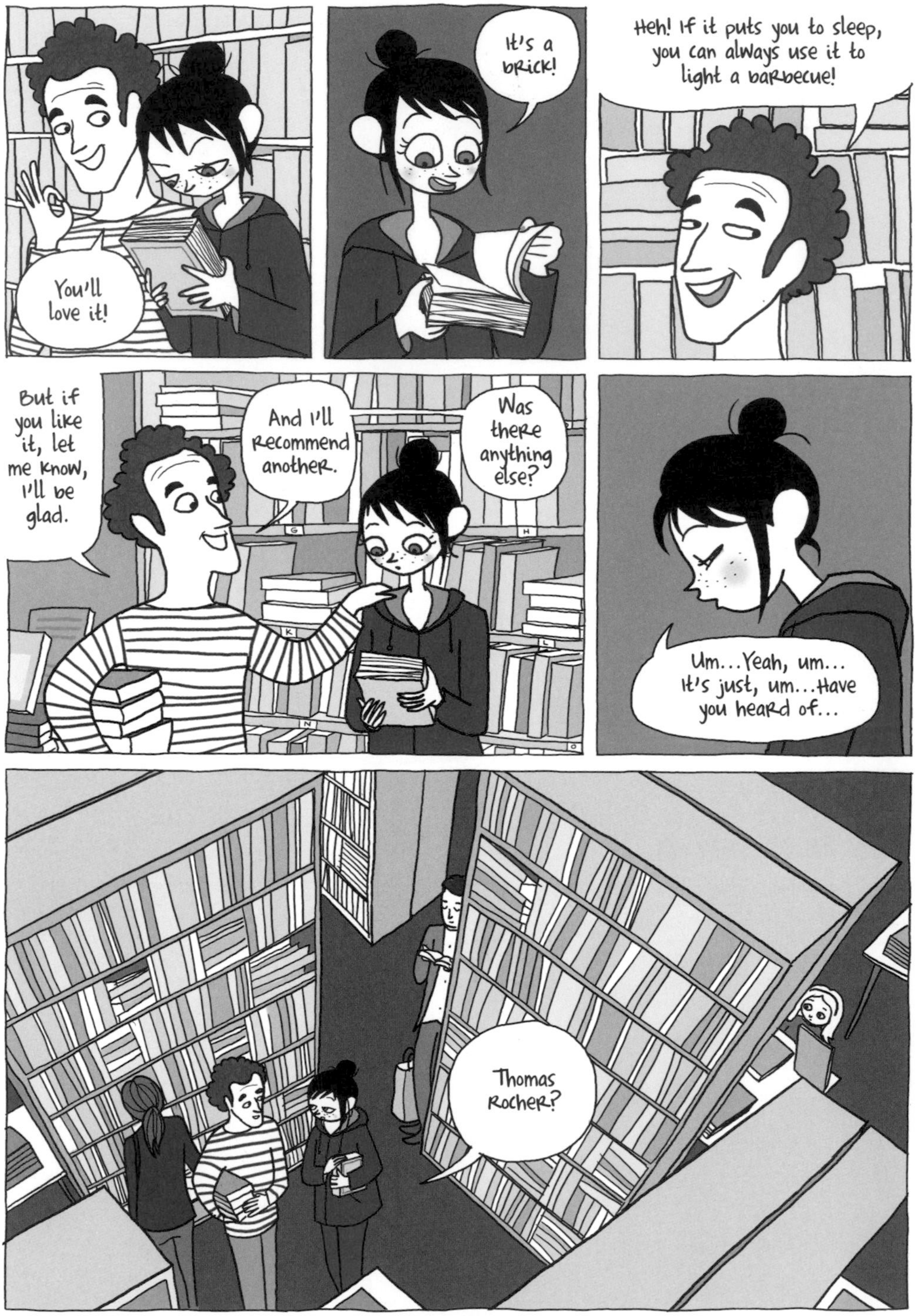
You'll love it!
It's a brick!
Heh! If it puts you to sleep, you can always use it to light a barbecue!
But if you like it, let me know, I'll be glad.
And I'll recommend another.
Was there anything else?
Um... Yeah, um... It's just, um... Have you heard of...
Thomas Rocher?

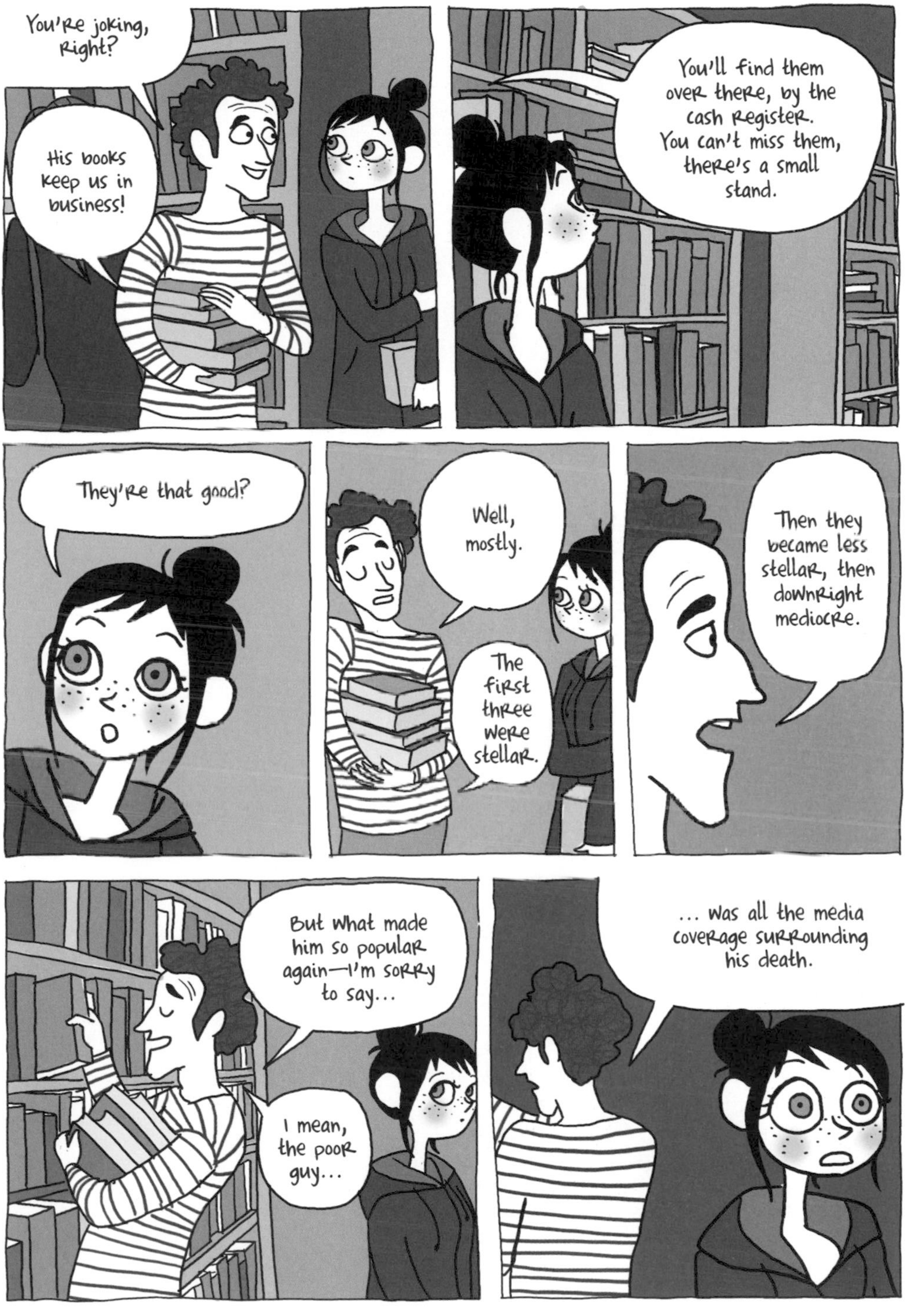
You're joking, right?
His books keep us in business!
You'll find them over there, by the cash register. You can't miss them, there's a small stand.
They're that good?
Well, mostly.
The first three were stellar.
Then they became less stellar, then downright mediocre.
But what made him so popular again—I'm sorry to say...
I mean, the poor guy...
... was all the media coverage surrounding his death.

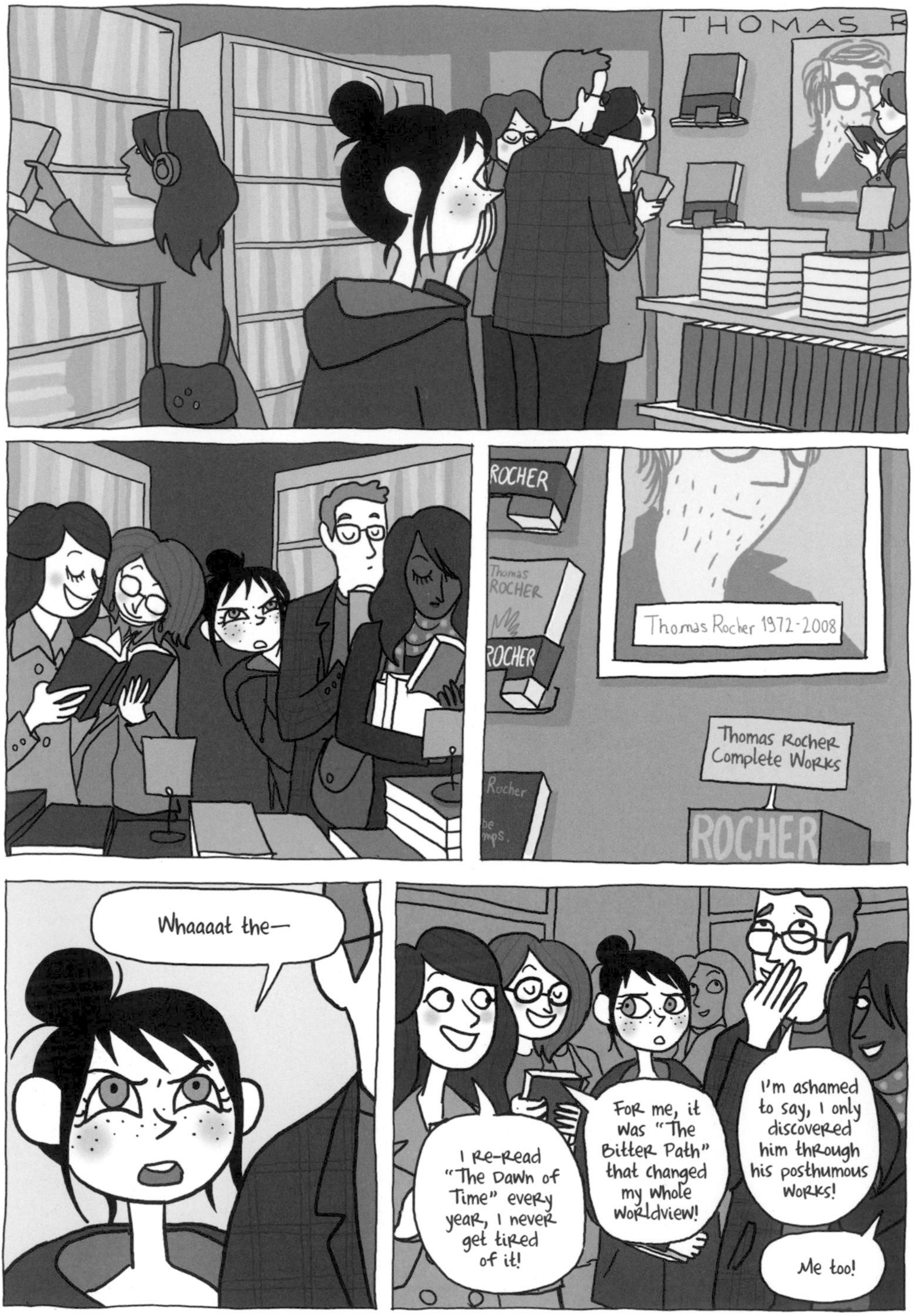
THOMAS R
ROCHER
Thomas ROCHER
ROCHER
Thomas Rocher 1972-2008
Thomas Rocher Complete Works
Rocher
ROCHER
Whaaaat the—
I re-read "The Dawn of Time" every year, I never get tired of it!
For me, it was "The Bitter Path" that changed my whole worldview!
I'm ashamed to say, I only discovered him through his posthumous works!
Me too!

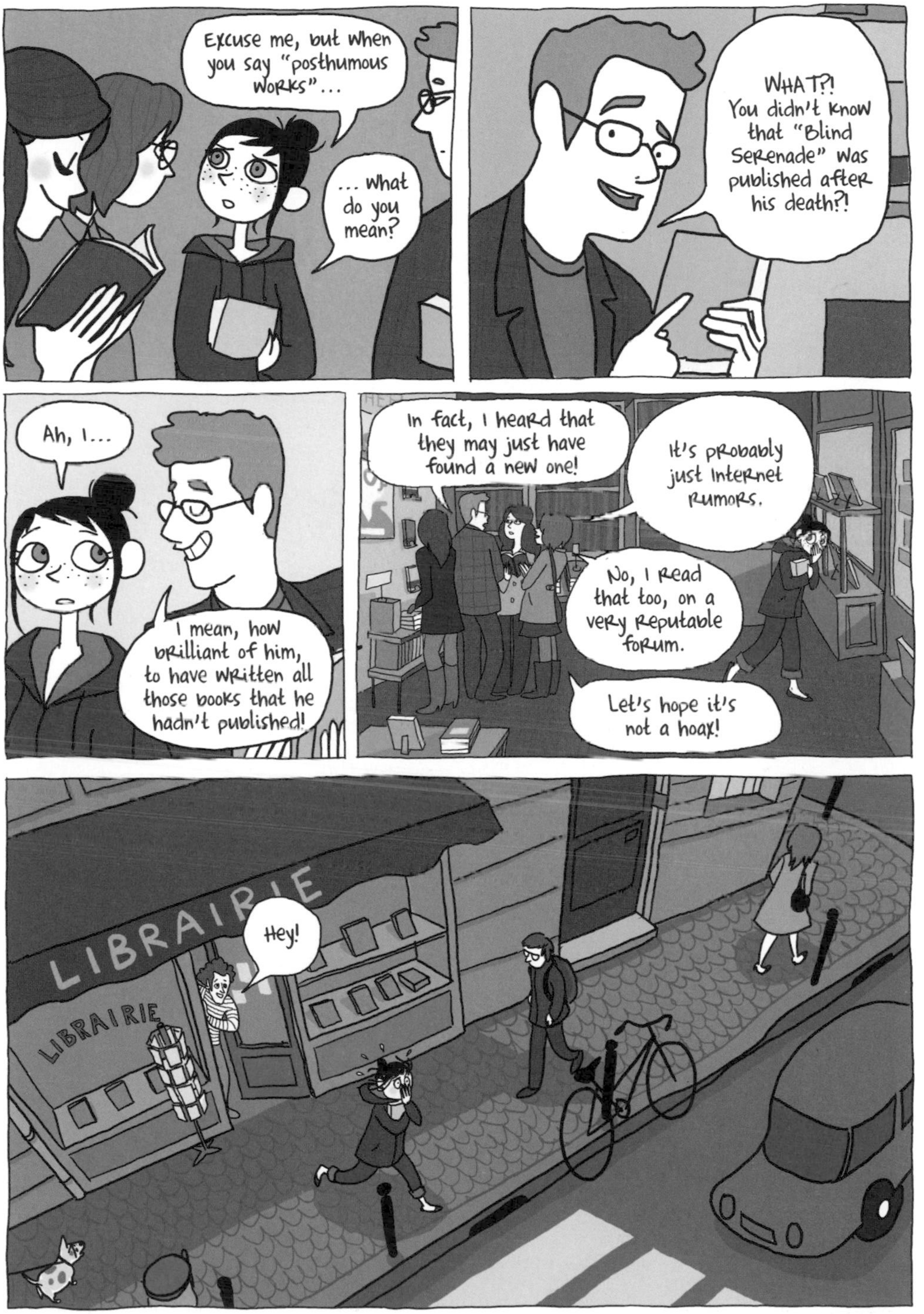
Excuse me, but when you say "posthumous works"...
... What do you mean?
WHAT?! You didn't know that "Blind Serenade" was published after his death?!
Ah, I...
I mean, how brilliant of him, to have written all those books that he hadn't published!
In fact, I heard that they may just have found a new one!
It's probably just internet rumors.
No, I read that too, on a very reputable forum.
Let's hope it's not a hoax!
LIBRAIRIE
LIBRAIRIE
Hey!

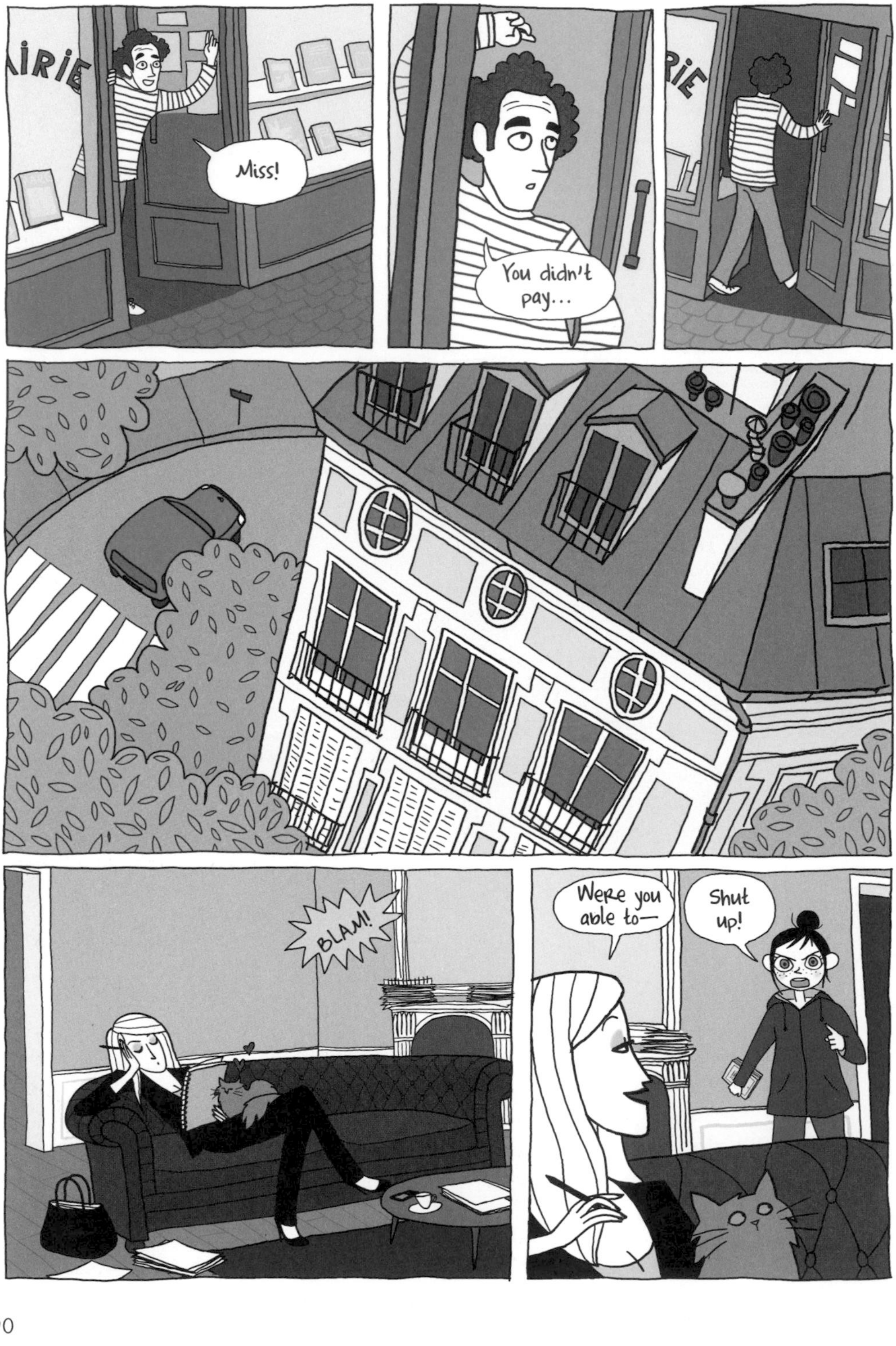

AIRIE
Miss!
You didn't pay...
RIE
BLAM!
Were you able to—
Shut up!

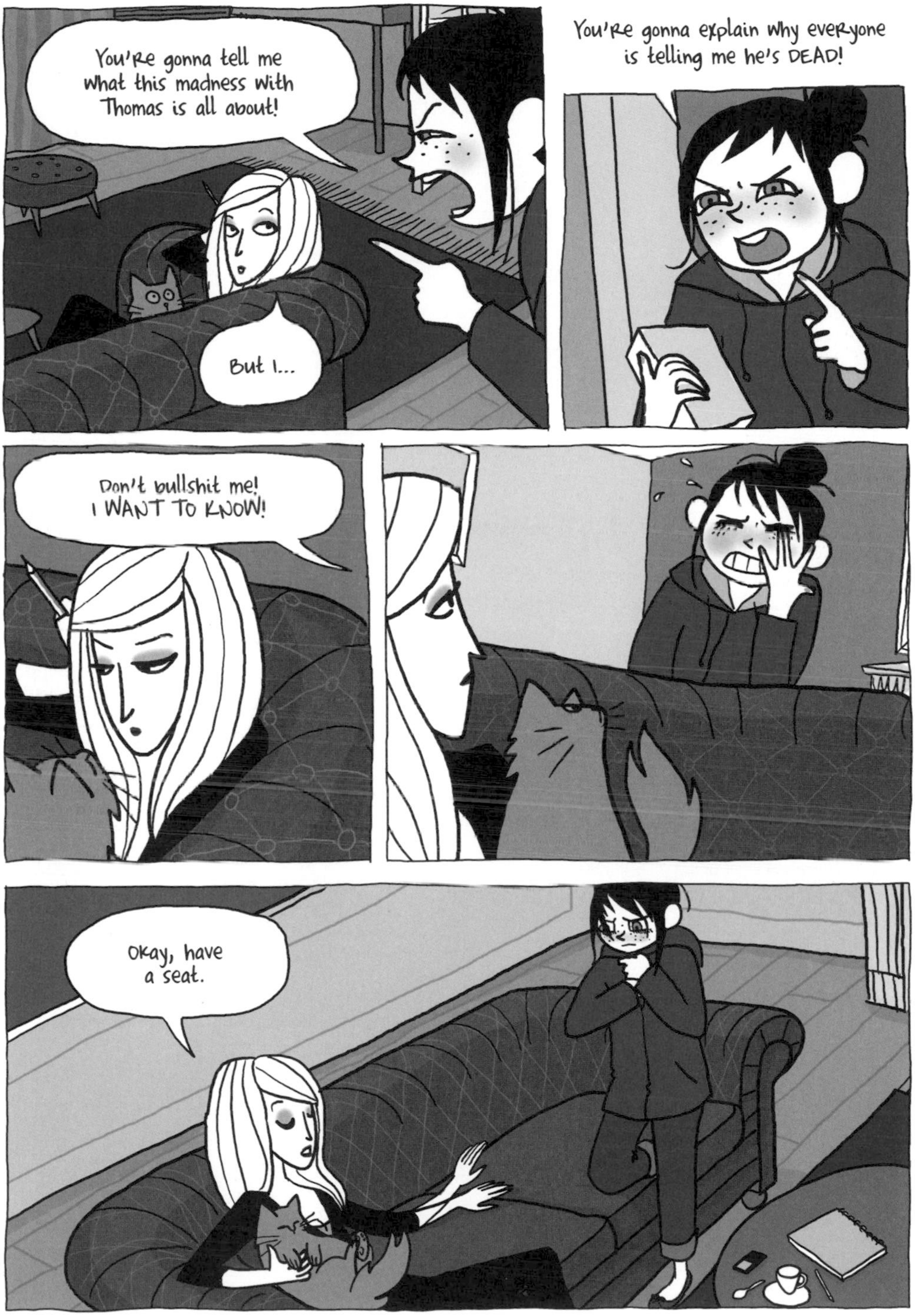
You're gonna tell me what this madness with Thomas is all about!
But I...
You're gonna explain why everyone is telling me he's DEAD!
Don't bullshit me! I WANT TO KNOW!
Okay, have a seat.

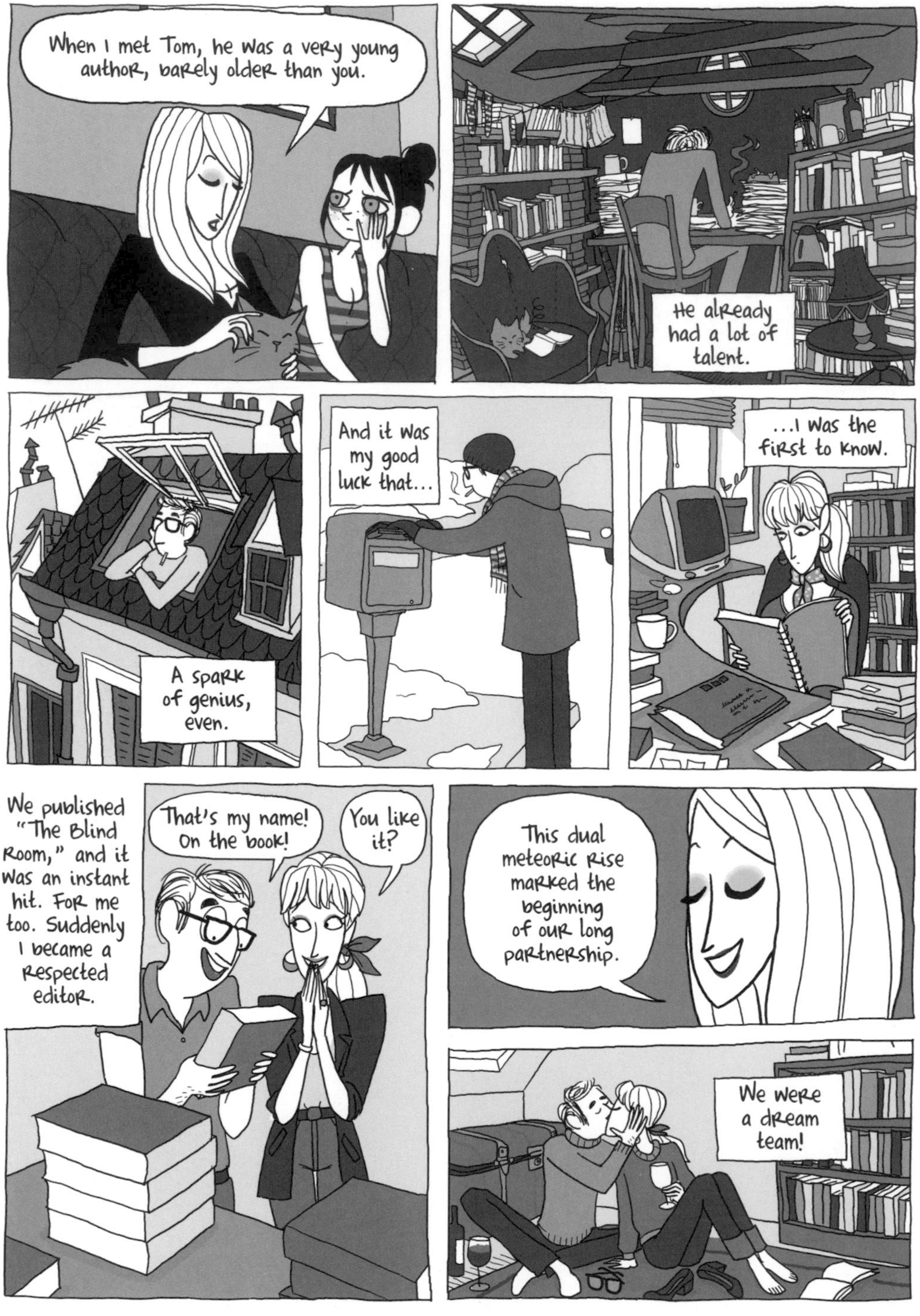
When I met Tom, he was a very young author, barely older than you.
He already had a lot of talent.
A spark of genius, even.
And it was my good luck that...
...I was the first to know.
We published "The Blind Room," and it was an instant hit. For me too. Suddenly I became a respected editor.
That's my name! On the book!
You like it?
This dual meteoric rise marked the beginning of our long partnership.
We were a dream team!

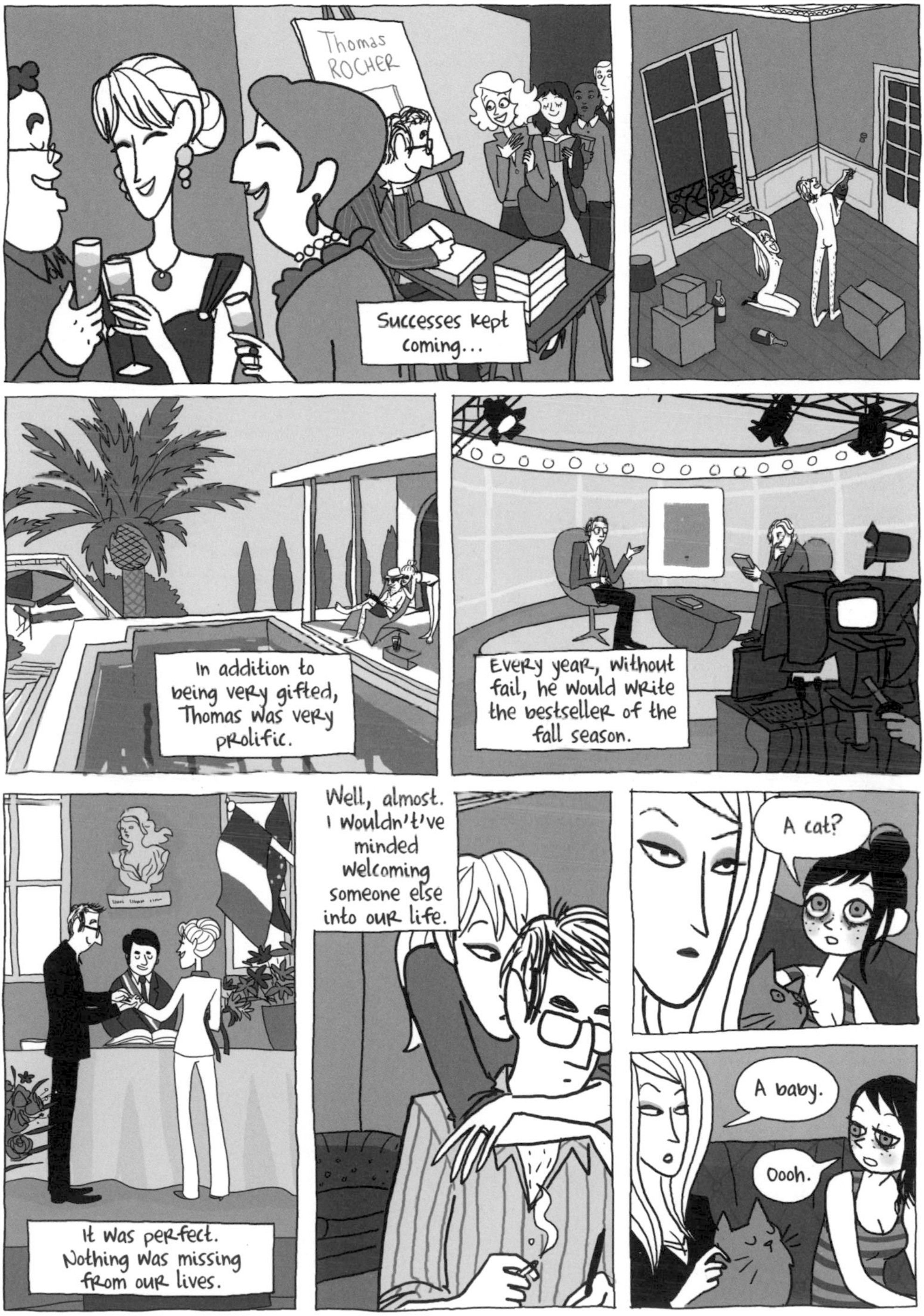
Thomas ROCHER
Successes kept coming...
In addition to being very gifted, Thomas was very prolific.
Every year, without fail, he would write the bestseller of the fall season.
It was perfect. Nothing was missing from our lives.
Well, almost. I wouldn't've minded welcoming someone else into our life.
A cat?
A baby.
Oooh.

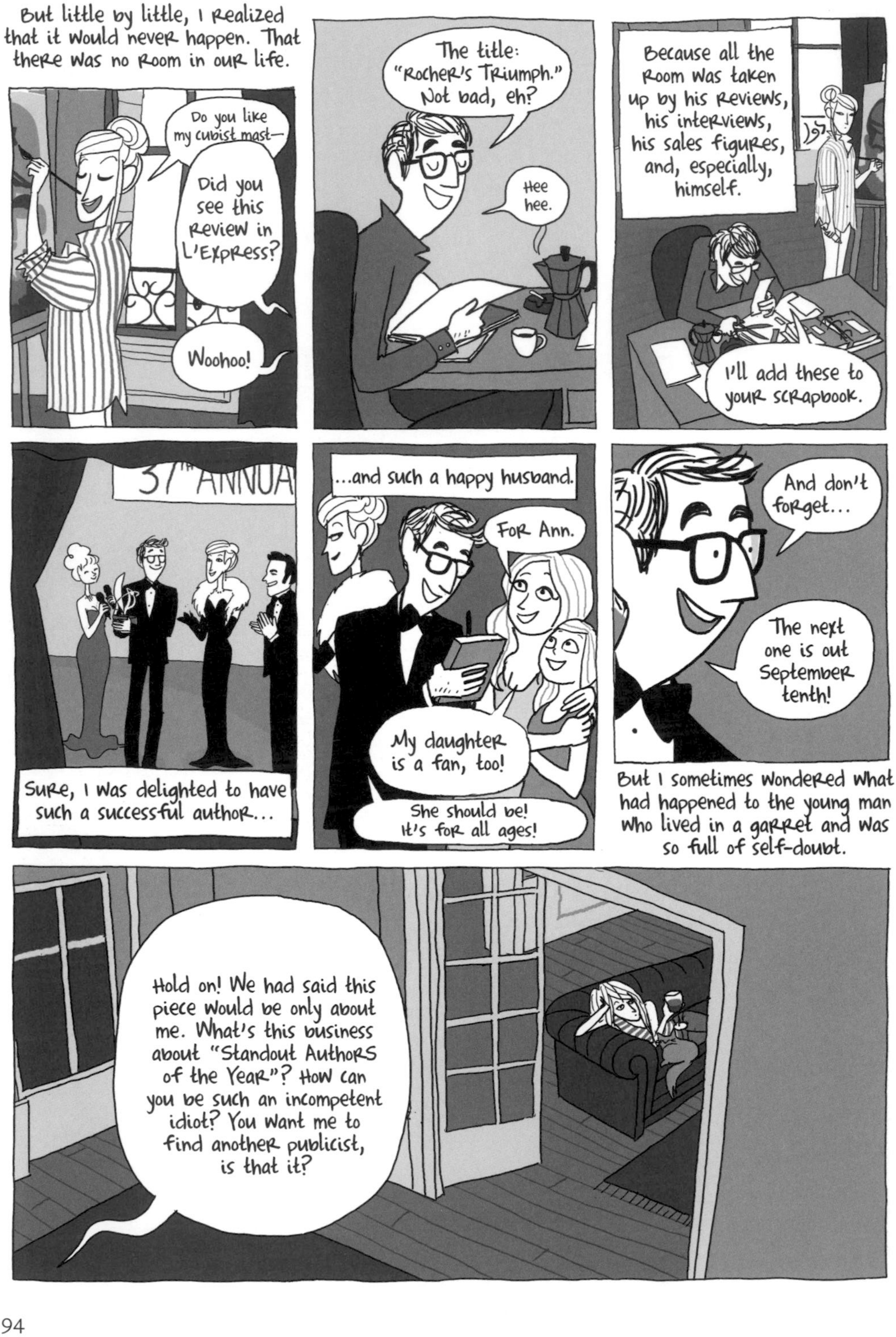

But little by little, I realized that it would never happen. That there was no room in our life.
Do you like my cubist mast—
Did you see this review in L'Express?
Woohoo!
The title: "Rocher's Triumph." Not bad, eh?
Hee hee.
Because all the room was taken up by his reviews, his interviews, his sales figures, and, especially, himself.
I'll add these to your scrapbook.
37TH ANNUA
Sure, I was delighted to have such a successful author...
...and such a happy husband.
For Ann.
My daughter is a fan, too!
She should be! It's for all ages!
And don't forget...
The next one is out September tenth!
But I sometimes wondered what had happened to the young man who lived in a garret and was so full of self-doubt.
Hold on! We had said this piece would be only about me. What's this business about "Standout Authors of the Year"? How can you be such an incompetent idiot? You want me to find another publicist, is that it?

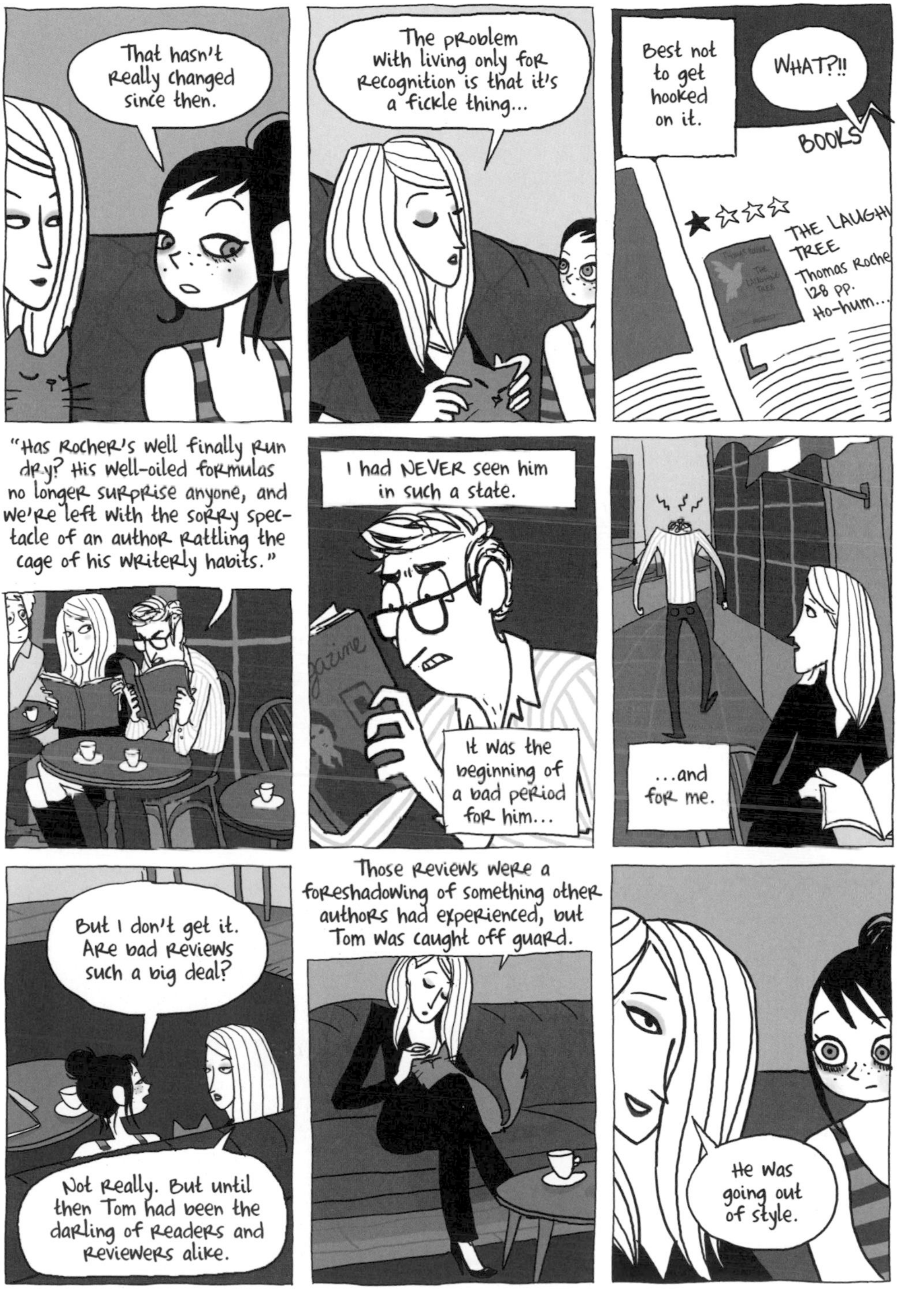
That hasn't really changed since then.
The problem with living only for recognition is that it's a fickle thing...
Best not to get hooked on it.
WHAT?!!
BOOKS
THE LAUGH
TREE
Thomas Roche
128 pp.
Ho-hum...
"Has Rocher's well finally run dry? His well-oiled formulas no longer surprise anyone, and we're left with the sorry spectacle of an author rattling the cage of his writerly habits."
I had NEVER seen him in such a state.
It was the beginning of a bad period for him...
...and for me.
But I don't get it. Are bad reviews such a big deal?
Not really. But until then Tom had been the darling of readers and reviewers alike.
Those reviews were a foreshadowing of something other authors had experienced, but Tom was caught off guard.
He was going out of style.

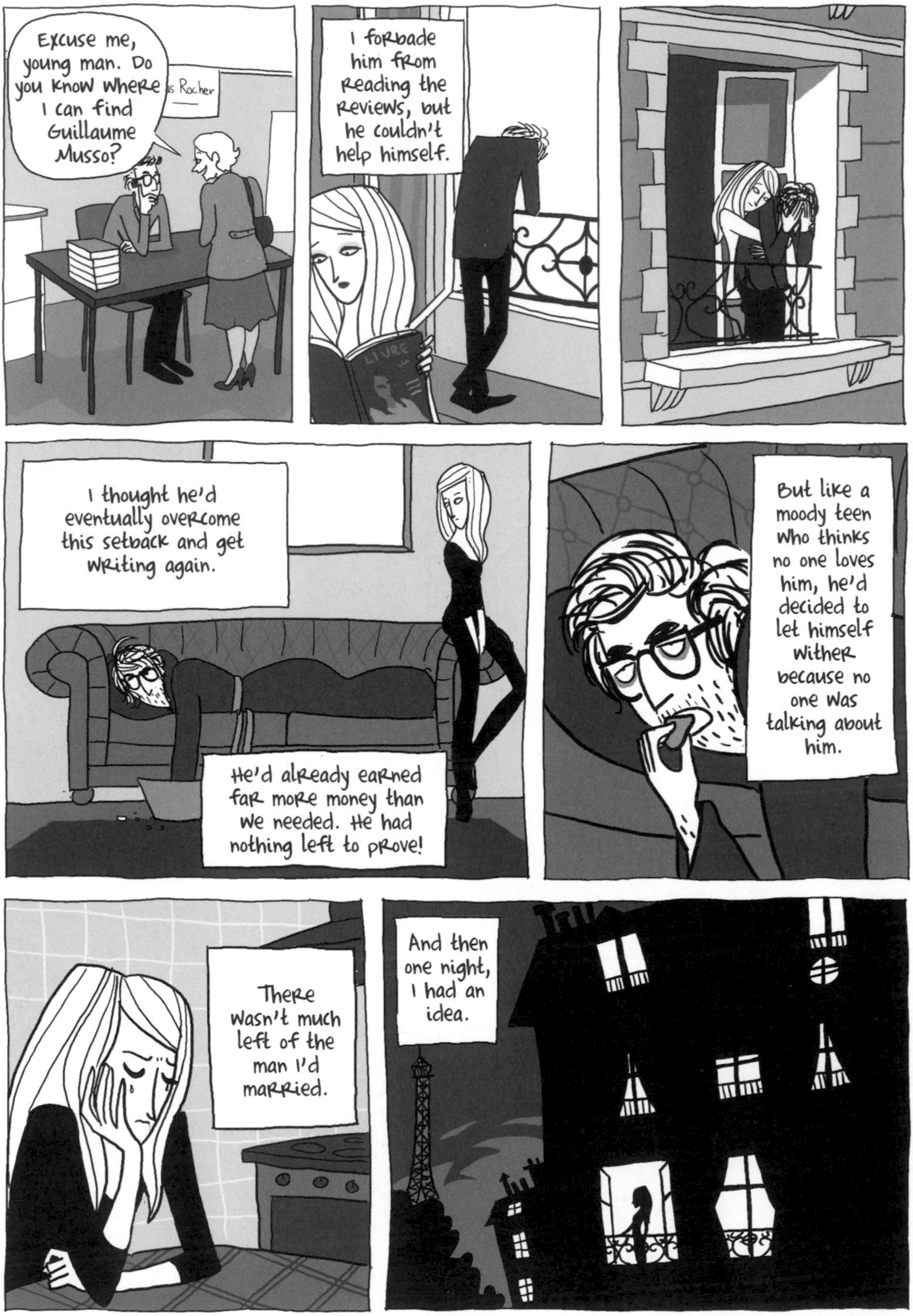

Excuse me, young man. Do you know where I can find Guillaume Musso?
Rocher
I forbade him from reading the reviews, but he couldn't help himself.
LIVRE
I thought he'd eventually overcome this setback and get writing again.
He'd already earned far more money than we needed. He had nothing left to prove!
But like a moody teen who thinks no one loves him, he'd decided to let himself wither because no one was talking about him.
There wasn't much left of the man I'd married.
And then one night, I had an idea.

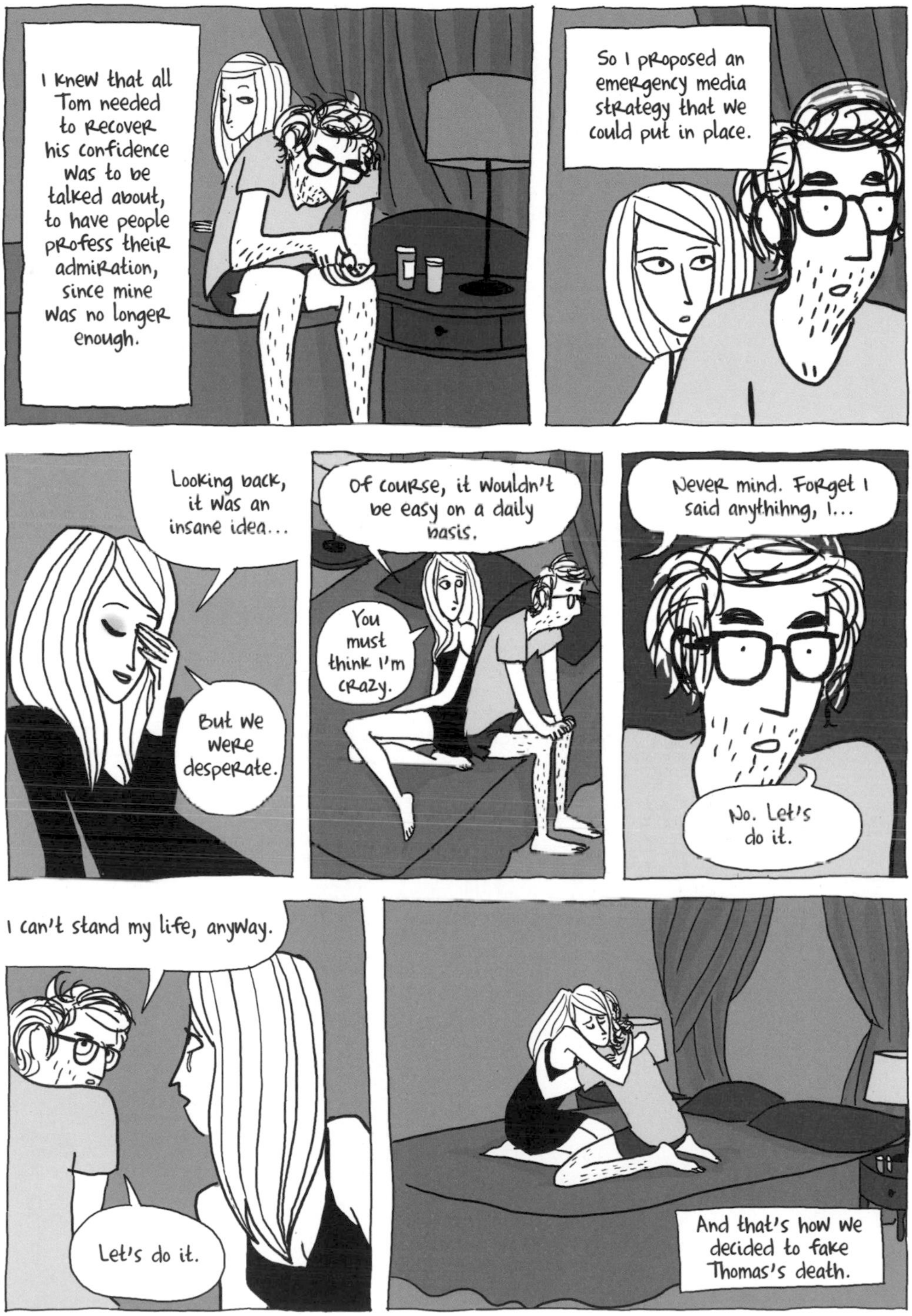
I knew that all Tom needed to recover his confidence was to be talked about, to have people profess their admiration, since mine was no longer enough.
So I proposed an emergency media strategy that we could put in place.
Looking back, it was an insane idea...
But we were desperate.
Of course, it wouldn't be easy on a daily basis.
You must think I'm crazy.
Never mind. Forget I said anythihng, I...
No. Let's do it.
I can't stand my life, anyway.
Let's do it.
And that's how we decided to fake Thomas's death.

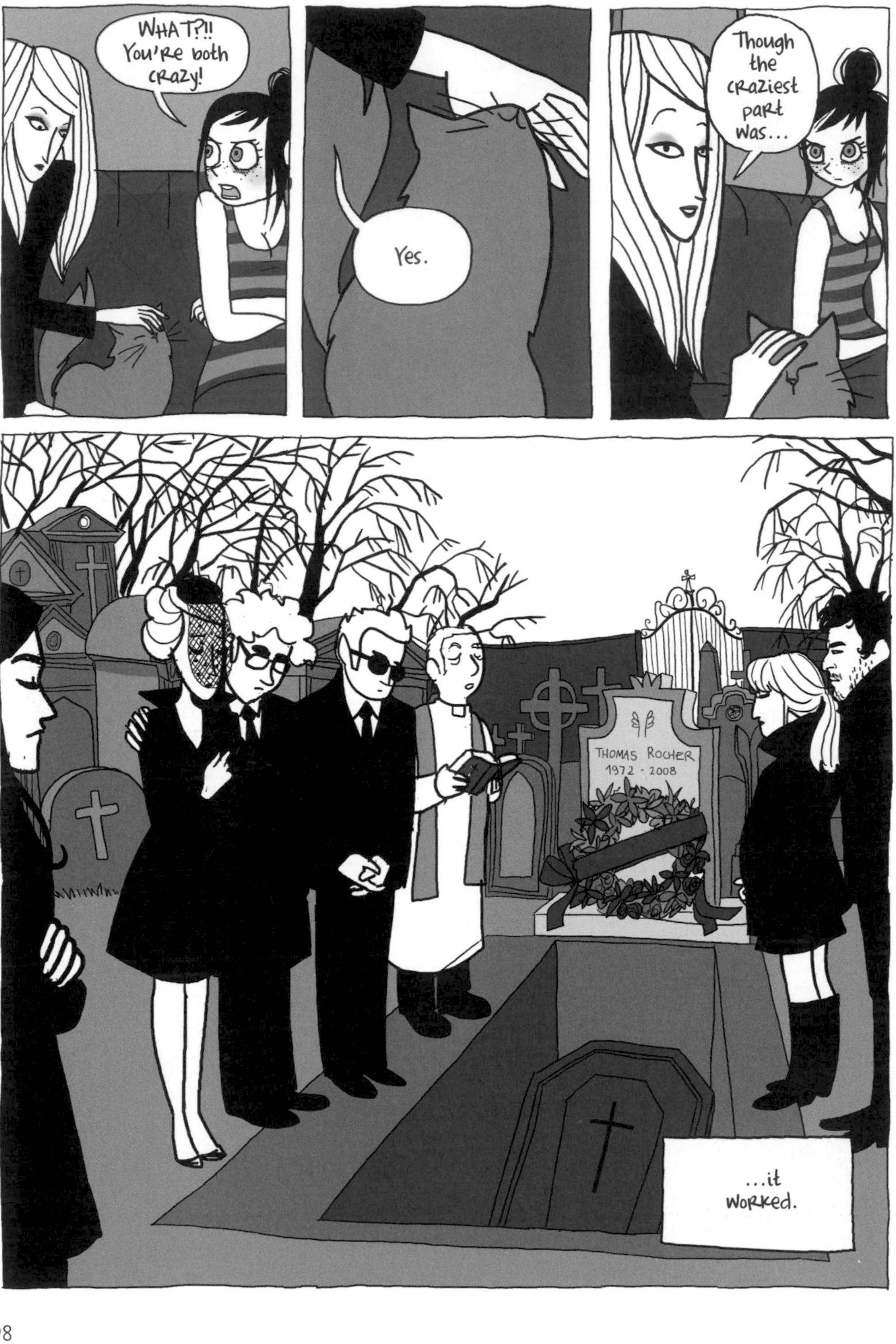

WHAT?!! You're both crazy!
Yes.
Though the craziest part was...
THOMAS ROCHER 1972 - 2008
...it worked.

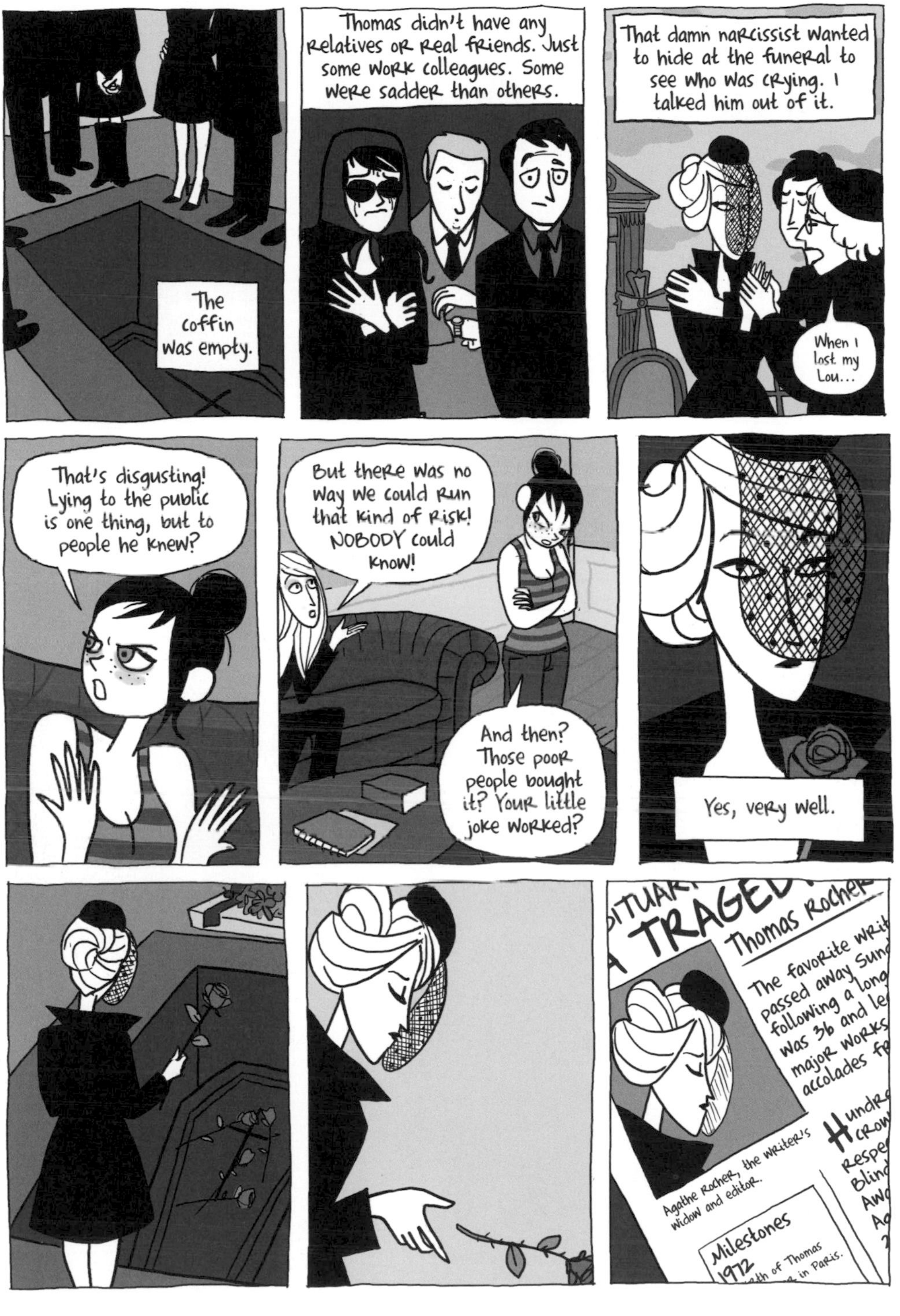
The coffin was empty.
Thomas didn't have any relatives or real friends. Just some work colleagues. Some were sadder than others.
That damn narcissist wanted to hide at the funeral to see who was crying. I talked him out of it.
When I lost my Lou...
That's disgusting! Lying to the public is one thing, but to people he knew?
But there was no way we could run that kind of risk! NOBODY could know!
And then? Those poor people bought it? Your little joke worked?
Yes, very well.
Thomas Rocher
Agathe Rocher, the writer's widow and editor.
Milestones
1972

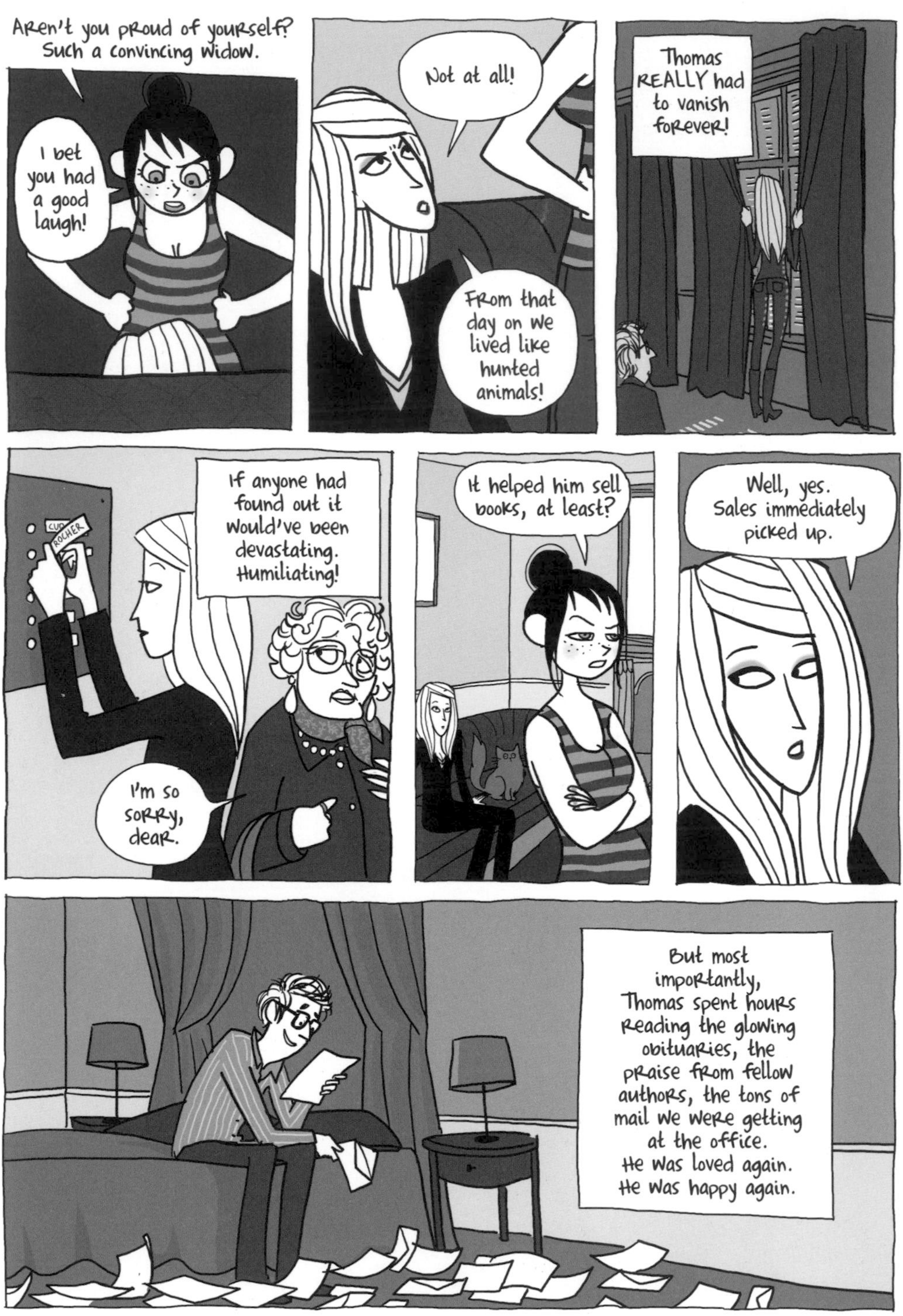
Aren't you proud of yourself? Such a convincing widow.
I bet you had a good laugh!
Not at all!
From that day on we lived like hunted animals!
Thomas REALLY had to vanish forever!
CUP
ROCHER
If anyone had found out it would've been devastating. Humiliating!
I'm so sorry, dear.
It helped him sell books, at least?
Well, yes. Sales immediately picked up.
But most importantly, Thomas spent hours reading the glowing obituaries, the praise from fellow authors, the tons of mail we were getting at the office.
He was loved again.
He was happy again.

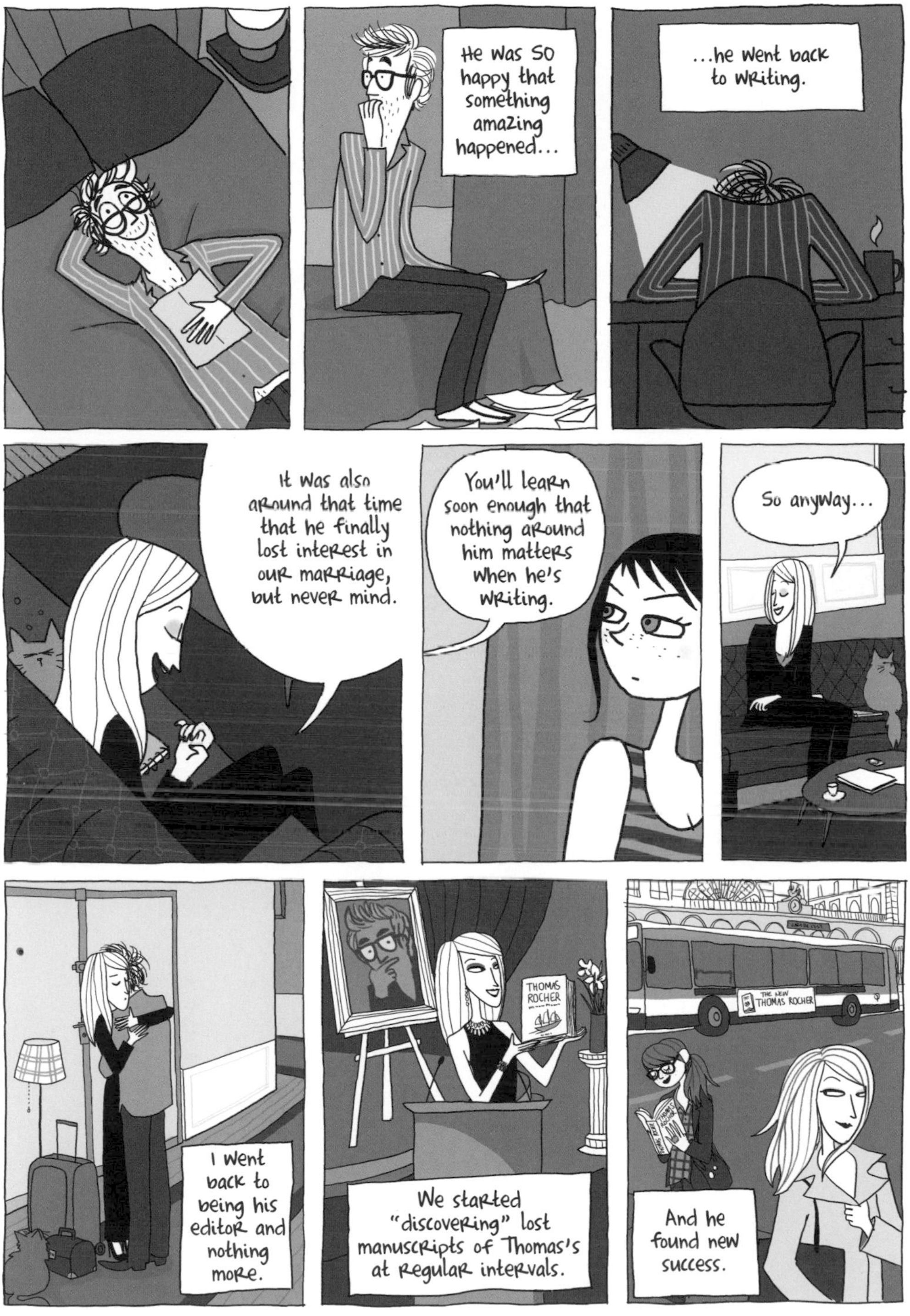
He was SO happy that something amazing happened...
...he went back to writing.
It was also around that time that he finally lost interest in our marriage, but never mind.
You'll learn soon enough that nothing around him matters when he's writing.
So anyway...
I went back to being his editor and nothing more.
THOMAS ROCHER
We started "discovering" lost manuscripts of Thomas's at regular intervals.
THE NEW THOMAS ROCHER
And he found new success.

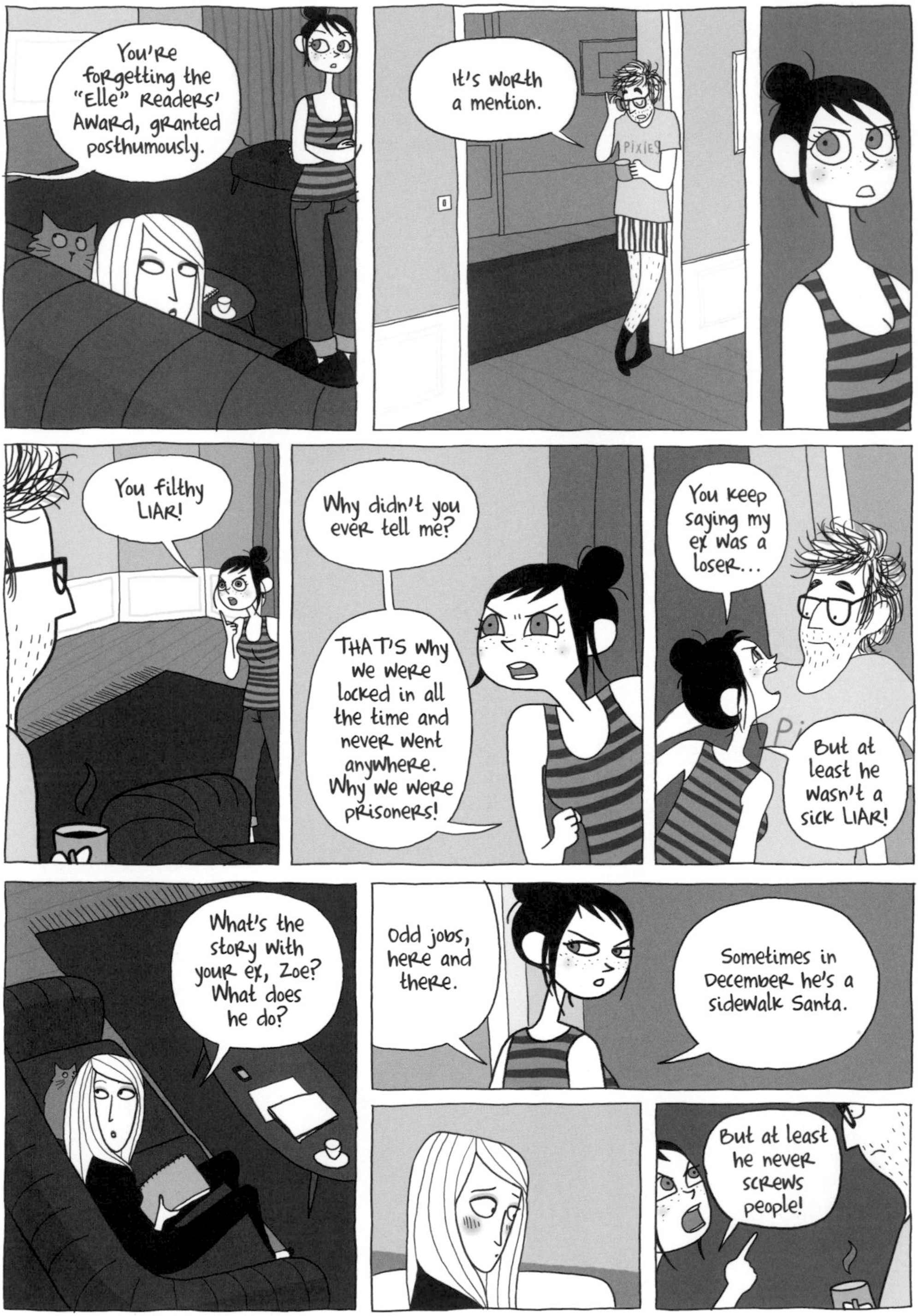
You're forgetting the "Elle" Readers' Award, granted posthumously.
It's worth a mention.
You filthy LIAR!
Why didn't you ever tell me?
THAT'S why we were locked in all the time and never went anywhere. Why we were prisoners!
You keep saying my ex was a loser...
But at least he wasn't a sick LIAR!
What's the story with your ex, Zoe? What does he do?
Odd jobs, here and there.
Sometimes in December he's a sidewalk Santa.
But at least he never screws people!

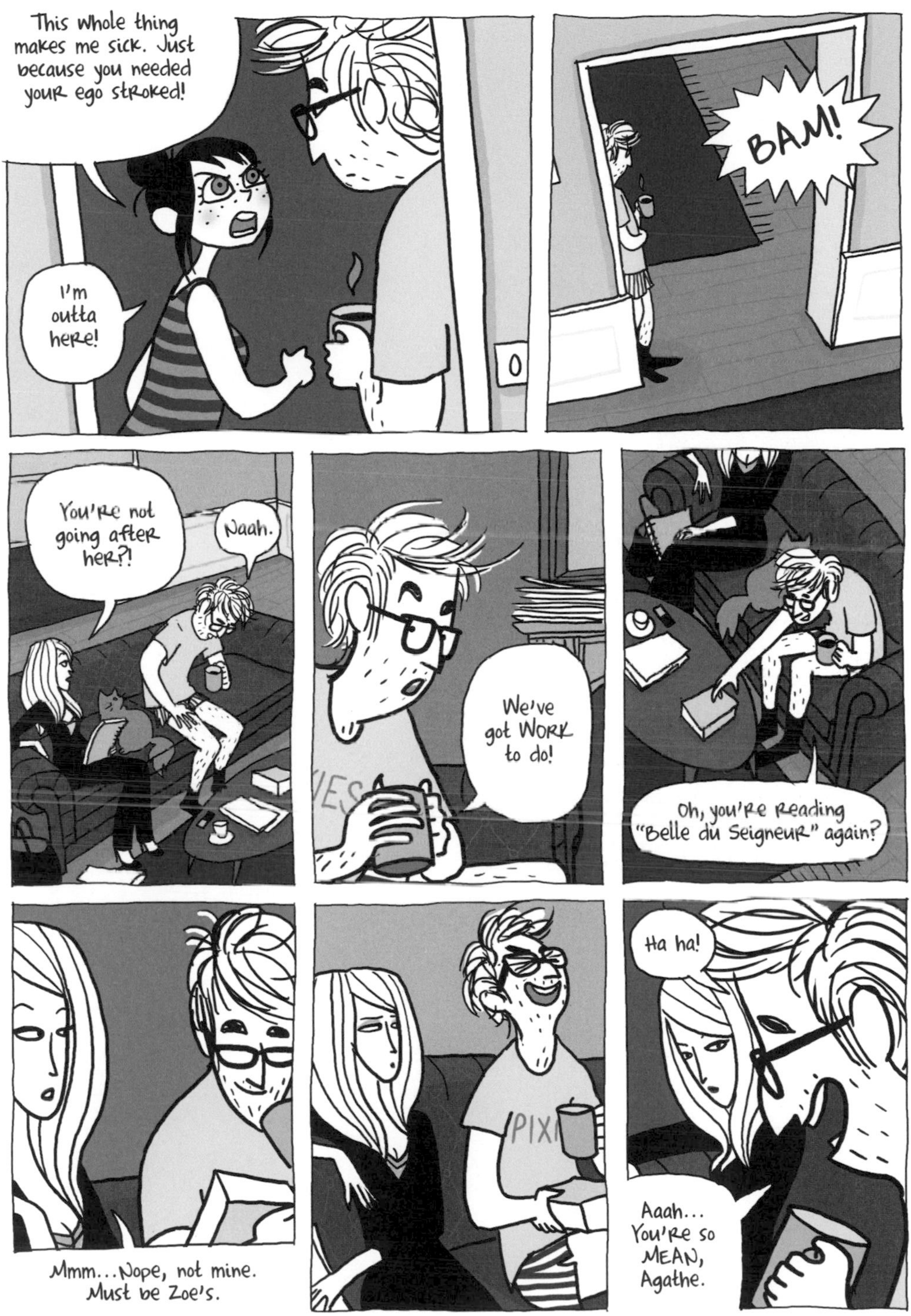
This whole thing makes me sick. Just because you needed your ego stroked!
I'm outta here!
BAM!
You're not going after her?!
Naah.
We've got WORK to do!
Oh, you're reading "Belle du Seigneur" again?
Mmm...Nope, not mine. Must be Zoe's.
Ha ha!
Aaah... You're so MEAN, Agathe.

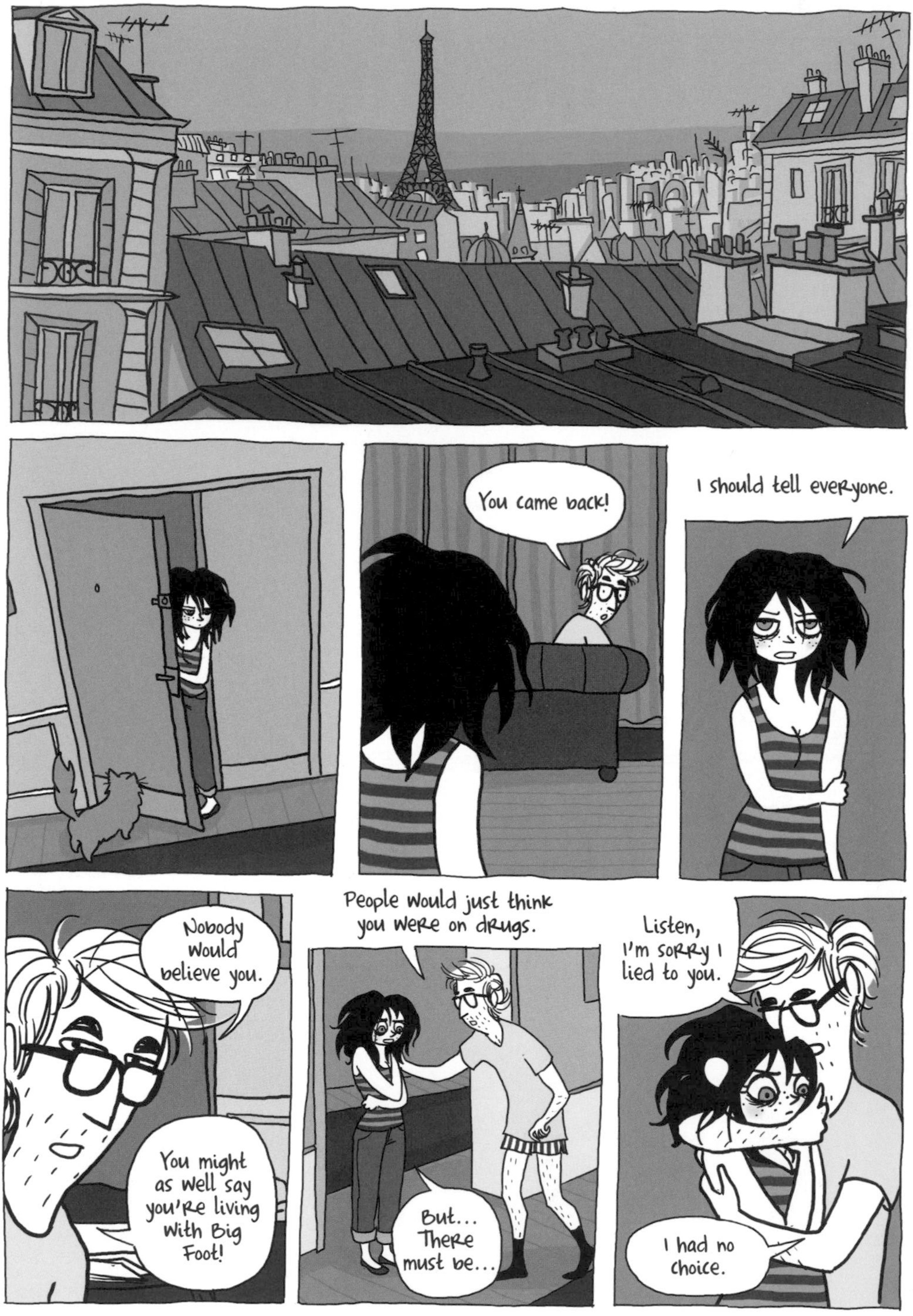

You came back!
I should tell everyone.
Nobody would believe you.
You might as well say you're living with Big Foot!
People would just think you were on drugs.
But... There must be...
Listen, I'm sorry I lied to you.
I had no choice.

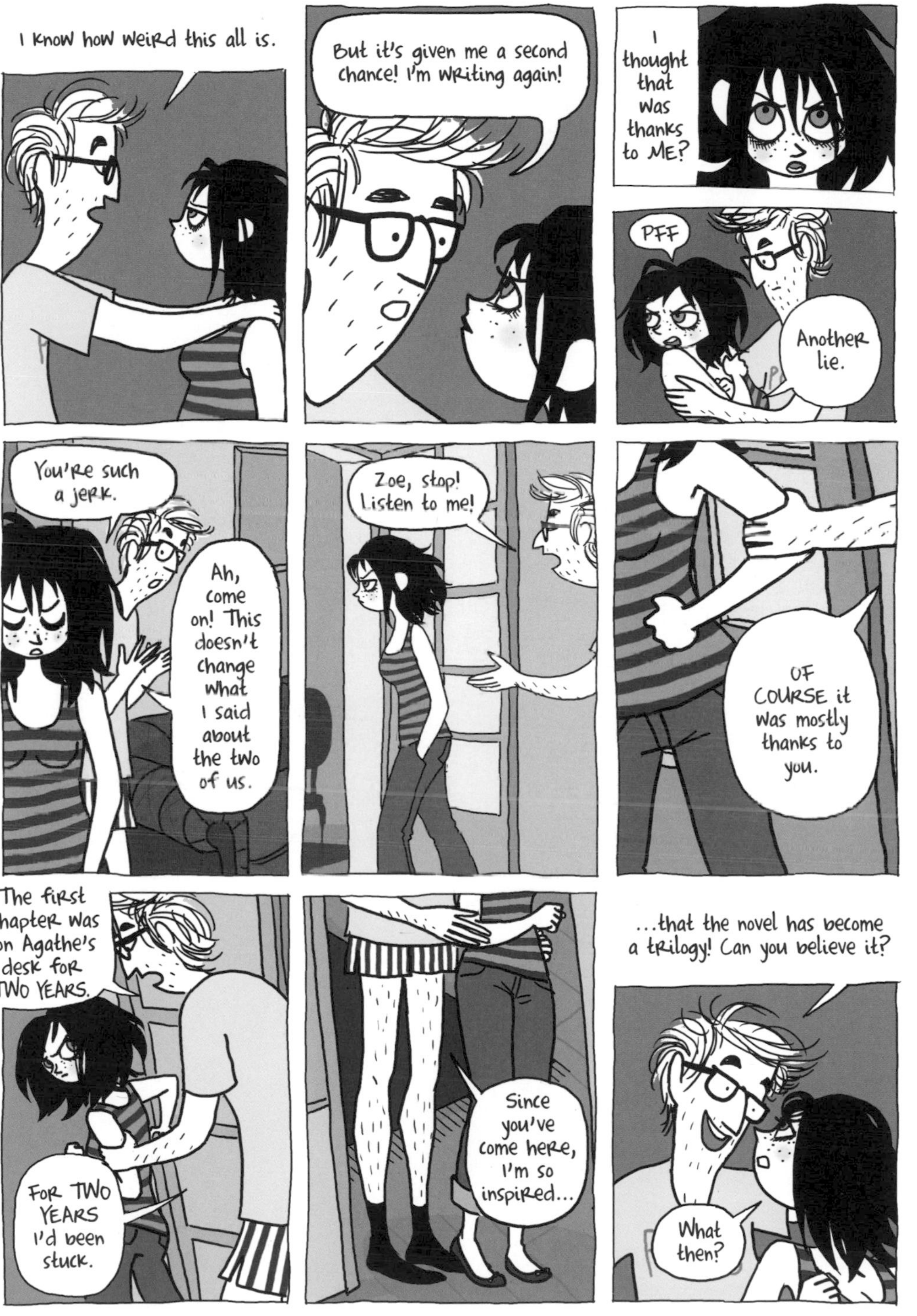
I know how weird this all is.
But it's given me a second chance! I'm writing again!
I thought that was thanks to ME?
PFF
Another lie.
You're such a jerk.
Ah, come on! This doesn't change what I said about the two of us.
Zoe, stop! Listen to me!
OF COURSE it was mostly thanks to you.
The first chapter was on Agathe's desk for TWO YEARS.
For TWO YEARS I'd been stuck.
Since you've come here, I'm so inspired...
...that the novel has become a trilogy! Can you believe it?
What then?

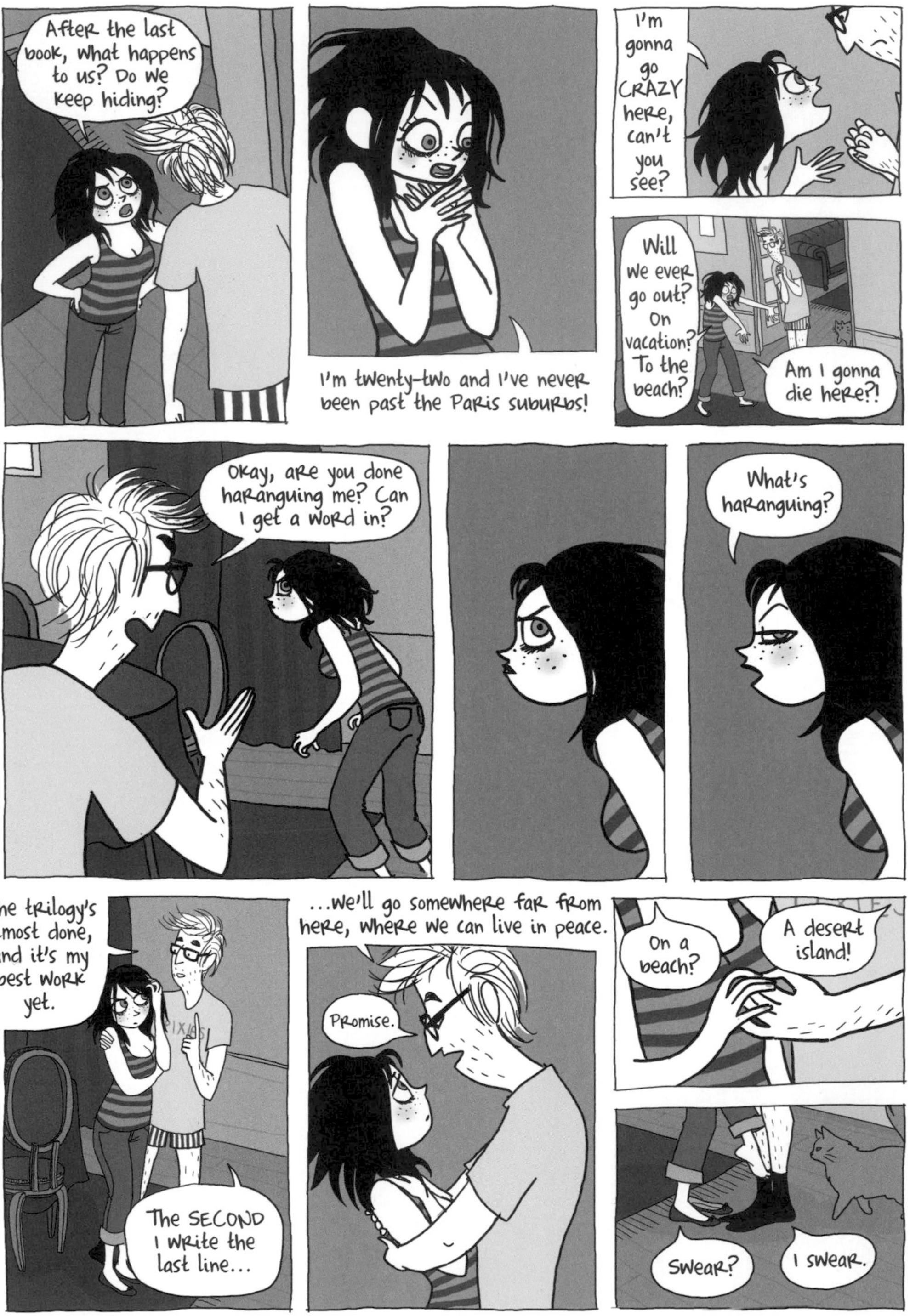
After the last book, what happens to us? Do we keep hiding?
I'm twenty-two and I've never been past the Paris suburbs!
I'm gonna go CRAZY here, can't you see?
Will we ever go out? On vacation? To the beach?
Am I gonna die here?!
Okay, are you done haranguing me? Can I get a word in?
What's haranguing?
The trilogy's almost done, and it's my best work yet.
The SECOND I write the last line...
...we'll go somewhere far from here, where we can live in peace.
Promise.
On a beach?
A desert island!
Swear?
I swear.

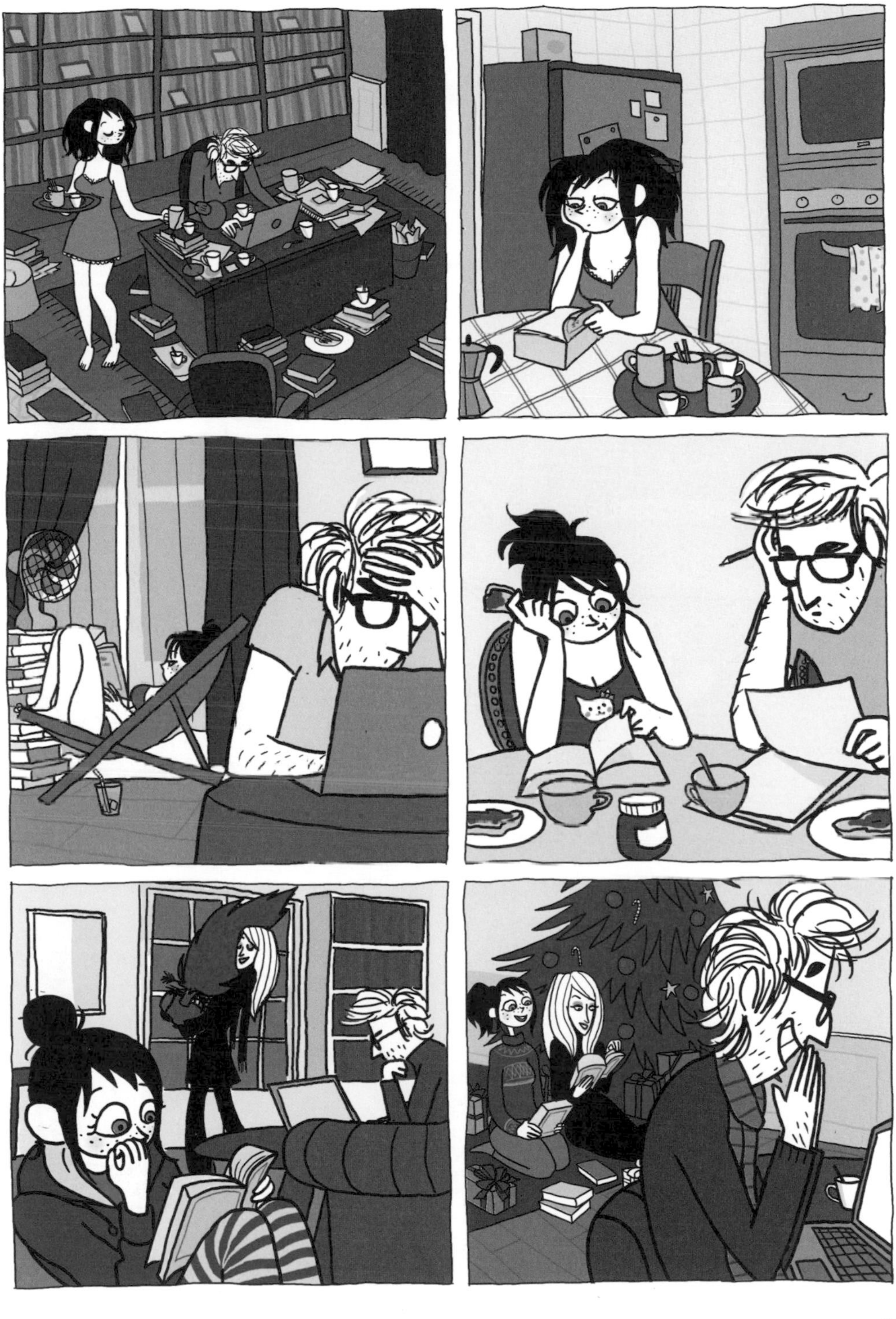

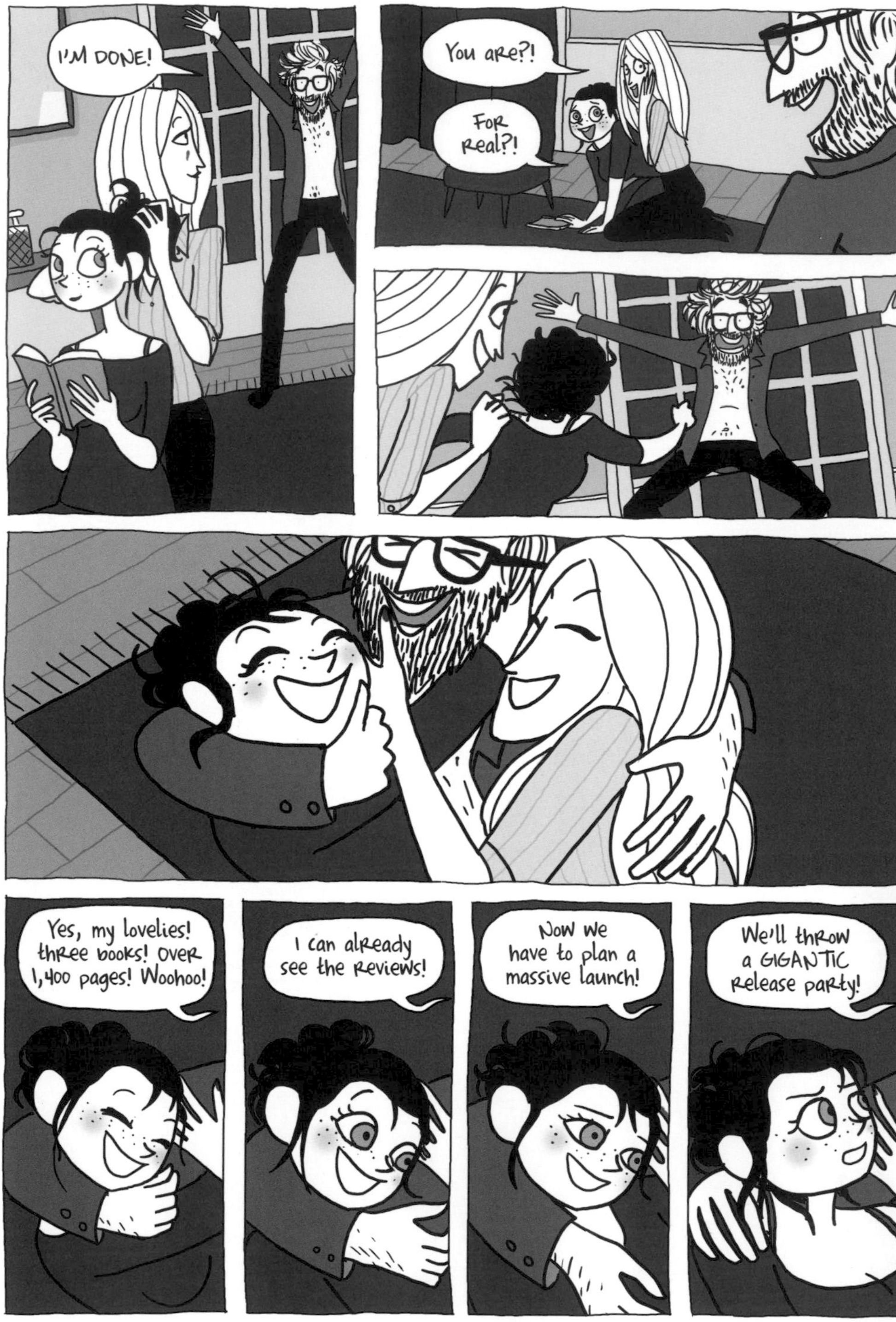
I'M DONE!
You are?!
For real?!
Yes, my lovelies! three books! Over 1,400 pages! Woohoo!
I can already see the reviews!
Now we have to plan a massive launch!
We'll throw a GIGANTIC release party!

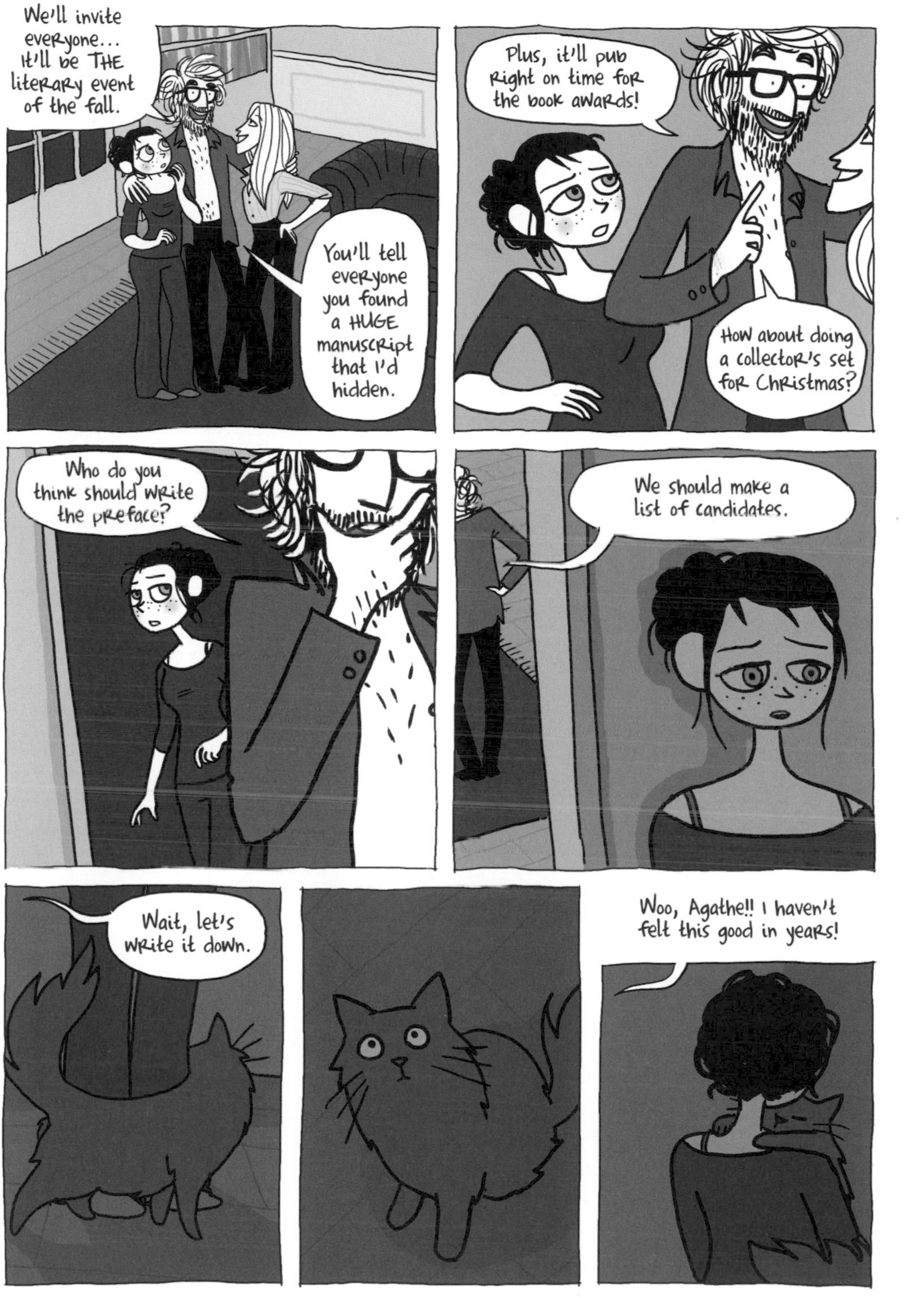
We'll invite everyone... It'll be THE literary event of the fall.
You'll tell everyone you found a HUGE manuscript that I'd hidden.
Plus, it'll pub right on time for the book awards!
How about doing a collector's set for Christmas?
Who do you think should write the preface?
We should make a list of candidates.
Wait, let's write it down.
Woo, Agathe!! I haven't felt this good in years!

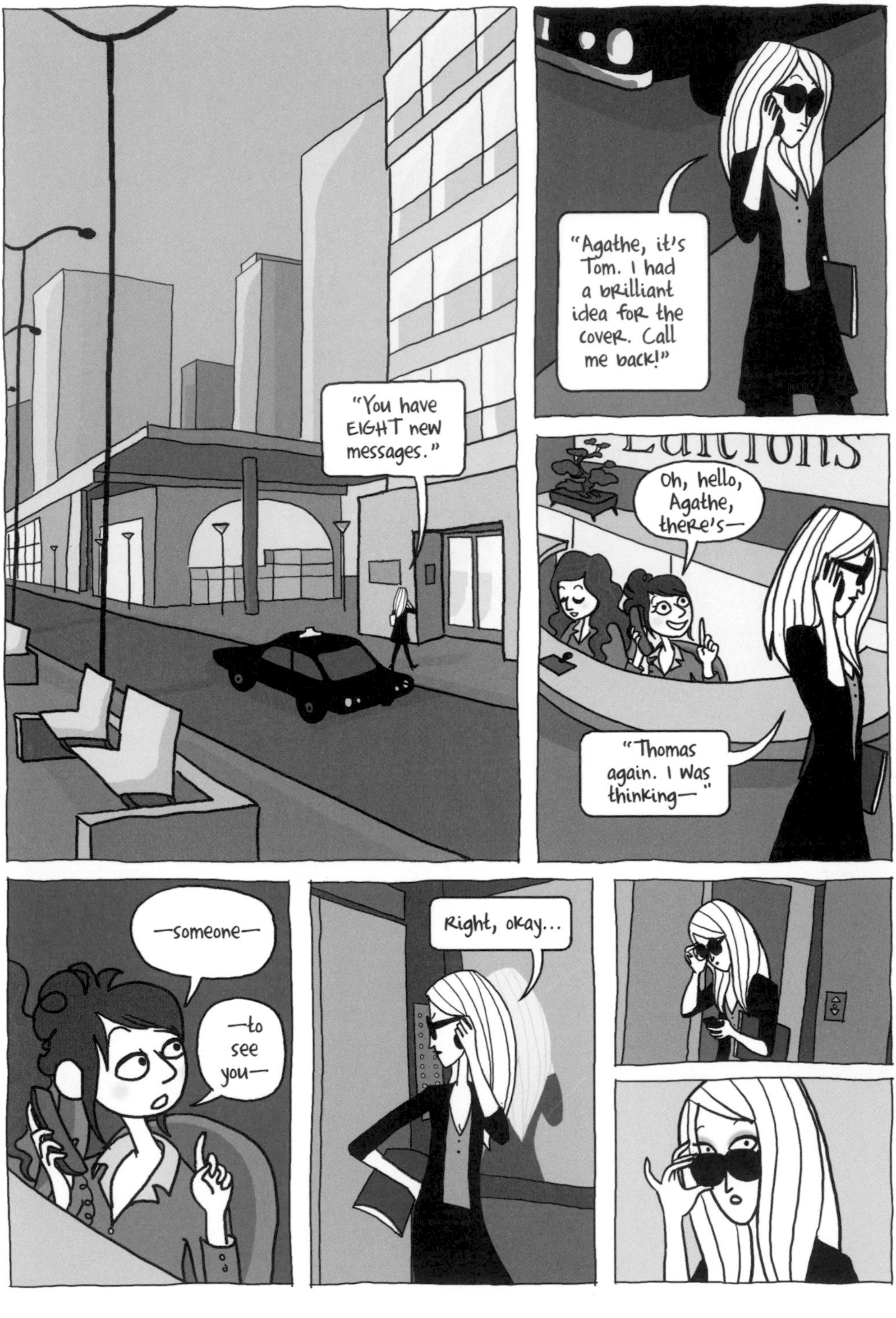
"You have EIGHT new messages."
"Agathe, it's Tom. I had a brilliant idea for the cover. Call me back!"
Editions
Oh, hello, Agathe, there's—
"Thomas again. I was thinking— "
—someone—
—to see you—
Right, okay...

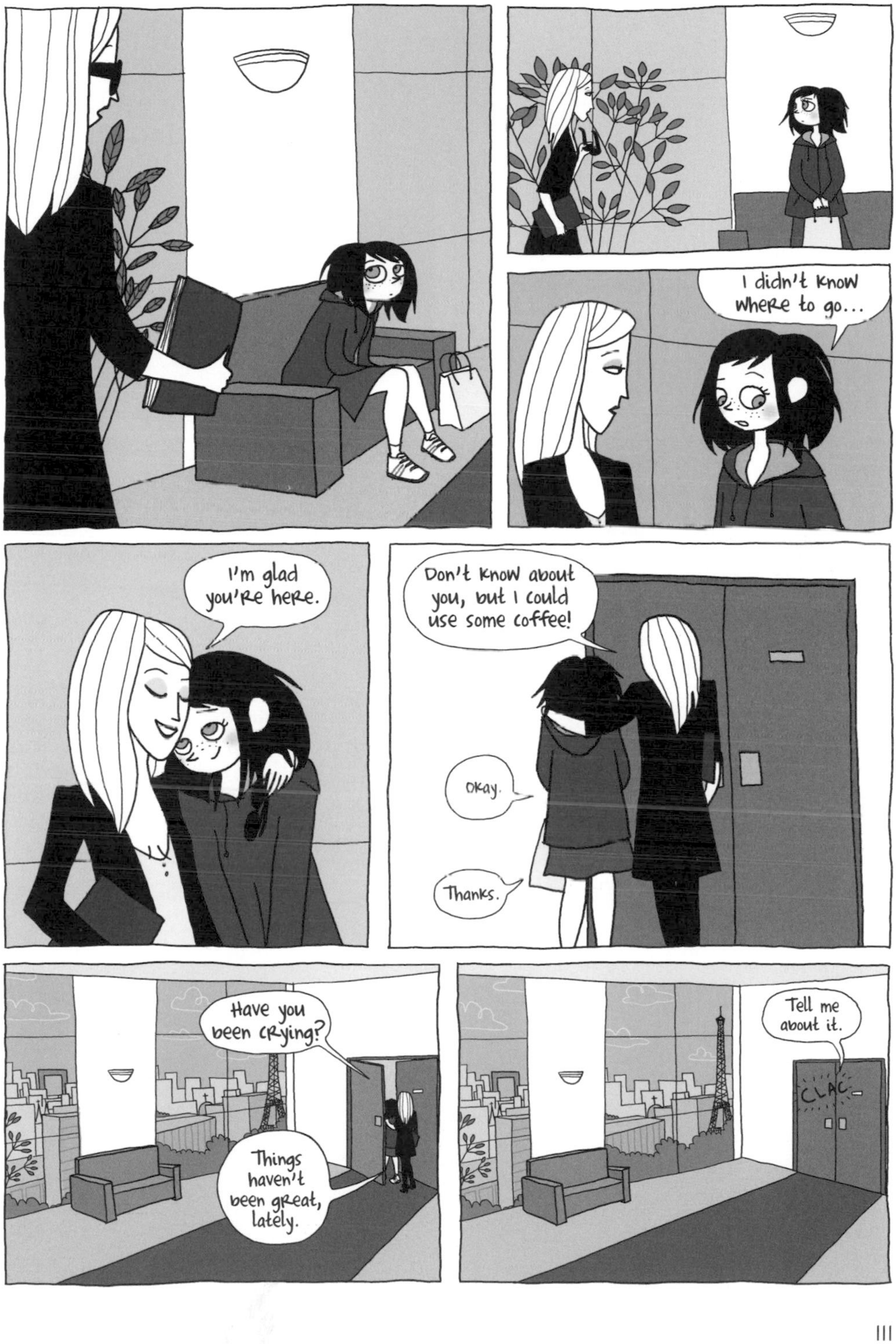
I didn't know where to go...
I'm glad you're here.
Don't know about you, but I could use some coffee!
Okay.
Thanks.
Have you been crying?
Things haven't been great, lately.
Tell me about it.
CLAC

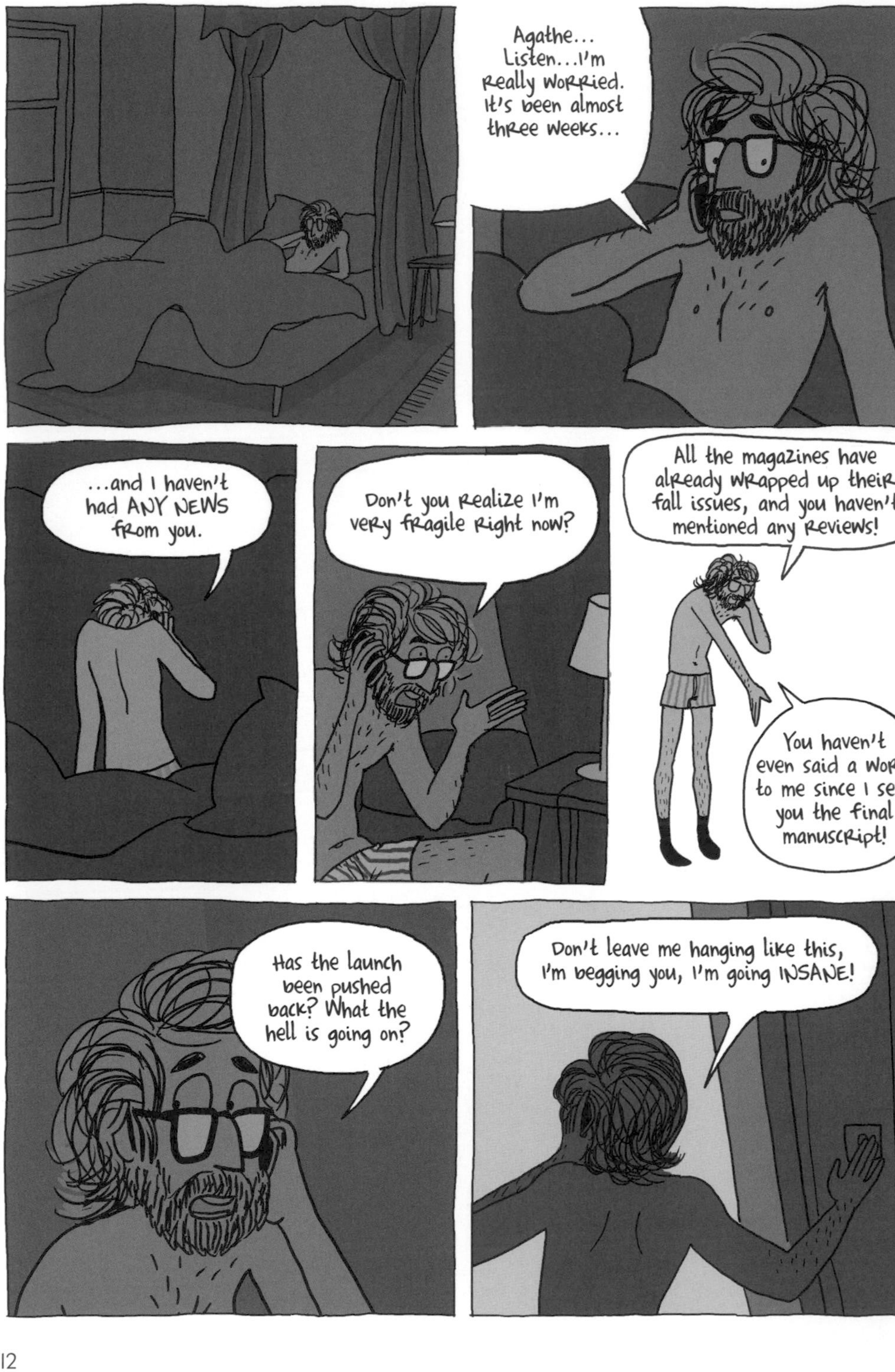
Agathe... Listen...I'm really worried. It's been almost three weeks...
...and I haven't had ANY NEWS from you.
Don't you realize I'm very fragile right now?
All the magazines have already wrapped up their fall issues, and you haven't mentioned any reviews!
You haven't even said a word to me since I sent you the final manuscript!
Has the launch been pushed back? What the hell is going on?
Don't leave me hanging like this, I'm begging you, I'm going INSANE!

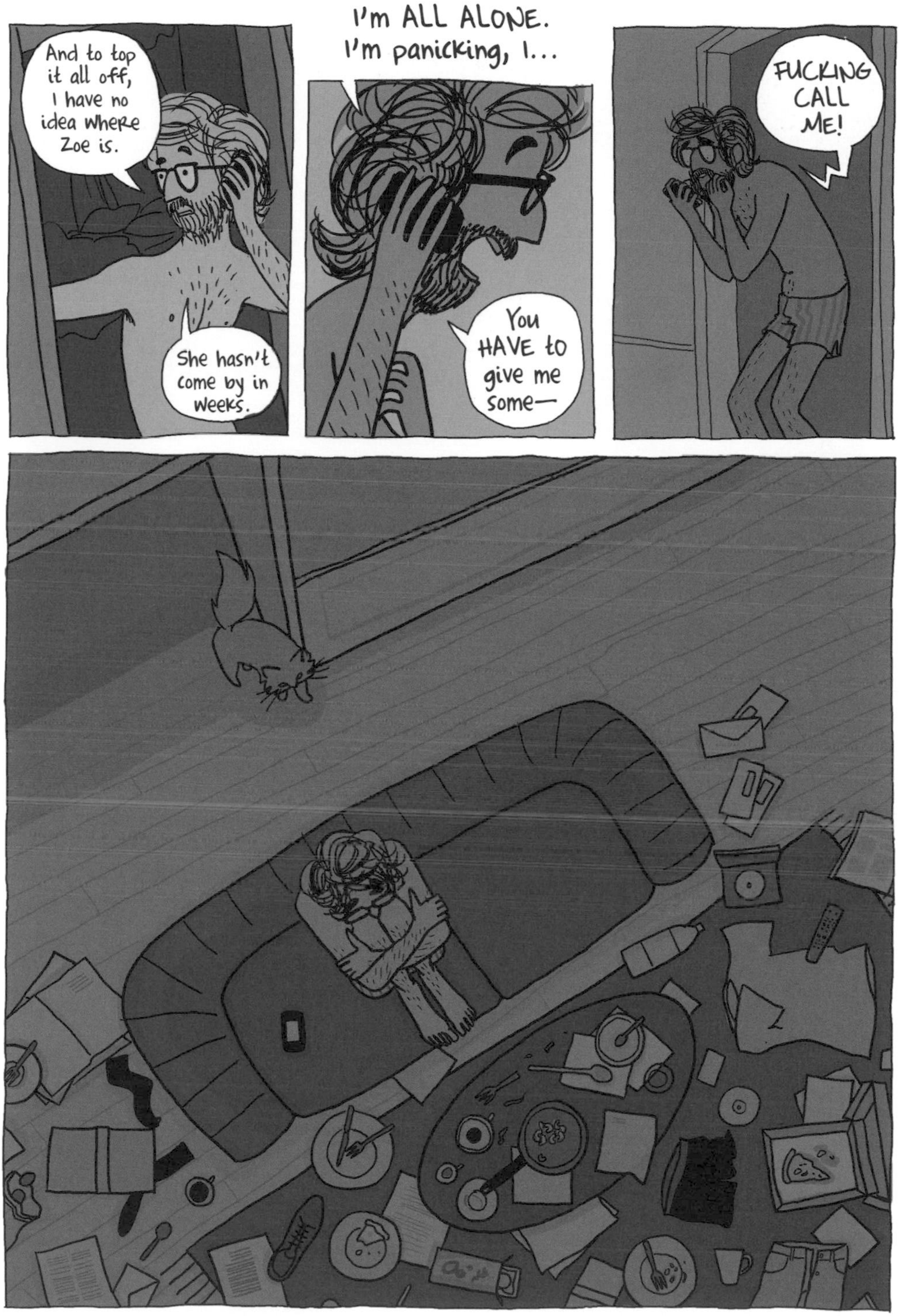
And to top it all off, I have no idea where Zoe is.
She hasn't come by in weeks.
I'm ALL ALONE. I'm panicking, I...
You HAVE to give me some—
FUCKING CALL ME!

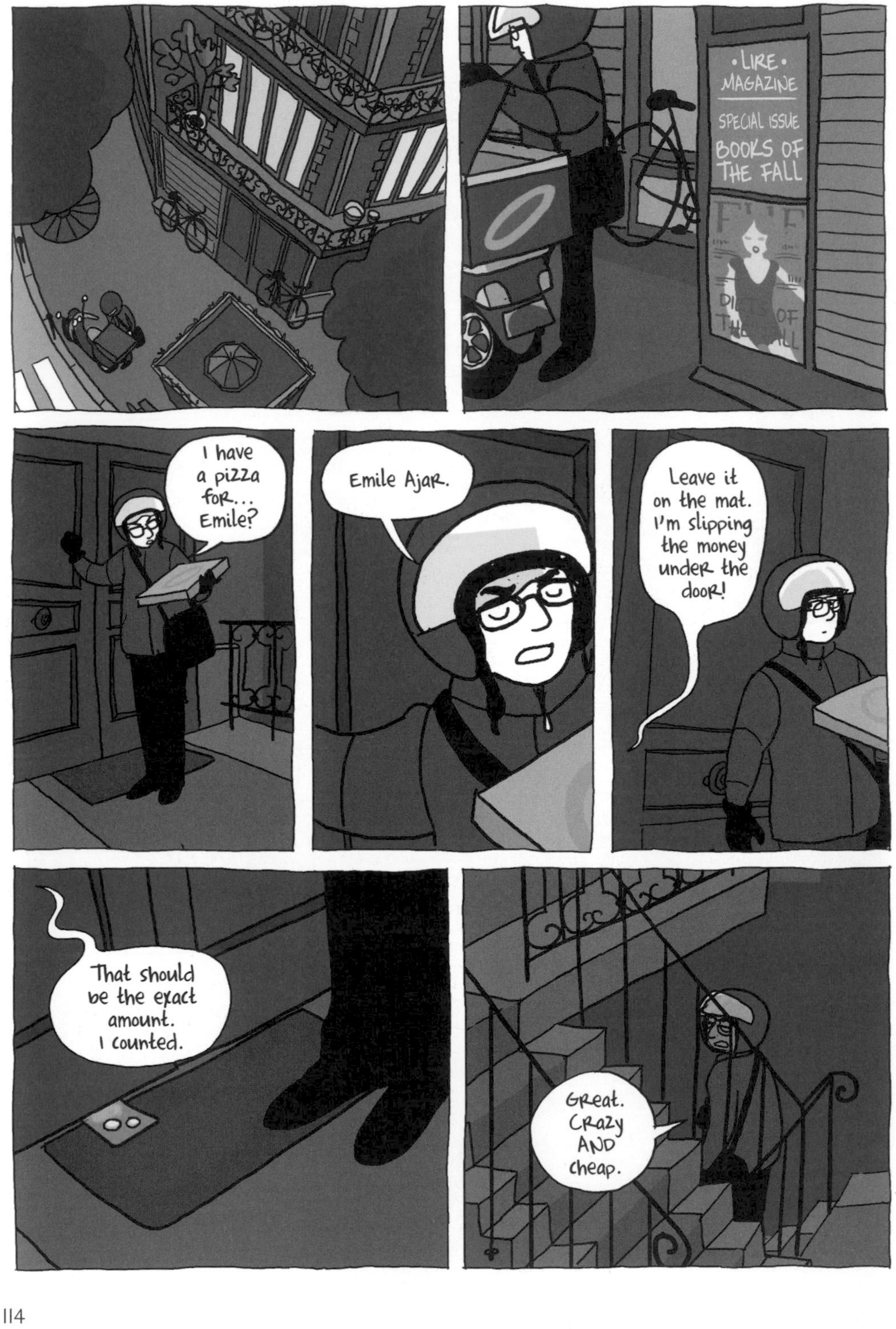
• LIRE •
MAGAZINE
SPECIAL ISSUE
BOOKS OF THE FALL
I have a pizza for... Emile?
Emile Ajar.
Leave it on the mat. I'm slipping the money under the door!
That should be the exact amount. I counted.
Great. Crazy AND cheap.

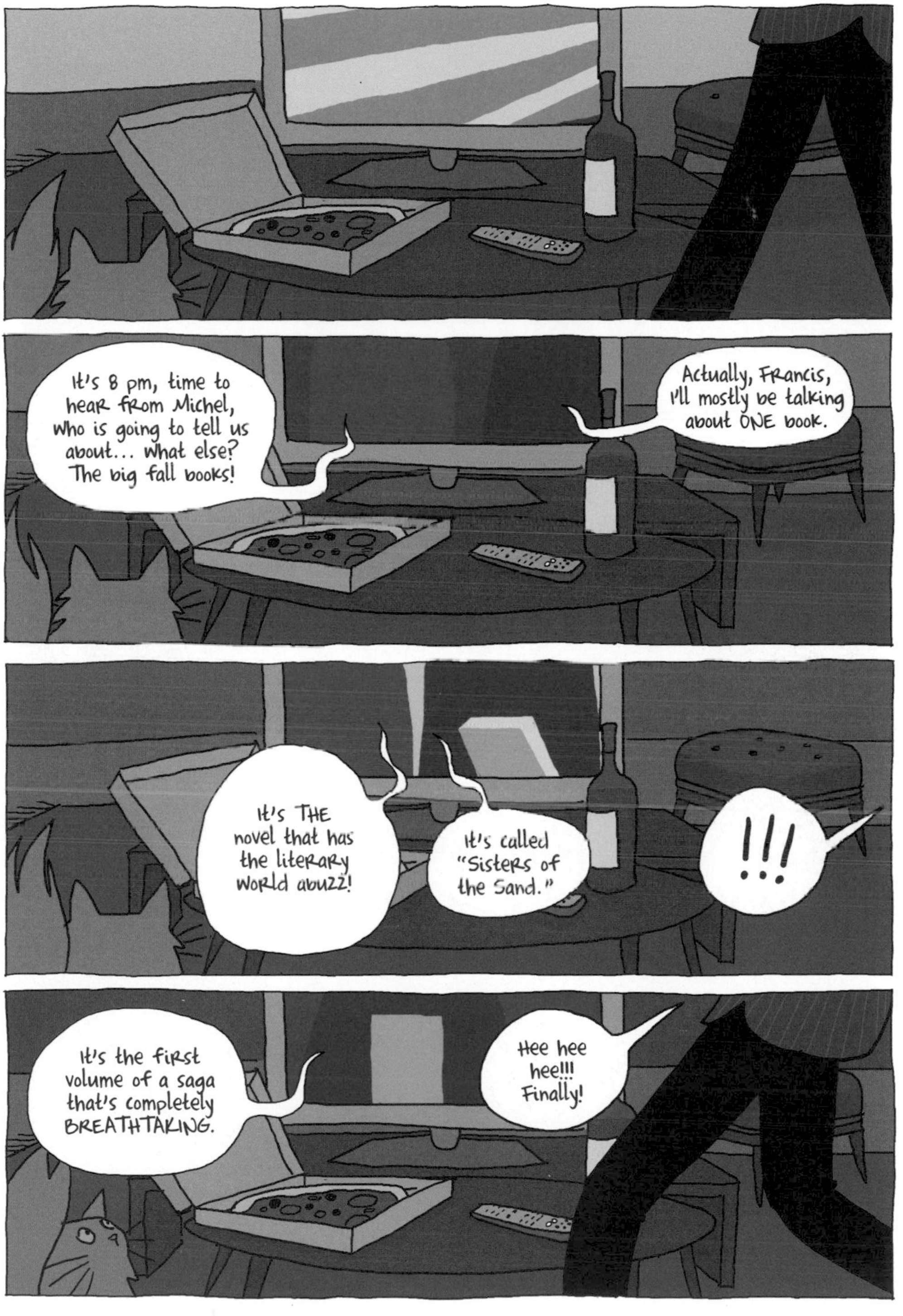
It's 8 pm, time to hear from Michel, who is going to tell us about... what else? The big fall books!
Actually, Francis, I'll mostly be talking about ONE book.
It's THE novel that has the literary world abuzz!
It's called "Sisters of the Sand."
!!!
It's the first volume of a saga that's completely BREATHTAKING.
Hee hee hee!!! Finally!

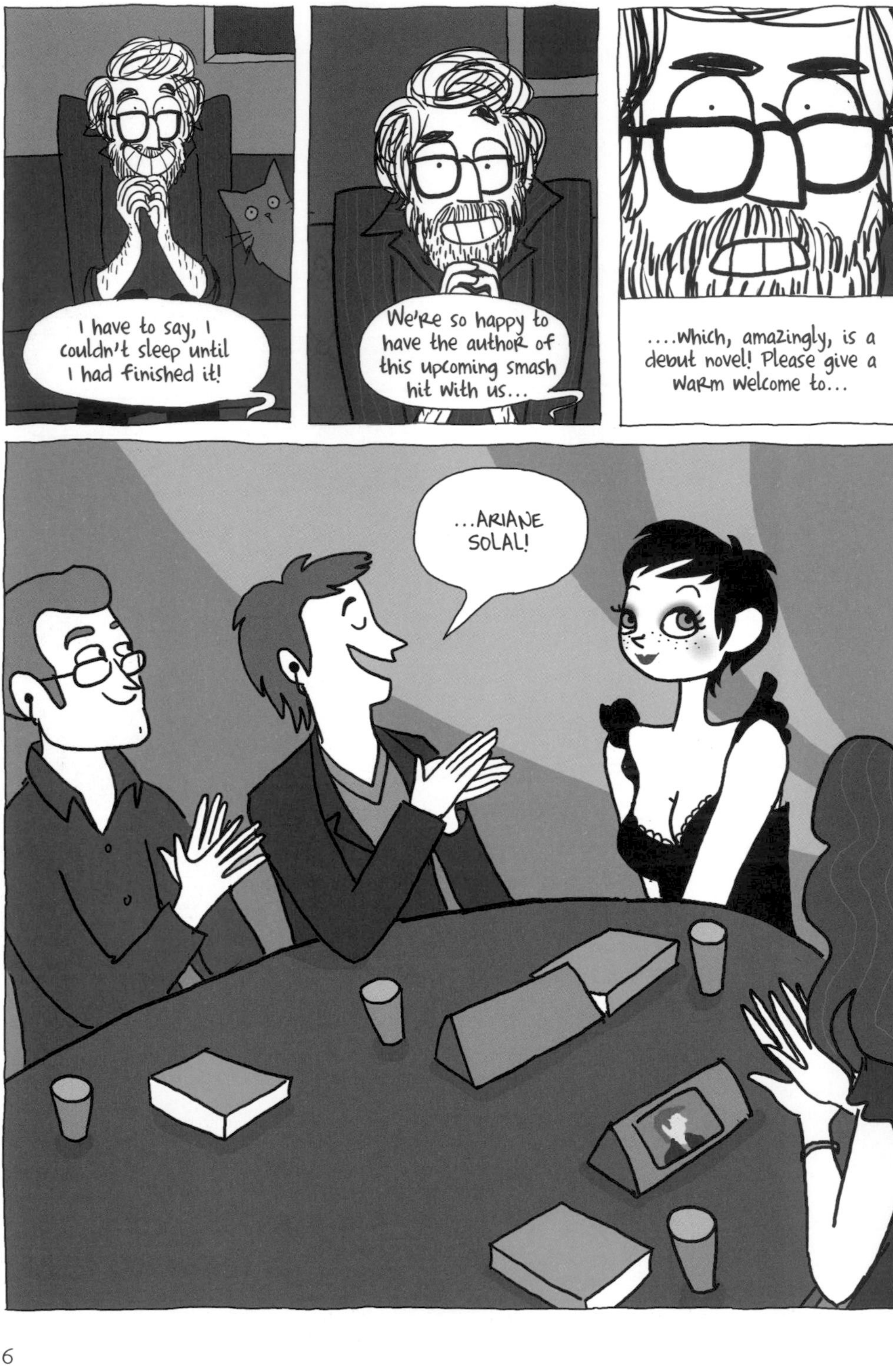
I have to say, I couldn't sleep until I had finished it!
We're so happy to have the author of this upcoming smash hit with us...
....Which, amazingly, is a debut novel! Please give a warm welcome to...
...ARIANE SOLAL!

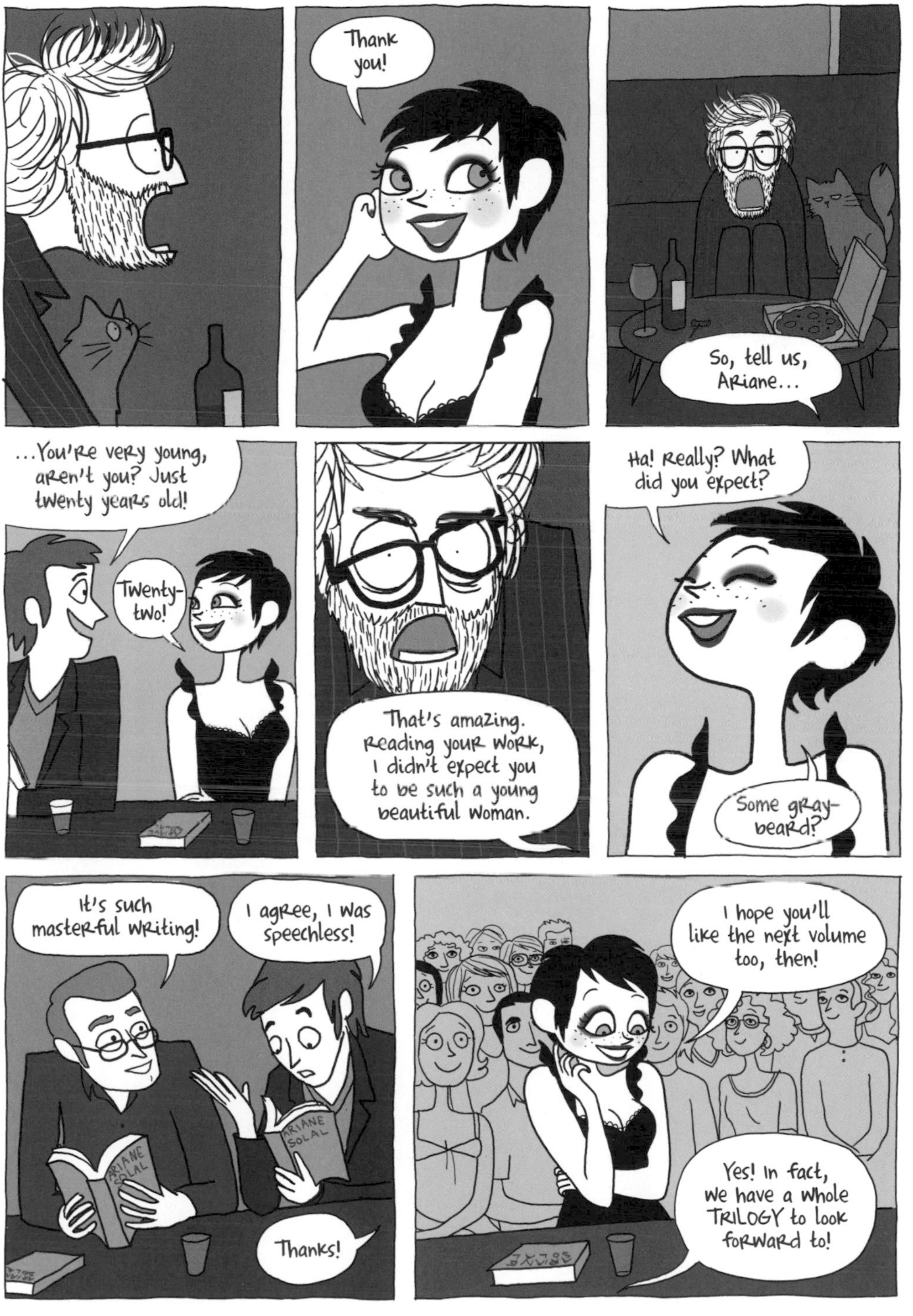
Thank you!
So, tell us, Ariane...
...You're very young, aren't you? Just twenty years old!
Twenty-two!
That's amazing. Reading your work, I didn't expect you to be such a young beautiful woman.
Ha! Really? What did you expect?
Some gray-beard?
It's such masterful writing!
I agree, I was speechless!
ARIANE SOLAL
ARIANE SOLAL
Thanks!
I hope you'll like the next volume too, then!
Yes! In fact, we have a whole TRILOGY to look forward to!

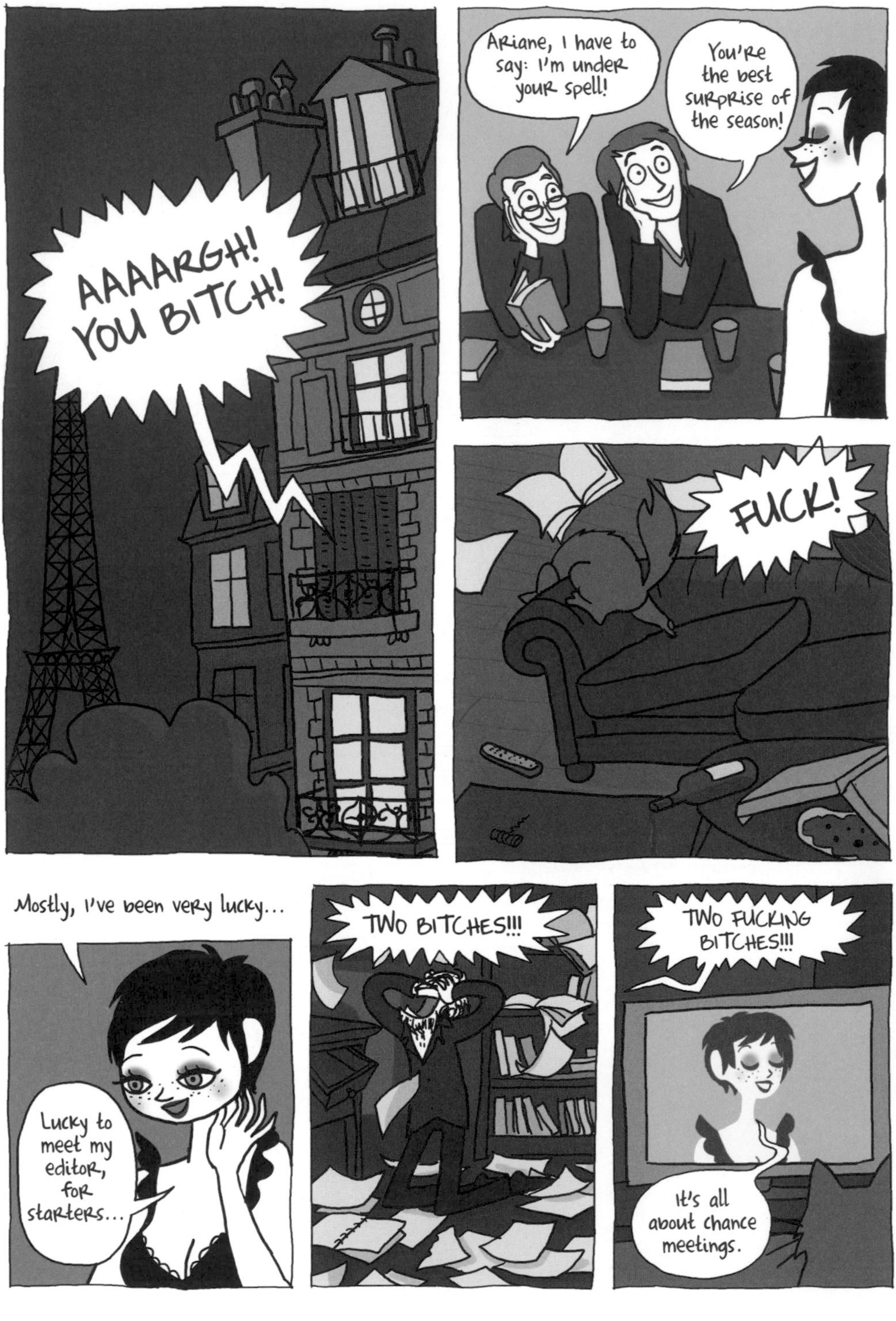
AAAARGH! YOU BITCH!
Ariane, I have to say: I'm under your spell!
You're the best surprise of the season!
FUCK!
Mostly, I've been very lucky...
Lucky to meet my editor, for starters...
TWO BITCHES!!!
TWO FUCKING BITCHES!!!
It's all about chance meetings.

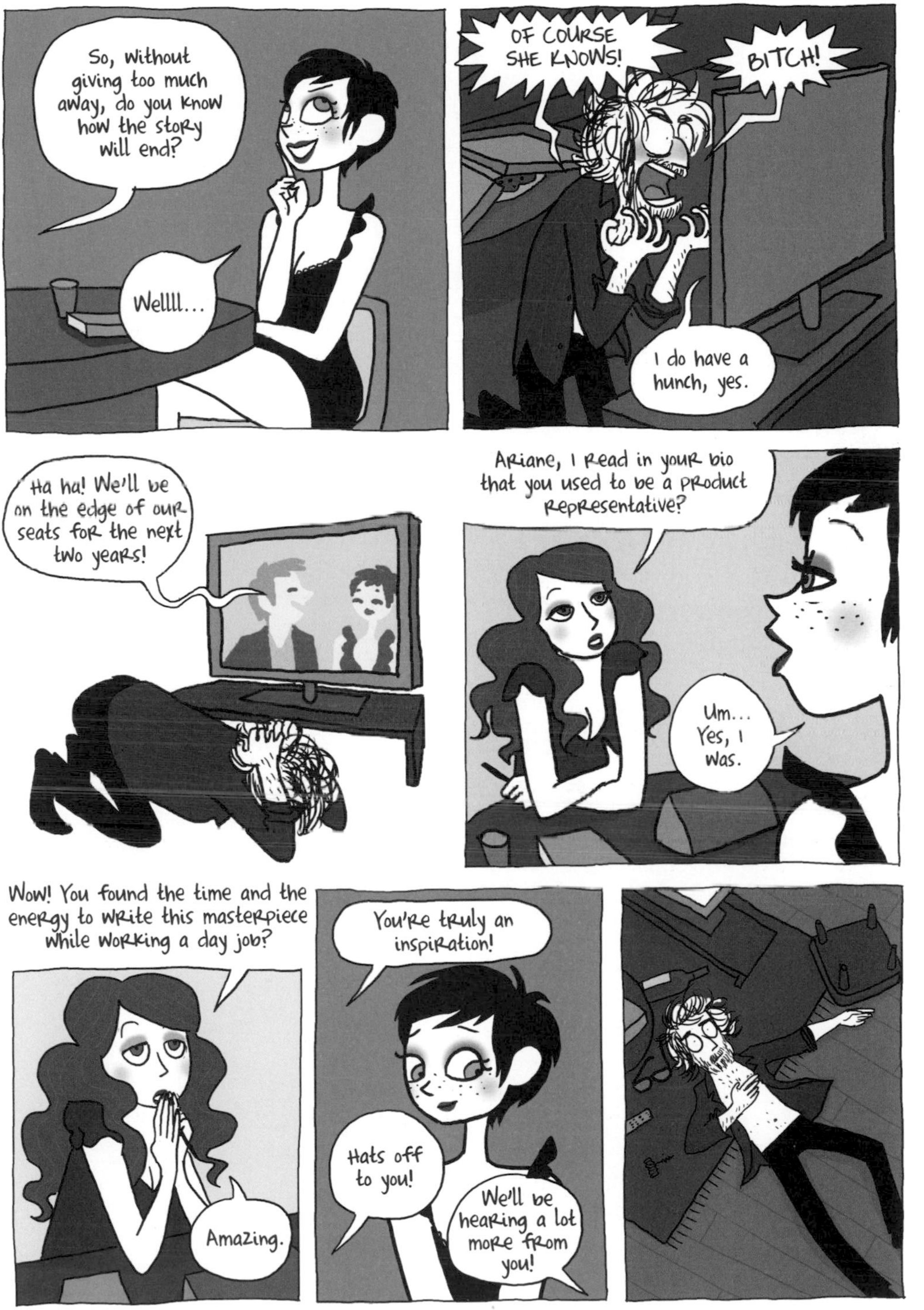

So, without giving too much away, do you know how the story will end?
Wellll...
OF COURSE SHE KNOWS!
BITCH!
I do have a hunch, yes.
Ha ha! We'll be on the edge of our seats for the next two years!
Ariane, I read in your bio that you used to be a product representative?
Um... Yes, I was.
Wow! You found the time and the energy to write this masterpiece while working a day job?
Amazing.
You're truly an inspiration!
Hats off to you!
We'll be hearing a lot more from you!

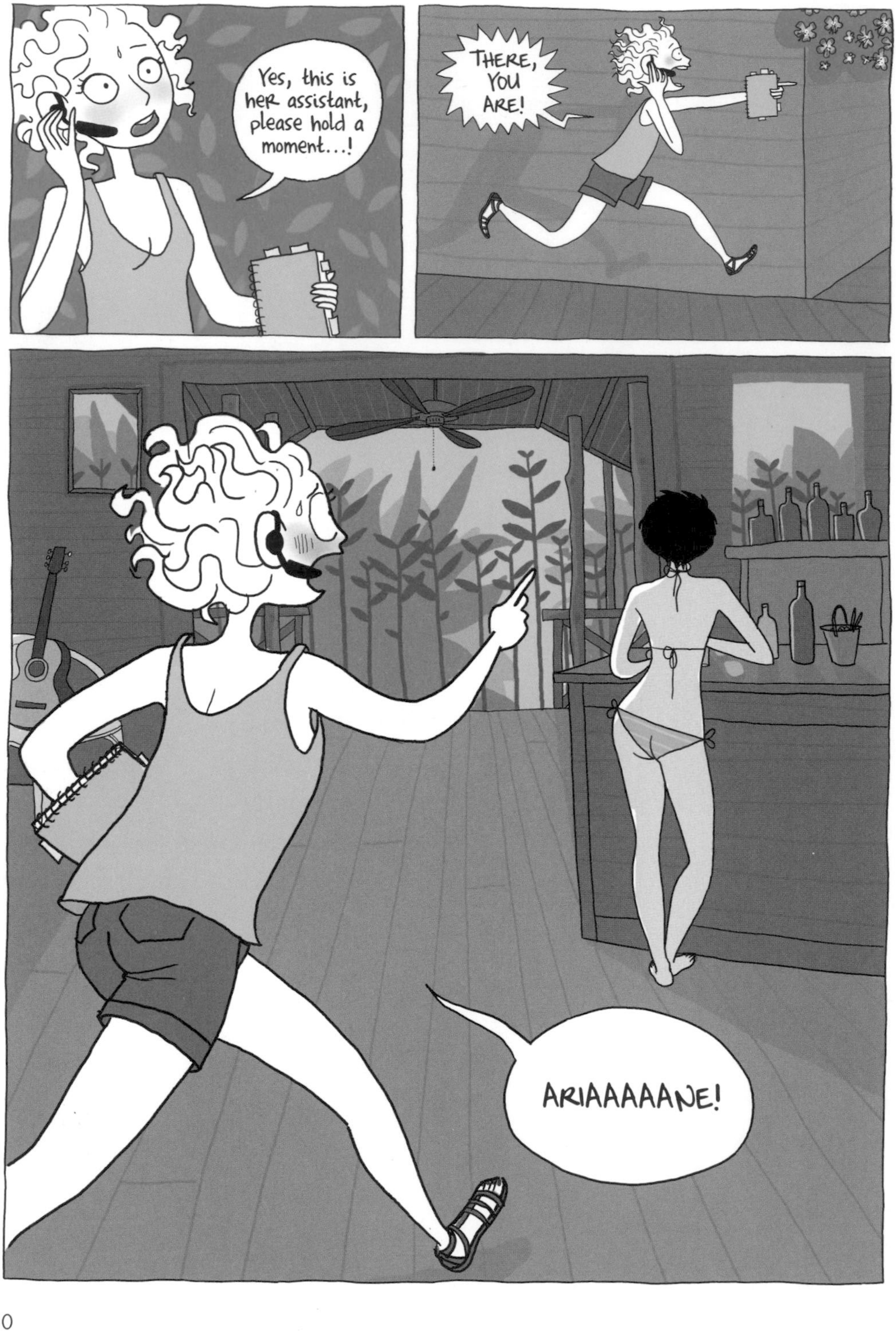
Yes, this is her assistant, please hold a moment...!
THERE, YOU ARE!
ARIAAAAANE!

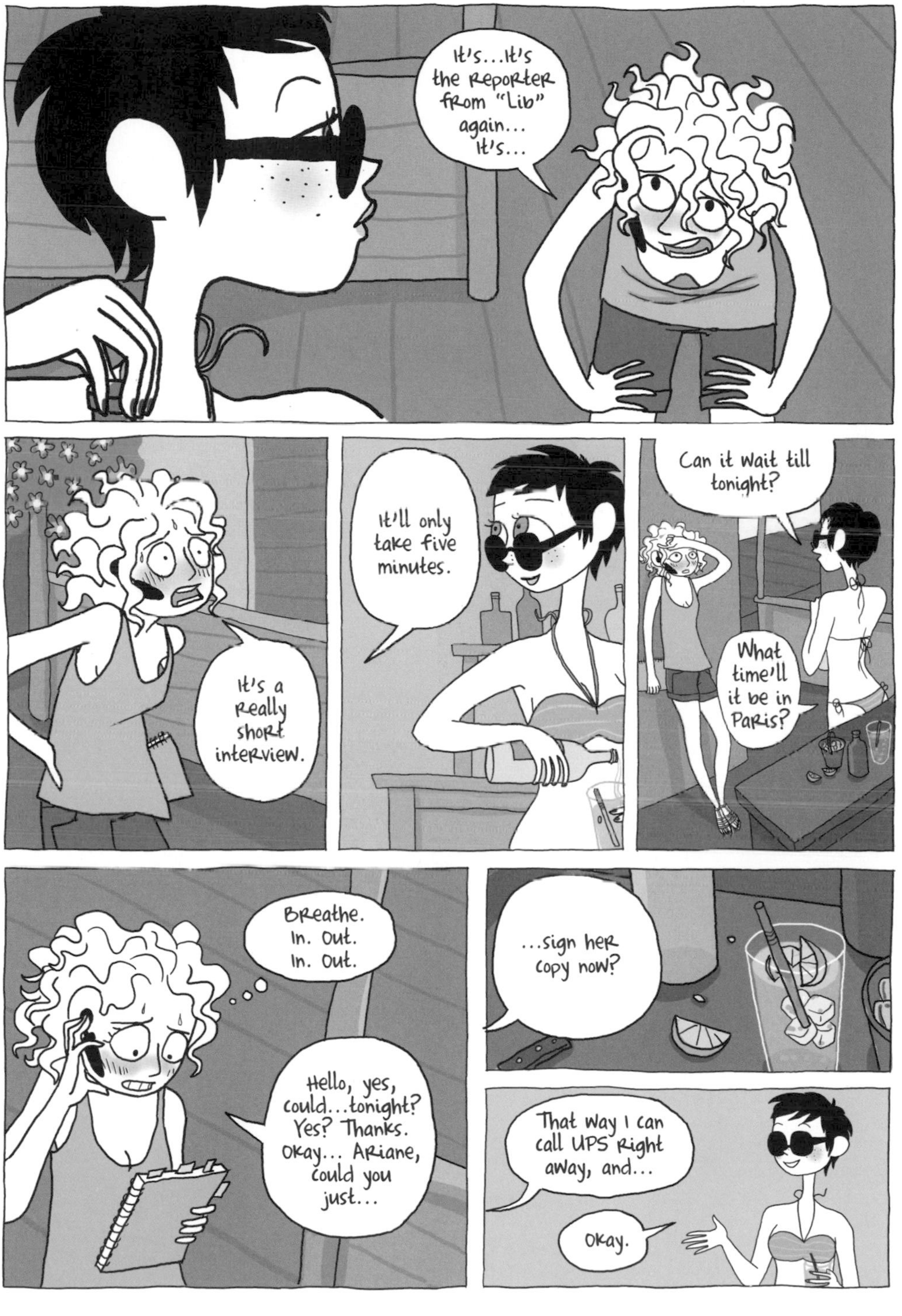
It's…It's the reporter from "Lib" again… It's…
It's a really short interview.
It'll only take five minutes.
Can it wait till tonight?
What time'll it be in Paris?
Breathe. In. Out. In. Out.
Hello, yes, could…tonight? Yes? Thanks. Okay… Ariane, could you just…
…sign her copy now?
That way I can call UPS right away, and…
Okay.

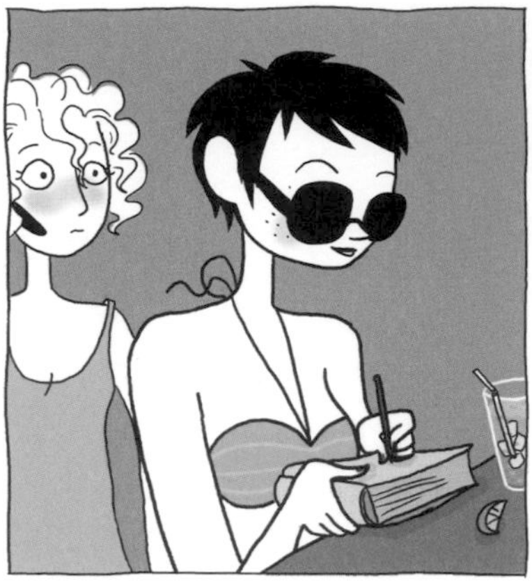

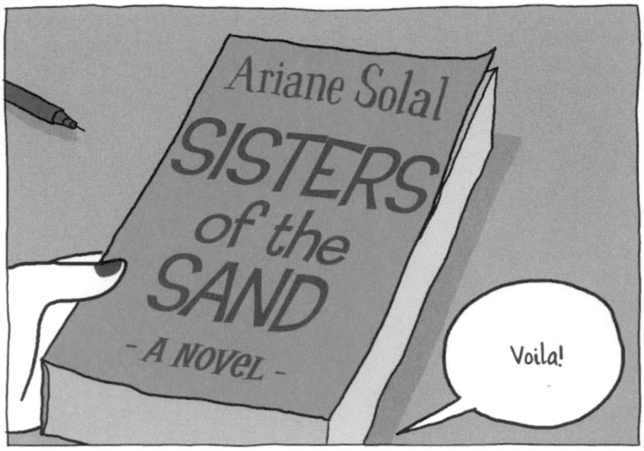
Ariane Solal
SISTERS of the SAND
- A NOVEL -
Voila!

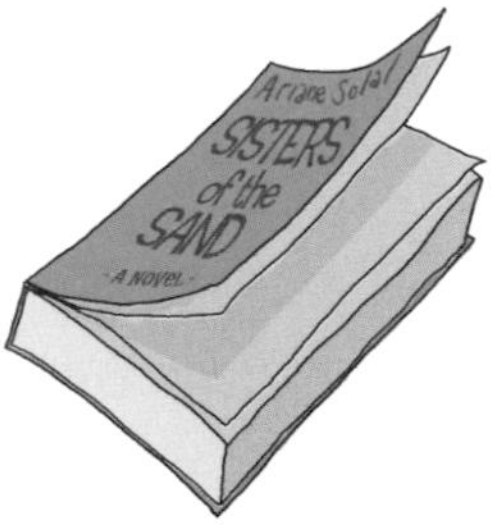
Ariane Solal
SISTERS of the SAND
- A NOVEL -

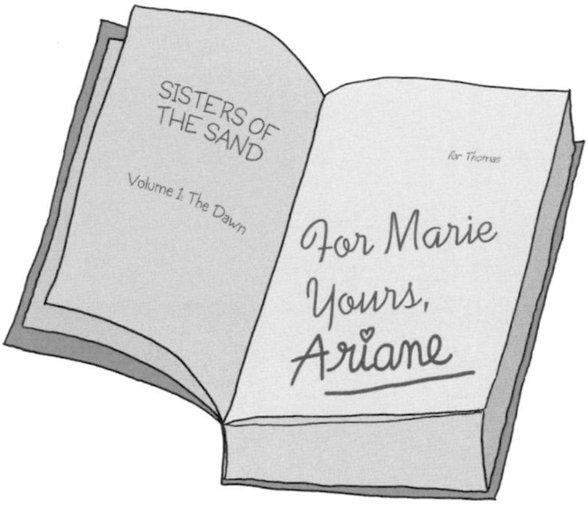
SISTERS OF THE SAND
Volume 1: The Dawn
for Thomas
For Marie
Yours,
Ariane

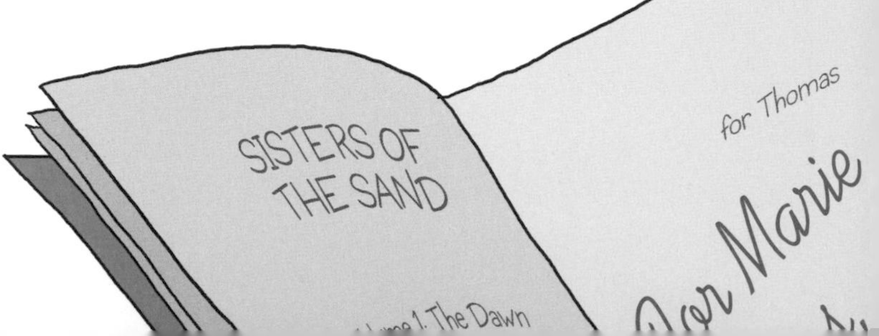
SISTERS OF THE SAND
for Thomas

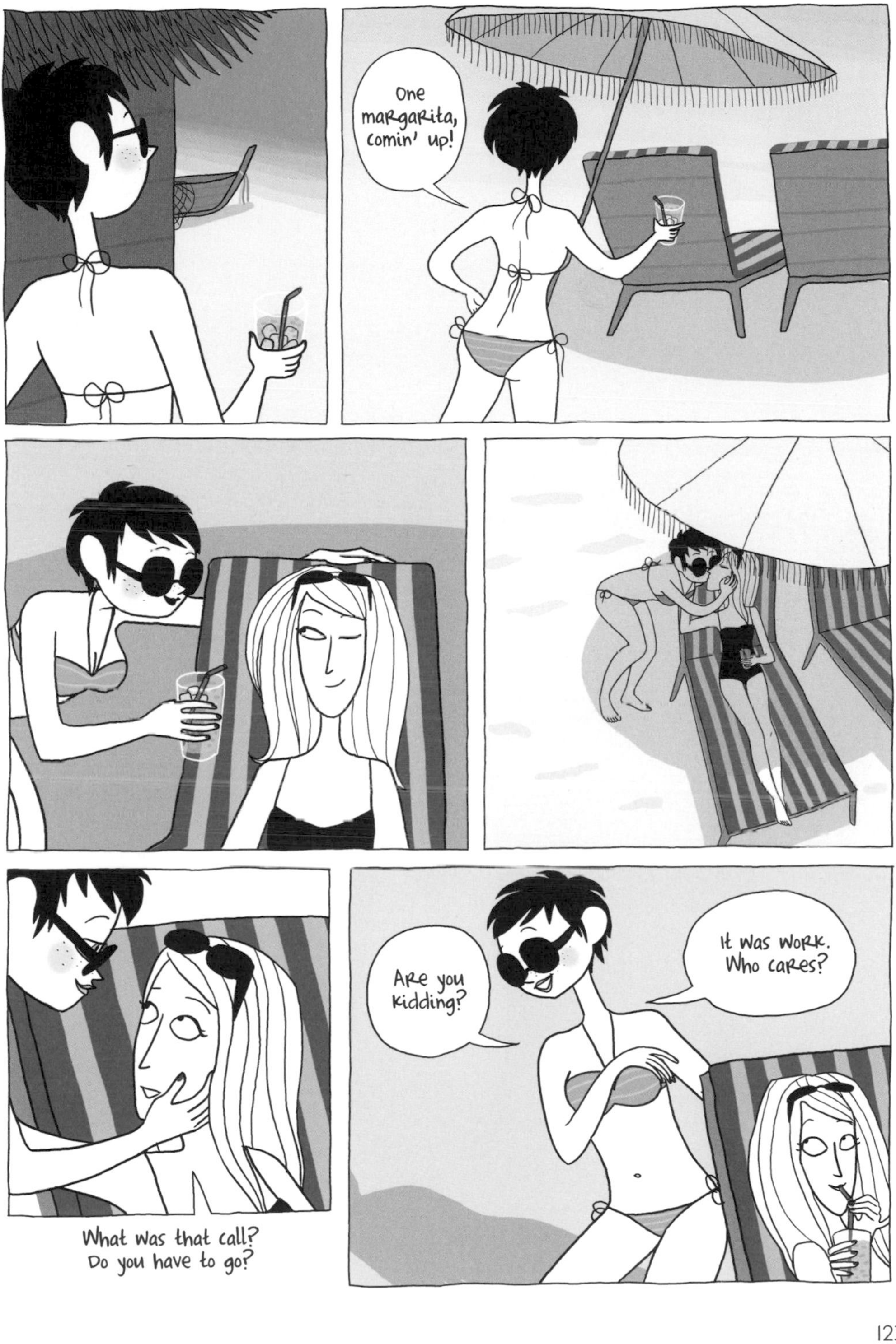
One margarita, comin' up!
What was that call? Do you have to go?
Are you kidding?
It was work. Who cares?

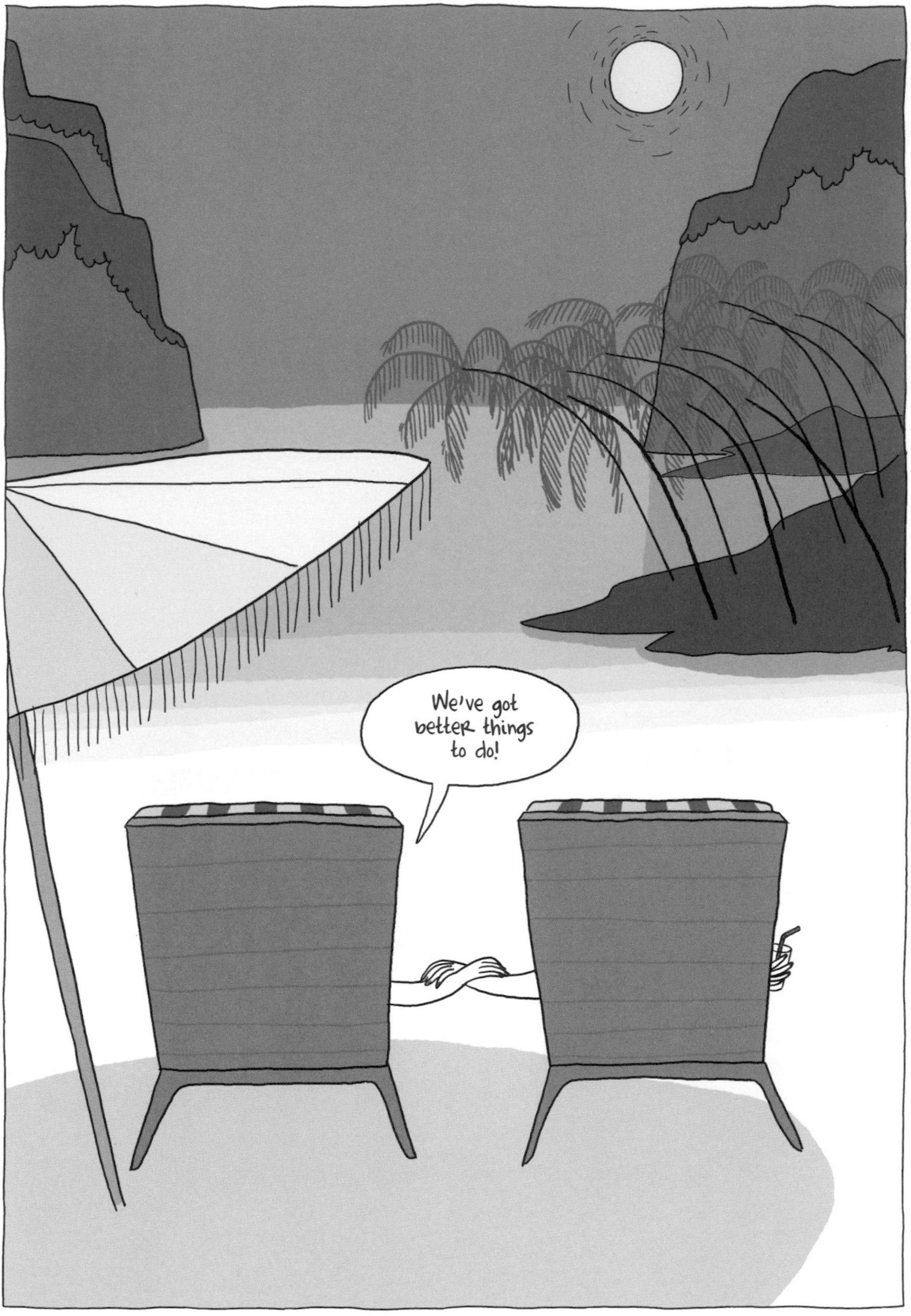
We've got better things to do!